AN EXCEL COMPANION
FOR
BUSINESS STATISTICS

David L. Eldredge

Murray State University

SOUTH-WESTERN College Publishing

An International Thomson Publishing Company

Team Director: David L. Shaut
Acquisitions Editor: Charles E. McCormick, Jr.
Production Editor: Deanna Quinn
Marketing Manager: Joseph A. Sabatino
Manufacturing Coordinator: Sue Kirven

ISBN: 0-538-89088-6 (package)

ISBN: 0-324-00771-X (book)

1 2 3 4 5 6 7 PN 4 3 2 1 0 9 8

Printed in the United States of America

I(T)P®
International Thomson Publishing
The ITP trademark is used under license.

BRIEF CONTENTS

CONTENTS

PREFACE

The computer software which is most commonly used for data analysis within business and industrial organizations is spreadsheet software. Current windows-based spreadsheet software comes with a number of built-in features for performing statistical analysis. Since the majority of the graduates of our business schools will use mainly spreadsheets for analysis in their subsequent careers, they will benefit from a familiarity with the use of these statistical features of spreadsheet software.

A few years ago, I concluded that if we as business statistics professors do not familiarize our students with these capabilities, they may never discover them. Accordingly, as an experiment in the Spring 1995 semester, I switched from the use of dedicated statistical software (e.g., Minitab, SPSS, SAS) to the use of spreadsheet software for my business statistics courses. The experiment was a success. I have used spreadsheet software as the sole software support for all the statistic courses I have taught since that time. Consequently, it pleases me to be able to share the results of some of my experiences through this manual with you.

What Is The Purpose Of This Manual? The title of this manual, *An Excel Companion for Business Statistics,* implies the three aspects of its purpose. First, it presents step-by-step instructions for using Excel for statistical analysis. The instructions are complimented by figures of computer screen captures. These show data input, menus, dialog boxes and statistical results. Second, it is designed to be used in conjunction with a textbook. For example, the manual does not include end-of-the-chapter exercises. Our intent is for you the student to work through a topic within this manual and then apply Excel to similar examples and exercises from your textbook. Third, it is focused on the area of business statistics. Although there are similarities in the application of statistical analysis to many areas, our orientation through examples is to the use of statistical analysis in business and industrial organizations.

Which Textbooks Does It Support? The manual has been designed to be used with most business statistics textbooks. This is possible for at least a couple of reasons. First, there is a large degree of consistency in many business statistics textbooks. The topics included and the organization of these topics is quite similar for many textbooks. Second, for those topics for which there is not consistency among textbooks, this manual uses a modular approach. As a result, it is relatively easy to identify the unit within this manual which corresponds to the topical coverage of a particular textbook.

Do I Need This Manual If My Textbook Covers Excel? A number of recently published business statistics textbooks incorporate the use of Excel within them. However, oftentimes the instructions provided are not in sufficient detail for those persons who do not have a good knowledge of Excel. This manual presents detailed instructions and many figures showing the computer screen as the user will see it. It just isn't possible within the confines of a business statistics textbook to provide this level of detail which is needed by some users. If the specific instructions and visual guidance provided within this manual were added to the typical business statistics textbook, its length would become substantial if not prohibitive.

Which Statistical Topics Are Supported By This Manual? The topics within this manual include most of those you will find within your textbook. The manual covers (1) the charts, graphs and numerical measures of descriptive statistics, (2) discrete and continuous probability distributions, (3) sampling distributions, (4) the point estimates, confidence intervals and hypothesis testing of introductory inferential statistics, (5) hypothesis tests utilizing the chi-square statistic, (6) the multivariate analysis approaches of the analysis of variance, regression analysis and time series forecasting, and (7) quality control charts. Chapter topics found within business statistics textbooks which are not supported within this manual include (1) probability concepts, (2) nonparametric statistics other than the chi-square statistic, (3) index numbers and (4) decision analysis.

Is Additional Software Required? No. Our approach is to use only the inherent capabilities of Excel. That is, we rely totally on the computing, charting, statistical analysis tools, statistical functions and other features which are included within Excel as it is distributed to customers. We do not rely on add-ins, special macro functions, or special worksheets. All you need is Excel in order to construct all the worksheets within this manual.

Which Versions of Excel Are Supported? The manual supports the three most recent versions of Excel for IBM-compatible personal computers. Each of these versions is known by various names. The earliest of these three is usually called Excel 5.0 for Windows 3.1 or Excel 5. The version which followed it is known as Excel for Windows 95 Version 7.0 , Excel 7.0 or Excel 7. Finally, the most recent version is named Excel 97 for Windows 95, Excel 8.0 or Excel 8. For simplicity and consistency, we will refer to these as *Excel 5*, *Excel 7* and *Excel 8* respectively within this manual. While these three versions are quite similar there are differences among them. This manual has been developed using Excel 7. However, we use boxed notes to draw your attention to any Excel 8 or Excel 5 differences which are important to our analyses. These will begin either with the words **Excel 8 Note** or **Excel 5 Note**.

What Level of Excel Knowledge Is Required? The primary purpose of this manual is to introduce you to the statistical capabilities of Excel. However, it is written assuming some readers will not have had prior experience with Windows and/or Excel. Accordingly, Chapter 1 includes a brief introduction to the Windows environment and an introduction to Excel. These sections are not a complete guide to either Windows or Excel. However, they present sufficient material for most persons to be able to begin using Excel for statistical analyses.

Should I Just Use the Worksheets Given On the Diskette? A diskette containing files of all the worksheets developed within this manual is included with it. However, if your objective is to learn to use Excel for solving statistical problems, you should follow the manual's instructions for developing the worksheets yourself. You will find this much more effective than just using worksheets developed by us. On the other hand, some of the worksheets require a considerable number of Excel operations to develop. Particular examples include the chi-square test of independence worksheet of Section 9.2 in Chapter 9 and the five quality control chart worksheets of Chapter 12. For such worksheets you may wish to forego the experience of developing them for the expedience of using those we have developed.

Will The Worksheets I Develop Always Look Like Those Shown In the Manual? As you work through the example analyses of this manual, you will develop your own Excel worksheets for performing the required computations and charting we demonstrate. Although your worksheets will generally resemble those given in the manual, you may detect differences. Some differences arise from additional editing and formatting which we have done in order to make the figures more understandable to the readers of this manual. In some instances we have enlarged charts and column widths, and others we have added borders to cells and used different font style such as italics or boldface. These sorts of cosmetic changes can be made by you but are not necessary for understanding the statistical analyses presented.

Acknowledgements

I need to thank a number of persons for bringing this project to completion. First, is Glen Garrett our ever faithful ITP Sales Representative at Murray State University for a number of years. I am grateful for Glen's friendship and service, and for suggesting me for a similar project which proceeded this one. Second, I would like to thank Ken Black of the University of Houston— Clear Lake for accepting me for that prior project. Also, for the suggestions he made for its improvement. Some of them are also included in this manual.

This manual has benefited from others that came before it. In particular, my friend Mike Middleton's *Data Analysis Using Microsoft Excel 5.0*, Kenneth N. Berk and Patrick Carey's *Data Analysis with Microsoft Excel 5.0 for Windows*, and John L. Neufeld's *Learning Business Statistics with Microsoft Excel*.

I would like to acknowledge the input from a number of "Business Stat" students at Murray State University. Their observations and recommendations in response to their use of the prior manual have been useful in a number of instances.

My thanks also goes to the project team at South-Western College Publishing under the direction of Acquisitions editor Charles McCormick, Jr. Their assistance has been helpful in the completion of this project.

Finally, your use of this manual may result in comments, criticisms and suggestions for improving it. I would greatly appreciate hearing of these from you.

David L. Eldredge
Dept. of Computer Science and Information Systems
Murray State University
P.O. Box 9
Murray, Kentucky 42071-0009

Dave.Eldredge@Murraystate.Edu

To my wife Judy, and to all my family for their love and support through the years.

CHAPTER 1. INTRODUCTION TO STATISTICS WITH EXCEL

The most powerful general-purpose managerial software available for data analysis in business and industry is spreadsheet software. Currently, the most widely used spreadsheet program is Microsoft Excel. Businesses and industries have used Excel throughout their organizations for their computational, charting and data management needs for years. Beyond these three uses, current versions of Excel include a number of features which provide the capability for easily conducting many statistical analyses. The purpose of this manual is to introduce you to these features which facilitate the computing and charting requirements of your study and use of statistics.

Versions of Excel are available for many types of computers under many operating systems. The Excel capabilities used in this manual are compatible with three versions: *Excel 7* and *Excel 8* (also called Excel 97) both under the Windows 95 operating system, and with *Excel 5* under the Windows 3.1 operating system (there wasn't an Excel 6). There are some differences between these three Excel versions. Our approach within this manual is to use Excel 7 and to draw your attention to any Excel 8 or Excel 5 differences which are important to our analyses. We will show these differences in the appropriate part of the manual within a boxed note. These boxes begin either with the words **Excel 8 Note** or **Excel 5 Note**.

We begin below in **Section 1.1** with a brief overview of some WINDOWS features for those persons who are unfamiliar with Windows. In **Section 1.2** we introduce EXCEL and provide some initial instruction in its use for those who are unfamiliar with it. These first two sections are not meant to be a complete guide to either Windows or Excel. They merely present enough material to get you started. To become proficient you will need to refer to other books and resources. One of these further resources can be the extensive on-line HELP SYSTEM provided by Excel. An introduction to it is presented in **Section 1.3**. This is followed in **Section 1.4** by an introduction to the features of Excel which we use in this manual to facilitate statistical analyses. These include DATA ANALYSIS TOOLS, STATISTICAL FUNCTIONS, the CHART WIZARD, the TRENDLINE feature for charts and the PIVOT TABLE WIZARD. We continue in **Section 1.5** with a presentation of a number of worksheet practices which will help to make your statistical worksheets more effective for you and any others who might use them. Finally, **Section 1.6** discusses the use of this manual as a companion to your study of a business statistics textbook.

1.1 USING WINDOWS

The first thing you need to know about Windows is how to start (or launch) the software. For most computer systems, Windows will start automatically when you turn on the computer and the computer monitor. If the system you are using is set up differently you may have to start Windows from the DOS prompt (such as *C:\>*). If your system displays the DOS prompt, you should use the keyboard to type **Win** and then press the **Enter** key on the keyboard. The result should be the Windows screen called the Windows desktop.

Excel under both the Windows 95 and Windows 3.1 operating systems is designed to be used with a computer mouse. The movements of the mouse in your hand causes the movement of a mouse pointer on the computer screen. The five mouse techniques you will be using to communicate with Excel are the following.

- **Point**—moving the mouse until the pointer is touching the element on the computer screen which you wish to select
- **Click**—quickly pressing and releasing the **left** mouse button
- **Double Click**—quickly pressing and releasing the **left** mouse button twice in rapid succession
- **Drag**—pressing and holding down the **left** mouse button while you move the mouse
- **Right Click**—quickly pressing and releasing the **right** mouse button once

After you have started Windows and understand the operation of the mouse, you are ready to start (or launch) Excel. In later chapters we will refer to the these steps as the **Start-Up Procedure.** The steps for the Start-Up Procedure depend on whether you are using Windows 95 or Windows 3.1.

START-UP PROCEDURE—WINDOWS 95

1. Point and click the **Start** button in the lower left corner of your Windows screen. The *Windows 95 menu* will open.
2. Point to **Programs** on the menu and a second nested menu will appear to the right of the Windows 95 menu.
3. Point to **Office 95** (or **Office 97** for Excel 8) on the menu and a third menu will appear to the right. (this step may not be necessary for your computer system).
4. Point and click the selection **Microsoft Excel** and the Excel window will appear.

START-UP PROCEDURE—WINDOWS 3.1

1. Start with the screen that is labeled **Program Manager** at the top.
2. Point and double click the selection **Microsoft Office** and a new window will open (this step may not be necessary for your computer system).
3. Point and double click the selection **Microsoft Excel** and the Excel window will appear.

Your resulting Excel window should be similar to that shown in Figure 1.1. If your window fills only a portion of the screen, you should change it to a full-screen presentation. To accomplish this click on the **Maximize Button** which is in the very top row called the Title Bar. It is the second button on the right for Windows 95 (see Figure 1.1) and is the first button on the right for Windows 3.1.

Although your window should generally resemble that of Figure 1.1, some of the details may differ. There are two primary reasons for these small differences. First, Excel allows modifications to be made to the appearance of its window. Second, there are some differences among the three versions of Excel. Figure 1.1 is for Excel 7.

Figure 1.1 Excel Window

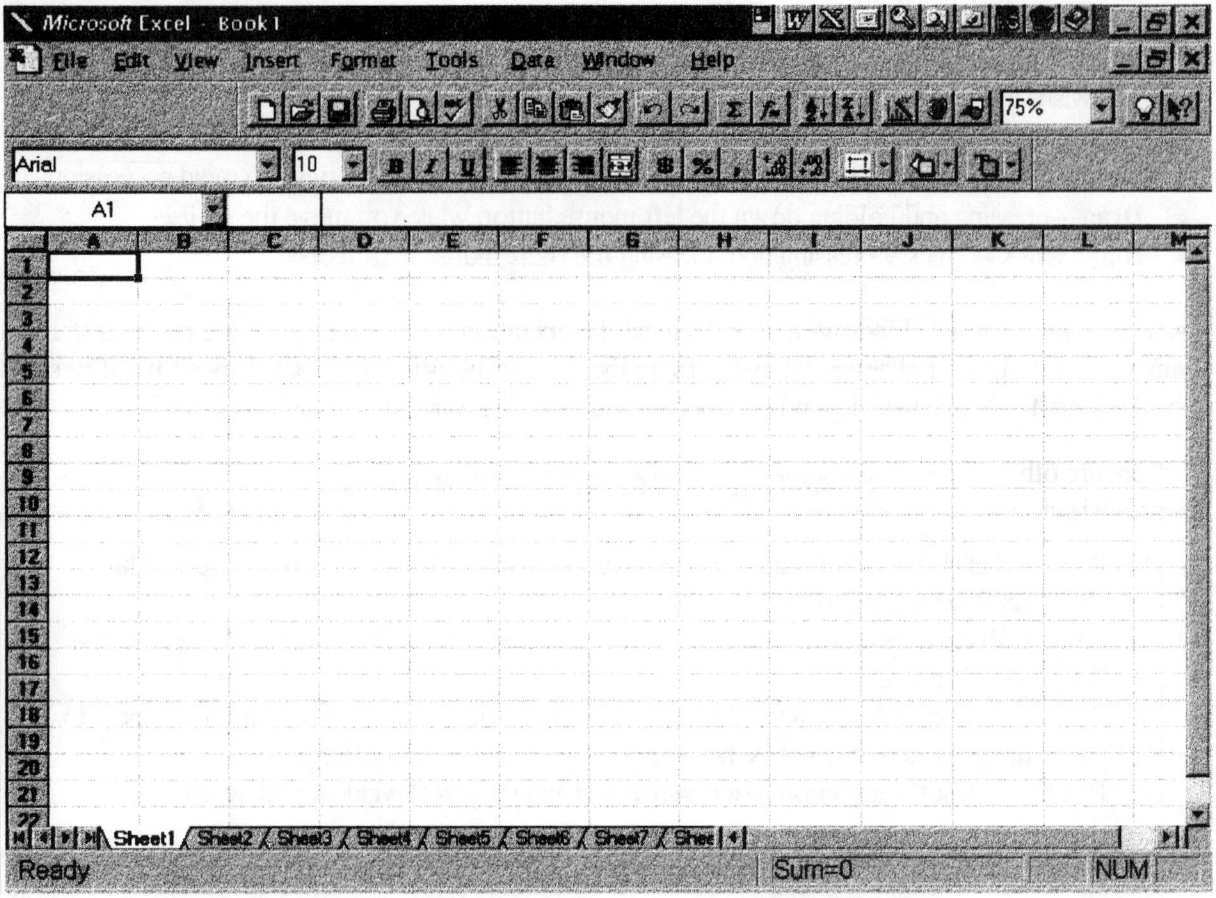

1.2 USING EXCEL

We will introduce Excel by discussing three major topics within this section. They include first a description of the parts which make up the Excel window. Next we will discuss the use of dialog boxes for communicating with Excel and last how to perform a number of Excel basic tasks.

1.2.1 The Excel Window

If this is your first look at an Excel window such as Figure 1.1, you may feel a sense of panic! How can you ever come to grasp the use of such a complex appearing presentation?

Three thoughts may help you overcome your feeling of panic. First, Excel has many capabilities which you will never need to use. Second, it has more than one way to complete most actions. Consequently, it is not necessary for you to know everything about Excel in order to make effective use of it. Third, the window is organized into lines starting at the top with a line labeled as *Microsoft Excel—Book1* on the left side. Our consideration of the window is simplified by starting at the top and considering the important aspects of each line one at a time.

The top line of the Excel window is called the **Title Bar.** The *Microsoft Excel* label refers to the computer software program being used and the label *Book1* is the default name for what Excel calls a *Workbook.* An Excel workbook is made up of one or more *Worksheets.* Each worksheet may be used to represent data and descriptive text, to perform computations and to display charts. A worksheet is divided into *columns* which are labeled as *A, B, C* and so on, and into the *rows* which are labeled as *1, 2, 3* and so on. The intersection of a row and a column forms a *cell* in which you can enter values, text, formulas or functions (special predefined formulas). The first of these worksheets within the *Book1* workbook is displayed in Figure 1.1. Additional worksheets are accessed by pointing and clicking on the tabs labeled **Sheet1**, **Sheet2** and so on at the bottom of the worksheet.

There are other names you may hear used when someone is referring to a workbook. These include spreadsheet, file and worksheet. However, the term *Spreadsheet* actually refers to the category of software which includes Excel, *File* refers to the workbook as saved on your computer's hard disk drive or on a diskette, and *Worksheet* is an element of an Excel workbook.

As you view the title bar of the Excel window note it includes the previously mentioned **Maximize Button.** In addition it includes the button for closing Excel. The **Close Button** is the first button on the right for Windows 95 and the first button on the left for Windows 3.1 (called the **Control Menu Box** for Windows 3.1).

The second line down in the Excel window is called the **Menu Bar.** It provides nine different menus usually starting on the left with the selection **File** and ending on the right with **Help.** Excel commands are organized into nine pull-down menus. You pull down (or open) a menu by pointing and clicking on a name on the menu bar. After you open a pull-down menu, you point and click to choose a command from the list of commands presented on it. We will be using items from the menu bar many times in the chapters to come. In addition to the nine menu selections, the menu bar includes buttons for maximizing and closing the Book1 workbook window. These are in addition to the buttons on the title bar for maximizing and closing the Excel program itself.

Excel includes thirteen (for Excel 5 and 7) or more (for Excel 8) of what it calls toolbars. Each toolbar includes buttons identified with icons (pictures) representing commands, and also boxes which list available options . The toolbars allow you to select frequently used commands and options more quickly than you can by using the menus. The third and fourth lines of Figure 1.1 show the two toolbars which are most frequently used and most frequently displayed in the Excel window. The first is the **Standard Toolbar** and the second is the **Formatting Toolbar.** To determine the purpose of each element of a tool bar, point to the icon or list box. A small descriptor of one or so words will appear below the toolbar element. These are called *ToolTips.* In addition to the short ToolTip descriptors, the very last line of the Excel window (labeled with the word *Ready* in Figure 1.1) displays an additional description of the purpose of the toolbar element. To select a command, point and click on the appropriate toolbar icon. To select an option from a toolbar list box, point and click on the down-pointing arrow on the right side of the box. A drop-down list will appear with the possible options. An option is selected by pointing and clicking on it.

The fifth line from the top in Figure 1.1 provides two pieces of information about the cell within the worksheet which is said to be the **Active Cell (or Cell Pointer)**. The active cell is that which is ready to have its contents either entered or modified. It is identified on the worksheet with a heavy border around it. In Figure 1.1 you will note that the active cell is cell A1. If you point and click on another cell in the worksheet, the active cell will change to the cell you clicked. The area on the right of the fifth line is called the **Formula Bar.** It shows the contents of the active cell and can be used for entering or editing the contents of the cell. To the left of the formula bar is the **Name Box**. It displays the cell address for the active cell.

Below the name box and formula bar is the active worksheet window. As previously mentioned, the worksheet window consists of rows and columns whose intersection define cells. The column letters above the cells and row numbers to the left of the cells provide an address (or name) for each cell. This row of letters starting with *A* and ending with *M* in Figure 1.1 and column of numbers starting with *1* and ending with *22* are called the **Worksheet Frame.** Directly below the worksheet on the left are the **Sheet Tabs.** As mentioned above, additional worksheets within the workbook are made active by pointing and clicking on the tabs labeled as **Sheet1**, **Sheet2** and so on.

Your worksheet may include more rows and/or columns than are displayed on the screen. In fact, the Excel worksheet can include up to 256 columns labeled as A though Z, then AA through AZ, BA through BZ and so on through to IV (eye-vee). In addition, it can have 16,384 rows (Excel 8 allows 65,536 rows) labeled 1 though 16,384. You will note that Figure 1.1 displays only columns A though M and rows 1 through 22. Your computer screen may display more or less columns and rows. The number shown depends on a number of considerations such as your version of Excel, the size of your monitor, the size of the window, the toolbars displayed and so on.

In order to display different areas of the active worksheet, the Excel window provides two scroll bars. The first is on the very right side of the worksheet itself. It is called the **Vertical Scroll Bar** and can be identified by the upward pointing arrow at its very top (to the right of the worksheet frame) and a downward pointed arrow at its very bottom. In order to view a lower part of the active worksheet, move the mouse pointer to the bottom arrow on the vertical scroll bar. Press and hold down the left mouse button. While you are performing this operation note that the row identifiers on the left of the worksheet are increased. A similar procedure using the top arrow on the vertical scroll bar will reverse the process.

The window also includes a **Horizontal Scroll Bar.** It is shown on the right in the row displaying the sheet tabs. The right pointing arrow at the right of the scroll bar can be used to scroll to right of the active worksheet. The left pointing arrow at the left of the scroll bar can be used to scroll back to the left.

The line below that displaying the sheet tabs and horizontal scroll bar displays the **Status Bar.** It includes three elements. The **Mode Indicator** on the left of the status bar indicates what Excel is prepared to do next and also provides prompts, explanations and guidance. To the right of the mode indicator is the **AutoCalculate Button** (not available in Excel 5). It provides the capability to obtain a quick sum of selected cells. Five other functions are available by right clicking in the AutoCalculate area. Finally, the right side of the status bar provides **Key Indicators** which show the status of some keys. For example, Figure 1.1 shows the *NUM (Num Lock)* key is engaged which means you can use the numeric keypad to enter numbers.

This completes our review of the elements of the Excel window. As you have explored these elements, you may have noted that the mouse pointer changes shape when it is moved from one part of the window to another. When the mouse pointer is within the worksheet, its shape is a block plus sign. When the pointer is over an icon, sheet tab or scroll bar, its shape is an upward pointing block arrow. When it is over the formula bar, its shape is an I-beam and so on. The mouse pointer can take on over a dozen different shapes. Generally the shape of the pointer indicates what action is to be taken by you.

1.2.2 Excel Dialog Boxes

Dialog boxes are displayed in the Excel window so you can enter information required by an Excel command. You may have noticed when you select a pull-down menu from the menu bar, the name of some of the commands on the menu are followed by ellipsis (...). These indicate that the command requires you to enter information through a dialog box. In addition, some of the commands accessed through toolbars will present a dialog box for obtaining additional information. Figure 1.2 presents an example Excel dialog box. If you wish to view this specific dialog box on your computer screen, click **Tools** from the menu bar and **Options** from the subsequent pull-down menu.

Like the Excel window, a dialog box may seem complex to you at first. However, Excel dialog boxes are all made up of a standard set of elements (or controls). In fact, the Windows program itself and all programs designed to be used with Windows are made up of these same standard elements. We have listed the eight standard elements in Table 1.1. The figure also gives a brief description and identifies example elements in Figure 1.2.

In our analysis procedures throughout this manual we will use these eight names to tell you how to respond to various dialog boxes. Accordingly, you may wish to refer back to Table 1.1 as you work through this manual. Perhaps a photocopy of this table for future reference would be helpful to you. At this point, see if you can locate on Figure 1.2 the examples listed in the right column of Table 1.1 .

Sometimes a dialog box will cover something you want to see on the screen. You can move it by pointing to the colored (usually green) title bar (labeled as Options in Figure 1.2) at the top of the box and dragging it with the mouse to a new position on the screen.

Figure 1.2 Elements of Dialog Boxes

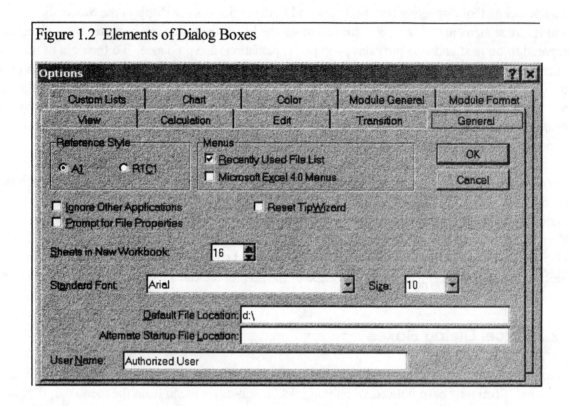

Excel 8 Note: Many dialog boxes include a *Collapse Dialog Box* button.   It has an upward pointing arrow and is located on the right side of text boxes. If you click it, the dialog box is collapsed and only the text box is displayed on top of the column headings. The required data can be entered into the text box by keying or dragging. Click the button with a downward pointing arrow on the right side of the text box and the original dialog box will be restored.

The dialog boxes for complex operations are presented as Wizards. A **Wizard** is a sequence of dialog boxes which simplifies the operation by guiding you through the process step by step. The title bar for each dialog box in the series designates it as *Step X of N*. The dialog box for each step asks you to enter information through the use of the dialog box elements of Table 1.1. Generally, Wizard dialog boxes include a command button labeled **Back** to go back one step and make revisions. Another command button is labeled **Next** which steps forward to the next step. Other are labeled **Help, Cancel, and Finish**. The Wizards you may use with this manual include the ANSWER WIZARD, the CHART WIZARD, the FUNCTION WIZARD and the PIVOT TABLE WIZARD.

Table 1.1 Dialog Box Elements

Element	DESCRIPTION	FIGURE 1.2 EXAMPLES
Tab	A button which resembles a file folder tab at the top of a dialog box. Clicking a tab switches to and displays a different page in the dialog box.	Ten **tabs** beginning with *View* and ending with *Module Format*
Text Box	A data entry area for text or numbers. Move the mouse pointer to the text box and it changes to the I-beam shape. Click and type the appropriate entry.	**Text Box** labeled as *User Name* with the entry *Authorized User*
List Box	A scrolling list of specified choices. Click on the up or down arrow on the right side of the list to scroll through it. Then click on your choice. The selected item appears in highlighted text.	Figure 1.2 does not include. Click on *Module Format* tab. Its dialog box includes a **list box** labeled *Code Colors*.
Drop-Down List Box	A list box which does not display its scrolling list until you click on the down arrow on the right side of its displayed text box. Click on your choice. The selected item appears in the text box above the list.	**Drop-down list box** labeled as *Size* with the entry *10*.
Command Button	A large rectangular button that executes or cancels a dialog box. In addition, some command buttons have ellipsis which indicate it will open an additional dialog box.	**Command buttons** labeled as *OK* and *Cancel*
Check Box	A square box for selecting an option. A check mark in a check box indicates the option is selected. Click on the check box to select or deselect the option. You can select more than one check box.	**Check boxes** under the label *Menus*. The check box labeled as *Recently Use File List* is selected and *Microsoft Excel 4.0 Menus* is not.
Option Button	A round button for selecting an option (also called a radio button). A dark circle in an option button indicates the option is selected. Click on the option button to select the option. To deselect an option, click on another option button. You can only select one option from a group of options.	**Option buttons** are under the label *Reference Style*. Of the two possible options *A1* is selected so *R1C1* is not.
Spinner	A box displaying a number with an up and a down arrow to the right of the box. Click on the arrows to make changes in the number by increments of one.	**Spinner** is labeled as *Sheets in New Workbook* and its current value is *16*

1.2.3 Excel Basic Tasks

Now that you have some familiarity with the Excel Window and with the use of dialog boxes, we will consider a number of basic Excel tasks. You will need to use all of these during the development of your worksheets for performing statistical analyses in this manual. Most of these tasks can be done in more than one way. Generally, we will take the approach of using the simplest way. For example, saving a workbook by clicking the **Save** icon instead of clicking **File** on the menu bar and then **Save** on the subsequent pull-down menu.

To begin you should go through the appropriate **Start-up Procedure** of Section 1.1. The result will be a blank worksheet similar to Figure 1.1. You are now ready to perform the following tasks.

1. **Moving Around a Worksheet.** Before entering or modifying the contents of a particular cell, you need to make that cell the *Active Cell (the Cell Pointer)*. You can select the cell to be active with either the mouse or the keyboard. To use the mouse point and click on the cell. Use the mouse to make cell B1 the active cell.

   If the cell is not currently displayed on the screen, the vertical and horizontal scroll bars can be used to display the area containing the cell, and then the mouse used to point and click. Now make cell M30 the active cell.

   In addition to the mouse, Excel allows the use of the keyboard to move around a worksheet. The most frequently used keys are (1) the four **arrow** keys which move one cell up, down, left or right, (2) the **Page Up (PgUp)** and **Page Down (PgDn)** keys which move up or down one full screen, (3) the **Home** key which moves to column A of the current row, and (4) the **Crtl** key and **Home** key pushed simultaneously which moves to cell A1. You should now try all four of these sets of keys for moving around the worksheet.

2. **Entering Text (Labels).** As previously mentioned, you may enter values, text, formulas and functions (predefined formulas) in each cell of a worksheet. Although text may be used as data, usually it is used to label or describe the data in a worksheet as we do here. Make cell B1 the active cell and use the keyboard to enter the worksheet title: **CHAPTER ONE WORKSHEET**. Press the down arrow to make cell B2 the active cell and key in **Your Name**. Select cell A3 by using the arrow keys or the mouse pointer. Key in **Today's Date**. Select cell D3 and enter a file name to use for saving the workbook, say, **FILE-ONE.xls**. Select cell A5 and key in the label **Numbers**. Your results should appear as shown in Figure 1.3.

3. **Entering Values (Numbers).** Values or numbers are the major entries in most worksheets. Select cell A6, key the number **1** and use the down arrow (or press the **Enter** key) to move the cell pointer to cell A7. Key the number **2** and move to cell A8. Continue down the column until you have entered the number **5**.

Figure 1.3 File-One Worksheet

	A	B	C	D	E	F
1		CHAPTER ONE WORKSHEET				
2		Your Name				
3	Today's Date			File: FILE-ONE.xls		
4						
5	NUMBERS			NUMBERS		
6	10			10		
7	2			2		
8	3			3		
9	4			4		
10	5			5		
11						
12	24			24		
13						

4. **Entering Formulas.**   Formulas provide the true power of spreadsheet software such as Excel. To demonstrate, select cell A12. Use the keyboard to enter **=A6+A7+A8+A9+A10** and press **Enter**. The value shown in A12 is 15, the sum of the values in cells A6 through A10. Change the value in A6 to **10** and notice A12 displays the new total. Select cell A12 again and notice that your equation is displayed in the formula bar. Formulas use the common mathematical symbols of + for addition, - for subtraction, * for multiplication, / for division and ^ for raising to a power.

5. **Copying Cell Contents.** You can copy text, values, formulas and functions from one cell to another, and from one worksheet to another. You can copy the contents of one cell at a time or the contents of a group of cells at one time. Click on cell A5 and drag through cell A10. Notice the range of cells are highlighted. Next click on the **Copy** icon (it looks like two sheets of paper with the top right corner turned down and is usually the eighth icon from the left on the standard toolbar—see Figure 1.1). This copies the contents of the selected cells to an Excel feature called the **Clip Board**. Next click on cell D5. Finally click on the **Paste** icon (it looks like a clip board and a sheet of paper and is usually the ninth icon from the left on the standard toolbar—see Figure 1.1). This copies the contents of the clip board to cells D5 through D10. Now repeat this process to copy the formula in cell A12 to cell D12. Now notice the contents of D12 as shown in the *formula bar*. The formula was copied but the cells in the formula were changed from A6 through A10 to D6 through D10. This is the result of a feature called **relative addressing** for cells which will be useful in future chapters. Another form of addressing called **absolute addressing** will be discussed later in this manual.

6. **Saving a Workbook.** Put a diskette in the disk drive which is appropriate for your computer system. For this discussion, we will assume it is drive A. Point and click on the **Save** icon (it looks like a diskette and usually is the third icon from the left on the standard toolbar—see Figure 1.1). A dialog box entitled *Save As* will appear. You must complete two actions. First click on the

arrow to the right of the drop-down list box labeled *Save in,* and click on the **3½ Floppy (A:).** Second, click in the far left of the text box labeled *File Name.* Use the **Delete** key to eliminate the default file name given and then key your file name, **FILE-ONE** (Excel will add the extension or suffix *.xls*). Finally, click on the **Save** command button. The light on the A drive should come on briefly as your file is saved to the diskette in that drive.

7. **Closing a Workbook.** For Windows 95 click the **Close button** (first button on the right of the *menu bar*) or for Windows 3.1 double click the **Control menu box** (first button on the left of the *menu bar*). Alternatively for both Windows 95 and 3.1, you can click **File** on the menu bar and then **Close** from the subsequent pull-down menu. The result will be that the menu bar, the toolbars and so on will continue to be shown on the screen but the worksheet will be deleted from the screen. If you had not saved the workbook just before you tried to close it, a dialog box would have opened reminding you to save your workbook. If you wished to now work on a new workbook, you would click the **New Workbook** icon (it looks like a single piece of paper with its upper right corner turned down and is usually the first icon from the left on the standard toolbar).

8. **Retrieving a Workbook.** The above steps have had you create a worksheet, save it to a diskette and than erase it from the computer's memory. We now will read it back into the memory from the diskette file. Click on the **Open** icon (it looks like an open file folder and is usually the second icon from the left on the standard toolbar). In the resulting dialog box click on the arrow to right of the drop-down list box labeled as *Look in* and click on **3½ Floppy (A:).** A list of files will be displayed in a box under the *Look in* list box and one (perhaps the only one) should be *FILE-ONE.xls*. Click on **FILE-ONE.xls** and then on the **Open** command button. Your workbook will be loaded into the computer and its first worksheet will appear on the screen.

9. **Printing a Worksheet.** You also will want to print your worksheets. Click on the **Print** icon (it looks like a printer and is usually the fourth icon from the left on the standard toolbar). Your worksheet will be printed.

    You can improve the readability of your worksheet by including on your printout the worksheet frame (the row and column headings) and the worksheet gridlines. To select these two options before printing, click on **File** from the menu bar and click on **Page Setup** from the pull-down menu. The Page Setup dialog box which then appears has dialog tabs. Click on the **Sheet** tab. Use the mouse pointer to place a check in the **Gridlines** check box and the **Row and Column Headings** check box. Finish by clicking the **OK** command button. Now select the print icon to print these revised worksheet.

10. **Exiting Excel.** A three-step procedure is recommended for exiting Excel. First save the workbook again (number 6 above). Second, close the workbook (number 7). Third exit Excel. For **Windows 95** click the **Close button** (first button on the right of the *title bar*). For **Windows 3.1** double click the **Control Menu Box** (first button on the left of the *title bar*). Alternatively for both, you could click on **File** from the menu bar and then **Exit** from the subsequent pull-down

menu. The result will be a return to the Windows screen.

11. **Exiting Windows.** This operation also depends on the version of Windows you are using.

- **Windows 95**—click the **Start** button in the lower right corner of the window, click on **Shut Down** in the subsequent Windows 95 dialog box, select the option button labeled **Shut down the computer?** in the next dialog box and click on the **Yes** command button.

- **Windows 3.1**—double click the **Control Menu Box** on the upper left of the *Program Manager* title bar. Alternatively, single click the **Control Menu Box** and then on **Close** from the subsequent pull-down menu.

1.3 USING HELP

It is not possible for most persons (perhaps any person) to remember all the commands, menus, buttons, tools, functions and other details of using Excel. The developers of Excel have anticipated this problem and provide a number of on-line (available as you are using Excel) aids for helping your memory. We will discuss four of these.

The first of these is the previously mentioned **ToolTips**. These are displayed when you move the mouse pointer to an icon or button and do not press a mouse button for a second or two. A descriptor of one or more words will then be displayed near the icon or button. In addition, the very last line of the Excel window provides an additional description of the purpose of the toolbar element.

A second help device is the **Help button** which is usually on the very right of the standard toolbar. Its icon is a question mark and a upward pointing block arrow (see Figure 1.1). If you click on this button once, the mouse pointer will change to the shape of the icon shown on the help button. Move the mouse pointer to a button on a toolbar and click the left mouse button. A help window will open which explains in more detail the use of the toolbar button you selected. If you again click the mouse button, the help window will disappear. This help function is also available for items on the pull-down menus which are accessed from the menu bar. First click the Help button, then a selection on the menu bar and finally click the item on the pull-down menu. Click again to close the help window.

Excel 8 Note: The **Help button** icon has been replaced by an icon for the **Office Assistant** (a question mark within a yellow balloon). The Office Assistant is an animated graphic which can display on-line help for a specific task, search on-line help for specific topics and provide user tips.   On the other hand, the *Help button* for Excel 8 is accessed by selecting **Help** from the menu bar and than selecting **What's This?** from the pull-down menu.

The third help resource is the **Help system**. It can be accessed in two ways. First, you can double click the *Help button*. Second, you can click on **Help** on the menu bar, and then click on **Microsoft**

Excel Help Topics on the subsequent pull-down menu. The result will be a dialog box as shown in Figure 1.4.   The dialog box shows four tabs corresponding to the four available options of the help system. **Contents** displays a list of general topics and **Index** displays a comprehensive, alphabetical list of all help topics. **Find** allows you to search through all topics for a word or phrase. The fourth feature of the help system is the **Answer Wizard**. It provides you step-by-step prompts to assist your search for help.

Excel 8 Note: The content, index and find features of Figure 1.4 are accessed by selecting **Help** from the menu bar and **Contents and index** from the pull-down menu. The Answer Wizard feature is not present. Its function has been replaced by the Office Assistant discussed in the prior Excel 8 Note.

Excel 5 Note: Excel 5 does not include the Answer Wizard feature and the Find feature is called Search instead.

Figure 1.4 Excel Help System

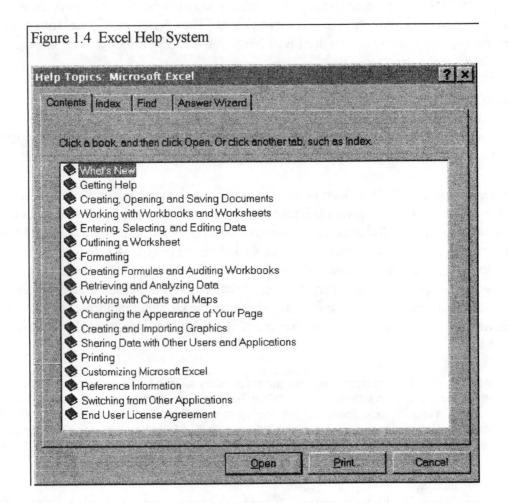

The fourth help resource we wish to mention is actually part of the Help system itself. It is the **Help for Lotus 1-2-3 users**. Some spreadsheet users are familiar with Lotus 1-2-3 but not familiar with Excel. To assist such persons, the developers of Excel allow you to enter Lotus 1-2-3 commands and functions, and obtain the equivalent for Excel. This system is accessed by clicking on **Help** on the menu bar. Next click on the selection **Lotus 1-2-3 help...** on the pull-down menu. The result will be a dialog box such as that shown in Figure 1.5. As you will note the dialog box provides instructions for its use.

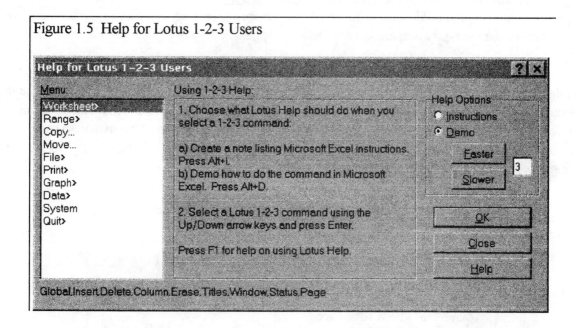

Figure 1.5 Help for Lotus 1-2-3 Users

1.4 USING EXCEL'S STATISTICAL ANALYSIS FEATURES

The developers of Excel have provided a number of features which facilitate the computation and charting requirements for statistical analyses. Primary among these are the DATA ANALYSIS TOOLS and the STATISTICAL FUNCTIONS which are used throughout this manual. Additional features which are used in the appropriate parts of this manual include the CHART WIZARD, the TRENDLINE feature for charts and the PIVOT TABLE WIZARD.

1.4.1 Data Analysis Tools

Excel includes 18 data analysis tools for statistics beginning with ANOVA: SINGLE-FACTOR and ending with z-TEST: TWO SAMPLES FOR MEANS. We demonstrate the use of all but one of these within the following chapters of this manual. In addition, Appendix A presents a complete listing and description of all 18 statistical analysis tools. Utilizing a question-and-answer format, Appendix A addresses the following questions.

1. What Are The Data Analysis Tools?
2. Where Can I Find The Data Analysis Tools?
3. Are The Data Analysis Tools Available On The Computer I Am Using?
4. How Do I Use The Data Analysis Tools?
5. For What Analyses Are The Data Analysis Tools Used?

To access the data analysis tools, you should click on **Tools** on the menu bar and click on **Data Analysis** on the subsequent pull-down menu. The result will be the dialog box shown in Figure 1.6. It may happen that the pull-down menu for the computer you are using does not include the entry Data Analysis. If so, you will need to do some preparation before accessing the Data Analysis dialog box. The details of the necessary preparation are found in Appendix A under *Question 3* in the above list.

From the dialog box of Figure 1.6, you click on the tool you wish to use. If the one you wish to use is not displayed in the list box, you click on the vertical scroll bar arrow to scroll to it. After you have selected the tool you wish to use, click the **OK** button. The result will be a second dialog box allowing you to enter the specific ranges and values for your data analysis problem. You may wish to try selecting a tool and viewing its dialog box. For example, refer to Figure 2.3 in Chapter 2 to see the dialog box for the HISTOGRAM data analysis tool.

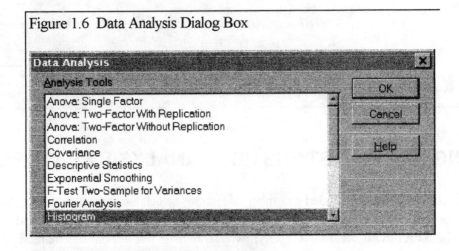

Figure 1.6 Data Analysis Dialog Box

The discussion in Appendix A of *Question 5* in the above list gives a short description of the use of each of the statistical tools. In addition, it classifies the tools into six categories beginning with *Descriptive Statistics* and ending with *Time Series Forecasting*. The chapter(s) within this manual which demonstrate each statistical tool is(are) also noted.

You may wish to explore the purpose and use of some of these tools at this time through the Help System. First, select the analysis tool of interest from the Data Analysis dialog box (Figure 1.6). Then in the subsequent dialog box click on the **Help** command button.

1.4.2 Statistical Functions

There are hundreds of built-in functions (predefined formulas) in Excel. Seventy-one (80 for Excel 8) are classified as **Statistical** beginning with **AVEDEV** and ending with **ZTEST**. We use many of these within this manual. In addition, Appendix B presents a complete listing and description of all the statistical functions. Again we use a question-and-answer format and address the following.

1. What Are The Statistical Functions?
2. How Do The Statistical Functions And The Data Analysis Tools Differ?
3. How Do I Use The Statistical Functions?
4. For What Analyses Are The Statistical Functions Used?

The Statistical Functions both supplement and duplicate the analysis capabilities of the Data Analysis Tools. However there are a number of differences which are presented in the discussion in Appendix B of *Question 2* of above list. The primary difference is that the results from the Tools usually are numbers and the results from the Functions are formulas.

Access to the statistical functions is facilitated by the FUNCTION WIZARD. It has an icon on the standard toolbar labeled with the symbol *fx*. Click on the icon and the dialog box of Figure 1.7 will be displayed. Next click on the category of **Statistical** in the list box on the left. As a result the right list box will present the 71 (80 for Excel 8) statistical functions. You can scroll through the list to find the function you wish to use. Next click on the function you wish to use and a second dialog box will be shown. For example, refer to Figure 3.8 of Chapter 3 to see the dialog box for the function VARP which computes the population variance.

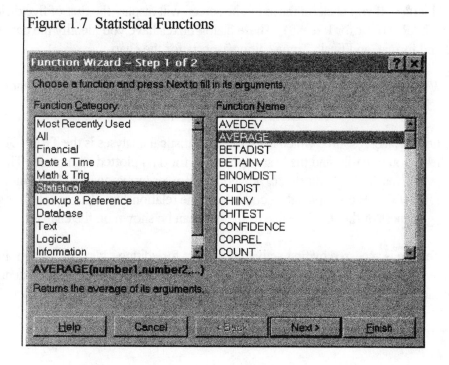

Figure 1.7 Statistical Functions

The discussion in Appendix B of *Question 4* in the above list gives a short description of the use of each of the statistical functions. In addition, we have classified the functions into fifteen categories beginning with *Descriptive Statistics—Measures of Central Location* and ending with *Regression and Correlation—Exponential Regression Analysis.*

You will note in Figure 1.7 that a brief description of the function which is highlighted in the right list is given below the list on the left. Much greater detail about the selected function can be obtained by clicking on the **Help** button in the lower left corner of the dialog box. You may wish to explore this facility for one or more functions of interest to you.

1.4.3 Other Statistical Features

Graphs and charts are effective in summarizing and visually presenting statistical data. Excel's CHART WIZARD makes the development of graphs and charts somewhat easy. It provides 15 chart types (see Figure 2.8 of Chapter 2). Nine of them are two-dimensional and six are three-dimensional charts. In addition, each chart type has from four to ten different presentation formats.

> **Excel 8 Note:** The CHART WIZARD has been changed considerably. Although the wizard lists only 14 types of charts, it actually includes all 15 Excel 7 types plus six additional. The Excel 7 three-dimensional types are listed as chart *sub-types* for Excel 8. Also, the Excel 7 combination chart is listed as a *custom type* in Excel 8. Each of the 14 Excel 8 types has from two to seven different sub-types (presentation formats in Excel 7). Refer to Appendix C for further details of the chart wizard for Excel 8.

The CHART WIZARD is accessed through the standard toolbar. It has an icon depicting a small bar/column chart with a magic wand above it (no wand in Excel 8). It is usually just to the left of the icon of a world globe. If you click on the icon, the screen will display the first of five dialog boxes of the CHART WIZARD (four for Excel 8). These dialog boxes have you identify the data to be charted, the chart type and format, and finally some editing aspects for the chart.

The CHART WIZARD is presented in detail in Section 2.2 of the next chapter (Appendix C for Excel 8). In addition, it is used in Chapters 4, 10, 11 and 12.

A second additional Excel resource which is useful for statistical analyses is the TRENDLINE feature for charts. It helps you to easily find the best relationship for data plotted on a chart. The relationship can be one of five forms: linear, logarithmic, polynomial, power or exponential (see Figure 10.5 of Chapter 10). TRENDLINE computes the equation for the relationship. The equation together with a measure of the goodness of the fit of the line to the data can be shown on the chart.

The Trendline feature is accessed by first activating a chart for editing. Next the data points within the chart are selected for editing and **Trendline** is selected from the **Insert** menu on the menu bar. The specific procedural instructions are presented in Section 10.1 of Chapter 10. In addition, Trendline is used in Chapter 11.

Excel 8 Note: TRENDLINE is accessed from **Chart** on the menu bar. Select **Add Trendline** from the menu.

The third additional Excel feature for statistical analysis we use within this manual is the PIVOT TABLE WIZARD. A pivot table is a summary of a list of data. The PIVOT TABLE WIZARD is a series of four dialog boxes in which you identify the list of data, the structure of the pivot table and the format for the output. The summary presented can be data sums, counts, averages, maximums, minimums, standard deviations and so on. We demonstrate the PIVOT TABLE WIZARD in Section 9.3 of Chapter 9 to compute frequency count of data for qualitative variables.

1.5 USING GOOD WORKSHEET PRACTICES

The process of developing and maintaining an effective worksheet involves the activities of planning, building, testing and protecting .

Planning for the development of a worksheet requires that you take some time considering the worksheet before you sit down at the computer. You need to decide

1. What the purpose of worksheet is,
2. What the inputs are,
3. What the outputs are to be, and
4. What the intermediate computational, charting and data management requirements are.

Once you have identified these major elements of the worksheet, you should make a rough sketch of the layout of all these elements. An effective worksheet will usually have separate areas for different uses, and will have a vertical layout as opposed to horizontal. For example, the worksheet can begin with identification material, and below it might be an area which contains all the input data. The area devoted to computations might be below the input data and the final results below the computations. This order of identification material, followed by input, followed by computations and then by outputs might be reordered to meet the specific requirements for some your worksheets.

As you get into actually building the worksheet you may have to revise parts of this initial plan. The plan provides a starting place for building the worksheet.

Building the worksheet involves entering textual material (labels), values (numbers), formulas, functions, and charts. For your worksheet to be effective, you need to make sure it is understandable to you and to any others who have need to look at it. To accomplish this consider the following guidelines.

- Begin the worksheet with suitable **Identification Material**—(1) a title or short description of the worksheet, (2) your name, (3) the date and (4) the file name for saving the worksheet.
- Use labels to identify all inputs, intermediate results and final outputs.
- Use currency, comma and integer (whole numbers) format wherever appropriate.
- Use uppercase and lower case letters as you would in a written report.
- Use bold, italics and underlining where appropriate for emphasis.
- Generally put data in columns if it is appropriate.
- Use consistent alignment and formatting.
- Write clear formulas by perhaps dividing complicated computations into more than one cell.
- Add a Cell Notes to cells which need further explanations. (Click on **Insert** on the menu bar, click on **Note**, type your note and click on **OK**. The note will be displayed when the cell is active. It also can be printed.)
- Enlarge charts above the default size.
- Use the on-line help system to answer questions that might arise.

Testing the worksheet involves using input data for which the output values are known. These known output values are then compared to the worksheet output to determine if the formulas are correct. The test input values can be actual values for which the results are known or can be values for which the results can easily be calculated by hand. If the worksheet has optional computation procedures, all the possible options should be tested. Without a verification of your worksheet, you cannot be assured it is without errors.

Protecting your worksheet from hardware and software failures should begin as you are building the worksheet and continue through out its use. Protecting your investment of time and mental energy involves.

- Saving your worksheet to a diskette frequently as you are building it and after it is completed.
- Keeping a backup copy of your worksheet file on a second diskette separate from the first one.
- Keeping a printout of the worksheet .
- Keeping a second printout of the worksheet showing the formulas, the row and column headings and cell notes. (To display the formulas on the screen, click on **Tools** on the menu bar, click on **Options** and click on the **View** tab. Select the **Formula** check box and click on **OK**. Next to prepare for printing, click on **File, Page Setup, and Sheet**. On the Sheet dialog box check **Gridlines, Notes,** and **Row and Column Headings.** Then print the worksheet.)
- Not giving anyone (including your professor) your only diskette with your worksheet file.

It is safe to say that almost everyone will experience some problem which can be reduced by adhering to the above guidelines.

1.6 USING THIS MANUAL WITH YOUR TEXTBOOK

As stated in the first paragraph of this chapter, *The purpose of this manual is to introduce you to the (Excel) features which facilitate the computing and charting requirements of your study and use of statistics.* The built-in capabilities of Excel allow you to easily computerize many of the methods in the textbook you are studying.

This manual has been designed to be used as a companion to many business statistics textbooks. This is possible because there is a consistency in the organization and flow of most, although not all, of the material presented in business textbooks. The typical business statistics textbook will have the following organization.

1. A chapter or two of **introduction** covering the importance of statistics, some basic definitions, the types of data and sources of data.

2. One, two or three chapter presentation of **descriptive statistics** covering graphical and numerical methods.

3. One, two or three chapter presentation of **probability and probability distributions** both discrete and continuous.

4. A chapter or part of a chapter presentation of **sampling distributions**.

5. Three or so chapters covering **statistical inference** (estimation and testing) for means, proportions and variances for the one population and the two population situations.

6. A chapter on the **analysis of variance**.

7. One, two or three chapters on **regression analysis**.

8. A chapter or more on **time series forecasting** sometimes including a presentation of index numbers.

9. Perhaps a chapter on **nonparametric statistics**.

10. Perhaps a chapter on **decision analysis**.

In addition to these topics, a typical textbook may have a chapter on the uses of the **chi-square statistic** and another chapter on **statistical quality control**. The placement of these two chapters in the above sequence is not as consistent among textbooks.

If you open your textbook to the *Contents* listing at the front, you may notice your textbook adheres to the above sequence of topics to a large degree.

This manual also follows the above sequence. However, we did have some decisions to make with regard to the coverage of statistical inference for the one and two population situations (number 5 in the above list). Some textbooks cover point estimates and confidence intervals separate from hypothesis testing. Others lump them together. Some cover the statistical inference of means with that for variances. Others put the statistical inference for proportions with means. Some cover the one population and two population situations together, others do not. Our approach is to present these topics modularly so the manual can be used with any of these different textbook organizations.

We present one chapter for the statistical inference of means, one for proportions and one for variances. Within each of these three chapters the one population and two population situations are covered in separate sections. Each section has subsections for point estimates with confidence intervals and for hypothesis testing. Accordingly, you should be able to easily identify the part of this manual which matches up with topics in your textbook by referring to the *Contents* listing at the beginning of this manual.

We also had decisions to make for the placement of the chi-square chapter. We have elected to place the chi-square chapter after the chapters dealing primarily with single variable statistical analysis (through Chapter 8) and before those dealing with two or more variable statistical analysis. We do so since the chi-square chapter begins with single variable analysis and ends with two variable analysis.

Finally, the quality control chapter was tacked on the end. We did so since this seemed to be the most popular location for the textbooks we reviewed.

The resulting sequence of chapters for this manual is given in Table 1.2.

Since our intent is that this manual is to be used in conjunction with a statistics textbook, we have not included end-of-the-chapter exercises. Once you have worked your way through a topic within this manual, you should be able to apply Excel to similar exercises given in your textbook.

As you work through the example analyses of this manual, you will develop your own Excel worksheets for performing the required computations and charting we demonstrate. Although your worksheets will generally resemble those given in the manual, you may detect some small differences. The differences arise from additional editing and formatting which we have done in order to make the figures more understandable to the readers of this manual. In some instances we have enlarged charts and column widths, and others we have added borders to cells and used different font style such as italics or boldface. These sorts of cosmetic changes can be made by you but are not necessary for understanding the statistical analyses presented.

Table 1.2 Sequence of Topics for An Excel Companion for Business Statistics	
CHAPTER	TOPICS
1	Introduction to the use of Excel for statistical analysis
2	Graphical descriptive statistics
3	Numerical descriptive statistics
4	Discrete and continuous probability distributions, and sampling distributions
5	Statistical inference for means for one and two populations
6	Statistical inference for proportions for one and two populations
7	Statistical inference for variances for one and two populations
8	Analysis of variance
9	Chi-square statistic applications
10	Regression analysis
11	Time series forecasting
12	Quality control charts

CHAPTER 2. DESCRIPTIVE GRAPHS AND CHARTS

2.1 The HISTOGRAM Analysis Tool
    2.1.1 Frequency Distribution
    2.1.2 Histogram
    2.1.3 Ogive

2.2 The CHART WIZARD
    2.2.1 Frequency Polygon
    2.2.2 Bar/Column Chart
    2.2.3 Pie Chart
    2.2.4 Scatter Diagram

Descriptive graphs and charts are easily developed using two Excel features. The first is the HISTOGRAM Analysis Tool presented in **Section 2.1**. This tool first computes a frequency distribution for a data set of one variable and then uses the frequency distribution to create a histogram and an ogive. The second Excel feature for graphs and charts is the CHART WIZARD presented in **Section 2.2**. It provides the capability to create many different chart types. In Section 2.2 we demonstrate its use for creating frequency polygons, bar/column charts and pie charts for single variable data sets. In addition, we demonstrate its use for creating a scatter diagram for data with two variable.

2.1 THE HISTOGRAM ANALYSIS TOOL ——————————

The HISTOGRAM tool has the capability to create (1) a frequency distribution, (2) a histogram, (3) an ogive (a cumulative relative frequency polygon) and (4) a histogram sorted in descending frequency order (called a Pareto Chart). To demonstrate the development of a frequency distribution, a histogram and an ogive consider the following example.

To earn money for school expenses, the three daughters in the Waspork family decided to open and run a stand selling shaved ice cones near the shopping mall in their home town of Markay. Their father, Bip, constructed the stand and their mother, Krit, purchased the needed equipment. The girls have now been in business for 50 days. The 50 values of Table 2.1 are the number of cones sold each day.

Table 2.1 Number of Cones Sold Each Day									
42	30	26	36	32	32	34	26	57	50
30	55	58	30	37	58	50	64	30	52
53	49	40	33	30	43	47	46	49	32
50	61	40	31	32	30	31	40	40	60
52	74	28	37	23	29	35	43	25	54

2.1.1 Frequency Distribution ——————————

The first step in developing a frequency distribution is to specify the classes (intervals) for the distribution. The specification of the classes includes (1) the number of classes , (2) the width of the classes and (3) the beginning value for the first class. In Excel the classes are called bins. If the bins are not specified, Excel will automatically set the number of bins approximately equal to the square root of the number of values in the data set. In addition it will set the width of each of the classes equal to the difference between the largest data value and smallest data value divided by the number of classes. Finally, the beginning value for the first class will be set equal to the lowest data value. The result is a quick look at the frequency distribution for the data set. However, it oftentimes is difficult to interpret.

Consequently, it is strongly suggested that you specify the classes/bins for your data set. Begin by selecting the number of classes/bins to be between 5 and 20. Then find the largest and the smallest values in the data set. The class width should be approximately equal to the difference between the largest and smallest values divided by the number of classes/bins. However the interpretation of the results will usually be made easier if the width is a multiple of two, five or ten.

To demonstrate, suppose we select 5 bins for the fifty data values in Table 2.1. We then note that the largest value is 74 and the smallest is 23 so the difference is equal to 51. If we were to use five bins, the class width could be 51 / 5 = 10.2. However, if the number of classes is increased to six, the width could be reduced to ten. Furthermore, if the beginning value for the first bin is made 20 (not 23), the resulting six bins would be 20 to 30, 30 to 40, 40 to 50, 50 to 60, 60 to 70 and 70 to 80. Most persons would find these classes/bins easier to understand then the eight bins of 23 and less, 23 to 30.28571, 30.28571 to 37.57143, and so on which Excel would automatically set up for this example.

To specify the classes/bins in Excel we would enter into the worksheet the upper value for each class/bin. To obtain the six bins specified above for our example, we would enter the six values of 30, 40, 50, 60, 70 and 80 into the worksheet. Using these six values Excel would determine the frequencies for the bins of *30 and less, greater than 30 to 40, greater than 40 to 50,* and so to *greater than 70 to 80.* In addition, Excel would include an empty bin of *greater than 80.* Oftentimes you may want an empty bin at the beginning of the distribution also. This is the approach we demonstrate in Figure 2.1 where we have entered the seven values of **20, 30, 40, 50, 60, 70** and **80**. Using these seven values, the HISTOGRAM analysis tool would determine the frequencies for the 6 classes/bins we wanted plus an empty bin at the beginning for values of 20 and less and an empty bin at the end for values greater than 80.

The following steps describe how to use the HISTOGRAM analysis tool for this example.

1. Use the **Start-up Procedure** given in Section 1.1 of Chapter 1 to start Excel.

2. Open a new Excel worksheet and enter the **Identification Material** as discussed in Section 1.5 of Chapter 1. Specifically enter the worksheet title in cell B1, your name in B2, the date in A3 and the file name you wish to use in D3 such as CHARTS.xls.

3. Enter the label **No. Sold** in Cell A5 and the values for the 50 sales values from Table 2.1 in cells A6 through A55 as shown in Figure 2.1.

4. Enter the label **Bin** in Cell B5 and the values **20,30, . . ., 80** in cells B6 through B12.

5. Use the **Saving a Workbook** procedure (Step 6 in Subsection 1.2.3 of Chapter 1) to save your worksheet using the file name **CHARTS** (Excel will add the xls suffix). Saving your workbook after you have put some effort into it will frequently save you time and grief later.

6. From the menu bar select **Tools** and then **Data Analysis** from the subsequent pull-down menu as shown in Figure 2.1. The Data Analysis dialog box as shown in Figure 2.2 will then appear. Select **Histogram** from the scrolling list and then click on the command button labeled as **OK**. The Histogram dialog box will appear as shown in Figure 2.3. You now need to select the input and output options for HISTOGRAM.

Figure 2.1 Example Data and Tools Pull-Down menu

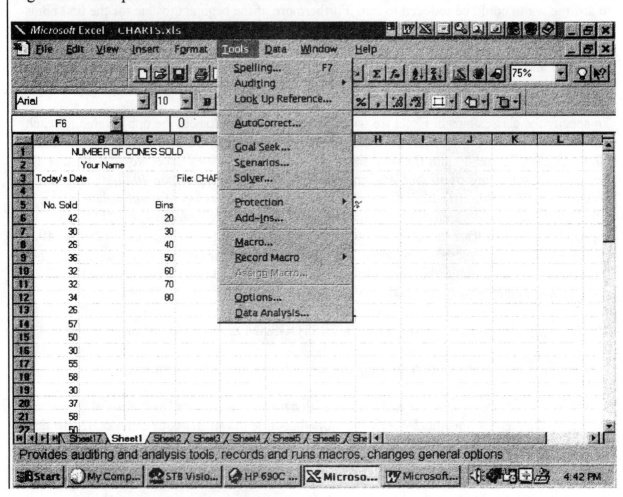

Figure 2.2 Data Analysis Dialog Box

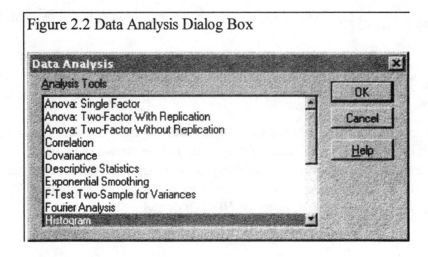

Figure 2.3 Histogram Analysis Tool Dialog Box

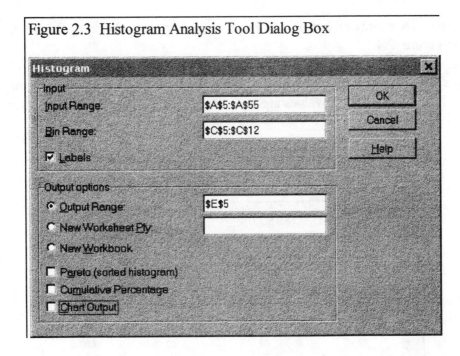

7. Move the pointer to the text box to the right of the label **Input Range** and click the left mouse button. Enter the range of cells for the data including the label in cell A5. You may either key the range **A5:A55** or click on cell A5 and drag to cell A55. (Note Excel automatically adds the $ signs to indicate absolute addresses if you use the drag operation.)

8. Move the pointer to the text box to the right of the label **Bin Range** and click the left mouse button. Enter the range of cells for the bins including the label in cell C5. You may either key **C5:C12** or click on cell C5 and drag to cell C12.

9. Move the pointer to the **Labels** check box and click the left mouse button once or twice to get a check mark in the box. This tells HISTOGRAM that the two ranges above include the labels in cells A5 and C5.

10. Move the pointer to the **Output Range** option button and click once or twice to get a dot in the button.

11. Move to the **Output Range** text box and click once and enter the cell address of E5 to specify the upper-left cell of for the Histogram output.

12. Sequentially move the pointer to the last three check boxes labeled as **Pareto (sorted histogram), Cumulative Percentage, and Chart Output** and click once or twice to **remove** the check mark from all three of these boxes (see Figure 2.3). The use of these selections is demonstrated in the following subsections.

13. Click on the **OK** command button and Excel will compute and display the frequency values shown in Figure 2.4.

These results show the frequency distribution using the six classes of *20 to 30* through *70 to 80*. In addition, they indicate that no values are *equal to or less than 20* and no values are *greater than 80.*

Figure 2.4 Frequency Distribution Results

	A	B	C	D	E	F	G	H
1	NUMBER OF CONES SOLD							
2	David L. Eldredge							
3	Date: August 10, 1997			File: CHARTS.xls				
4								
5	No. Sold		Bins		Bin	Frequency	Cumulative %	
6	42		20		20	0	.00%	
7	30		30		30	12	24.00%	
8	26		40		40	16	56.00%	
9	36		50		50	10	76.00%	
10	32		60		60	9	94.00%	
11	32		70		70	2	98.00%	
12	34		80		80	1	100.00%	
13	26				More	0	100.00%	
14	57							
15	50							
16	30							
17	55							
18	58							
19	30							
20	37							
21	58							

2.1.2 Histogram

The procedure for producing a histogram in addition to a frequency distribution is exactly like steps one through thirteen above with one exception.   The change involves Step 12. In order to additionally get a histogram, the check box for **Chart Output** should have a check mark in it. To demonstrate, again use the **Tools/Data Analysis/Histogram/OK** command sequence to call up the HISTOGRAM dialog box as you did for Figure 2.3. Your prior input and output selections may still be shown. It not reenter them. In addition, use the mouse button to add the check mark to the box for **Chart Output**. Click on **OK** and Excel will present a dialog box asking for permission to overwrite the output range. Select **OK** and the results of Figure 2.5 will appear.

If your analysis is only for your usage, the format of the histogram of Figure 2.5 may be satisfactory. However, if you wish to present your histogram to others, you may wish to edit it with more finished looking features.   As examples of possible editing, consider the following.

Figure 2.5 Histogram for Frequency Distribution

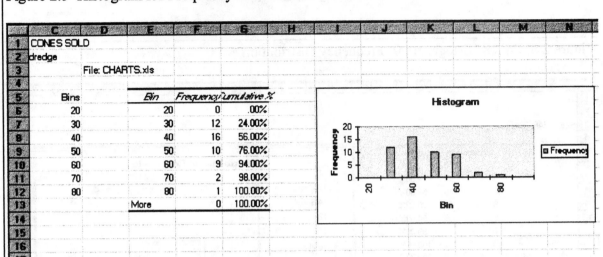

1. To enlarge the histogram, double click inside the histogram and a cross-hatched border (see Figure 2.6) will appear around the chart (**Excel 8:** single click and border is not cross-hatched). Point to the bottom sizing handle (the black square in the center of the bottom chart border) and the mouse pointer will become a two headed arrow. Drag the sizing handle to row 20. Point and drag the right center sizing handle (black square in the center of the right chart border) to column O.

2. To give the histogram a different title click on the current title, *Histogram*. Key a new title such as **Distribution of Cones Sold** and press the **Enter** key.

3. To change the X-axis title, click on the current title *Bin* and key in a new title such as **Class endpoint**. Press the **Enter** key.

4. Since only one set of data is plotted, a legend is not needed. Click on the legend box which contains the word **Frequency**. Press the **Delete** key.

5. Traditionally histograms do not have space between their bars although bar graphs do. To make this change move the pointer to just above the bars in the histogram and double click the left mouse button. Now select **Format** from the menu bar and then **Column Group** from the subsequent pull-down menu. Click on the **Options** dialog tab and change the **Gap Width** from 150% to 0% by pressing the down arrow on the Gap Width spinner. Click **OK**.

Excel 8 Note: For Step 5, first click on one of the bars. Small squares will appear on all the bars to show they are ready to be edited. Click on **Format** on the menu bar. Click on **Selected Data Series** from the pull-down menu. Click on the **Options** dialog tab. Use the **Gap Width** spinner to change from 150% to 0%. Click on **OK**.

The histogram which results from these five editing steps is as shown in Figure 2.6.

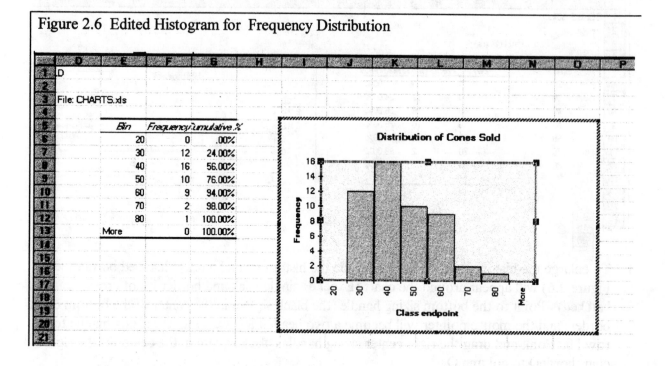

Figure 2.6 Edited Histogram for Frequency Distribution

2.1.3 Ogive

The procedure for adding an ogive to the output of the HISTOGRAM tool also requires changing only one input to the 13-step procedure of Subsection 2.1.1 above. Again the change involves Step 12. In order to compute the cumulative relative frequencies (cumulative percentages) the check box for **Cumulative Percentage** in the Histogram dialog box should have a check mark in it. To demonstrate, again call up the HISTOGRAM dialog box as shown in Figure 2.3. This time use the mouse button to add the check mark to the box for **Cumulative Percentage**. Click on **OK** and give permission to overwrite the output data. Excel will create a second chart on top of the first as shown in Figure 2.7.

If you would like, you can eliminate the first chart by clicking inside it but not inside the second chart. The sizing handles will appear for the first chart to indicate it has been selected. Next press the **Delete** key. Alternatively, you can use sizing handles for the second chart to expand it to cover all of the first chart as was done for Figure 2.7.

As you will note in the second chart, the cumulative percentages are given in column G. This chart is a combination of a histogram and a plot of the cumulative percentages. The axis for the histogram is on the left and the axis for the cumulative percentages of the ogive is on the right. Again you can edit the chart to give it a more finished look.

Figure 2.7   Histogram and Ogive for Frequency Distribution

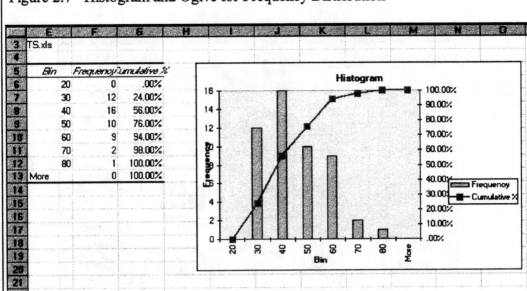

2.2 THE CHART WIZARD

The Excel feature called the CHART WIZARD can be used to create the fifteen types of charts shown in Figure 2.8. In Section 2.2, we demonstrate the use of seven of them. The **XY (Scatter)** chart is used to develop both a frequency polygon for the example problem of Subsection 2.2.1 and a scatter diagram for the example of Subsection 2.2.4. In Subsection 2.2.2 another example is introduced. It is used to demonstrate a **Bar** chart, a **3-D Bar** chart, a **Column** chart, a **3-D Column** chart, a **Pie** chart and a **3-D Pie** chart.

> **Excel 8 Note:** the Chart Wizard of Excel 8 has significant differences from those of Excel 7 and 5. The differences are such that to discuss them totally with notes would interfere with the flow of this manual. Accordingly, Appendix C presents Section 2.2 through the end of subsection 2.2.1 using the Chart Wizard for Excel 8.

2.2.1 Frequency Polygon

The XY (Scatter) chart can be used to create a frequency polygon for the *Cones Sold* example used throughout Section 2.1 above. You would proceed in the following manner.

1. Move the cell pointer to cell E25 and enter the label **Midpoint** and to F25 and enter the label **Frequency**.

2. In cells E26 through E33 enter the midpoints for the classes/bins of cells E6 through E13 as **15, 25, 35, . . . , 85**.

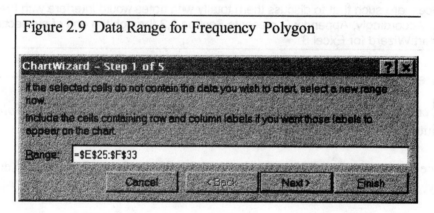

Figure 2.8 Chart Wizard Chart Types

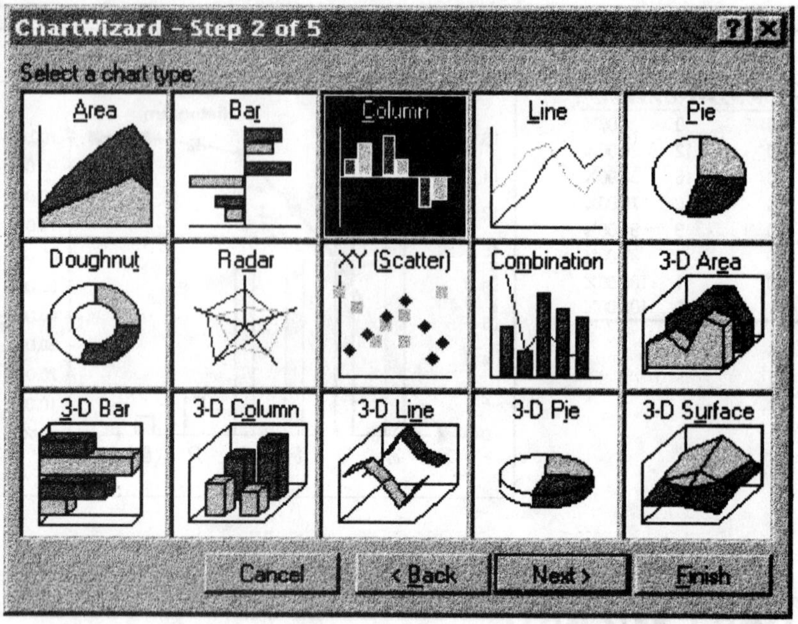

3. Copy the frequency values from cells F6 through F13 to cells F26 through F33. (You may wish to refer ahead to Figure 2.13 to see the results of Steps 1, 2 and 3.)

4. Move the pointer to the CHART WIZARD icon on the standard toolbar and click once.

5. The pointer will change to a small representation of a cross and a bar chart. Move it to cell H25 and click the mouse button. The *Chart Wizard Step 1* dialog box will appear as shown in Figure 2.9.

Figure 2.9 Data Range for Frequency Polygon

6. Enter the range E25:F33 in the **Range** text box by keying or by dragging. Click on the **Next** command button. The *Chart Wizard Step 2* dialog box will appear as previously shown in

Figure 2.8.

7. Use the mouse to select the **XY (Scatter)** chart and then select the **Next** button. The Chart Wizard Step 3 as shown in Figure 2.10 will appear.

8. Select format number **2** for Step 3 and click the **Next** button to obtain Step 4 as shown in Figure 2.11.

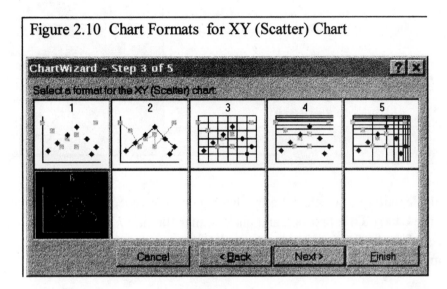

Figure 2.10 Chart Formats for XY (Scatter) Chart

Figure 2.11 Chart Wizard Step 4 for Frequency Polygon

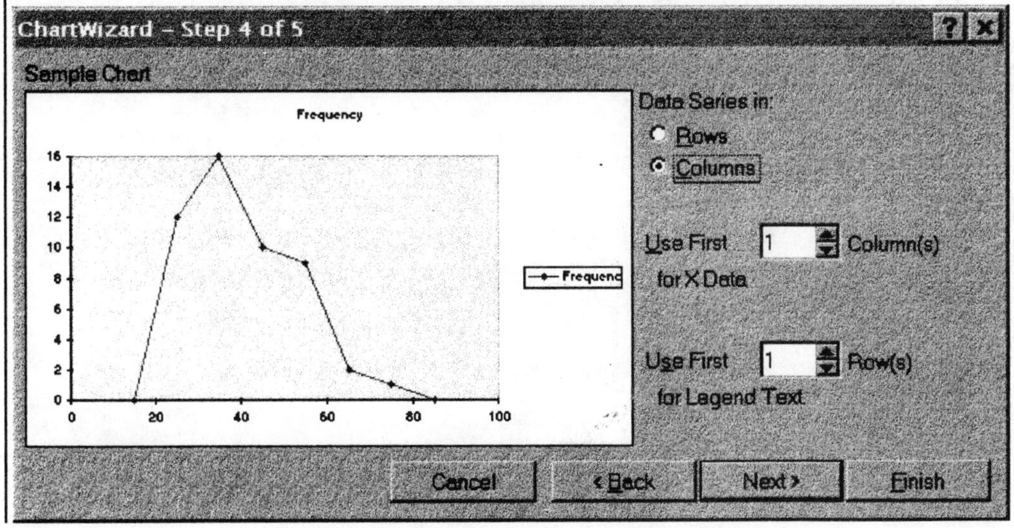

9. For Step 4, make sure the **Columns** option button is selected for **Data Series in** since the data are in columns. Click on the button once or twice to get a dot in it. Select **Next** to obtain Step 5 of Figure 2.12.

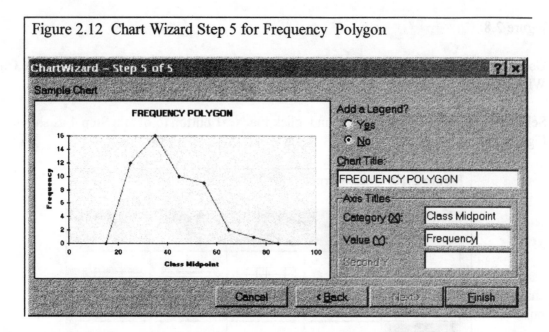

Figure 2.12 Chart Wizard Step 5 for Frequency Polygon

10. For the **Add legend** option select **No** by clicking once or twice on its button. Move the pointer to the **Chart Title** text box and click. Enter the title *FREQUENCY POLYGON*. Enter *Class Midpoint* for the **X-axis title** and *Frequency* for the **Y-axis title**. Select the **Finish** command button. The result will be as shown in Figure 2.13.

If you would like, you can enlarge the chart as you did to get Figure 2.6.

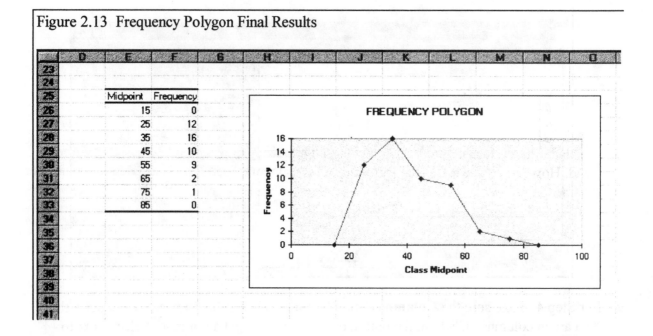

Figure 2.13 Frequency Polygon Final Results

2.2.2 Bar/Column Chart

The graphs and charts presented so far in this chapter included histograms, ogives and frequency polygons. These are used to display a frequency distribution for **quantitative** or numerical variables (measured on an interval or ratio measurement scale). For **qualitative** or categorical variables (measured on a nominal or ordinal scale) a bar/column chart or pie chart can be used to display the frequency distribution.

A bar/column chart is similar to a histogram. The height of the bars are proportional to the frequency for each class. However since the classes are not measured on a numerical scale, it is usual to have space between the bars.

As an example, let us revisit the three Waspork sisters who are running a stand selling shaved ice cones near the shopping mall in their home town. The sisters sell five flavors of shaved ice, cherry, grape, lime, orange and peppermint. During their first 50 days in business they sold a total of 2066 cones. Table 2.2 presents a tabulation of these sales by flavor. These data represent a frequency distribution for a qualitative or categorical variable. Consequently, the previous procedures of this chapter for developing a histogram, an ogive and a frequency polygon would not be appropriate.

Table 2.2 Cone Sales by Flavor

SHAVED ICE CONE FLAVOR	NUMBER OF CONES SOLD
Cherry	330
Grape	186
Lime	537
Orange	269
Peppermint	744
TOTAL	2066

The tabulation of sales data in order to obtain the frequency distribution of Table 2.2 can be done by hand. However, if the sales data are within an Excel worksheet, Excel has a feature which can determine the frequency distribution. The feature isn't the HISTORGRAM analysis tool because it only works for quantitative data. The feature is the PIVOT TABLE WIZARD. The use of it to tabulate a one variable frequency count is presented in Subsection 9.3.1 of Chapter 9.

Once the frequency distribution has been computed, it can be charted. The procedure for creating a bar/column chart for these data is quite similar to that used above to create a frequency polygon. We will continue with the Excel workbook from the prior example.

1. Click on the **Sheet 2** tab at the bottom of the window. This will allow you to create a second worksheet for this second example within the workbook entitled *CHARTS*.

2. Enter the data labels **Flavor** in cell A5 and **Number** in cell B5. Enter the names of the five flavors in cells A6 through A10 and the five frequency values in cells B6 through B10. As a check on your data entry, you can enter the equation **=SUM(B6:B10)** in cell B11 to see if the total is correct. Refer ahead to Figure 2.17 to see the results of this step.

3. Move the mouse pointer to the CHART WIZARD icon on the standard toolbar and click.

4. The pointer will change to a small cross and a bar chart. Move it to cell D5 and click the left mouse button. The *Chart Wizard Step 1* dialog box will appear as was previously shown in Figure 2.9.

5. Enter the range A5:B10 in the **Range** text box by keying or dragging. Click on **Next** to obtain the Step 2 dialog box as was previously shown in Figure 2.8.

6. Select the **Column** chart and click on the **Next** button to yield the dialog box shown in Figure 2.14 (for **Excel 8,** the equivalent figure is Figure 2.8 given in Appendix C).

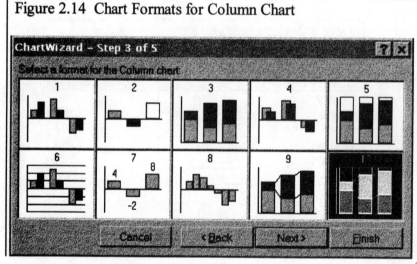

Figure 2.14 Chart Formats for Column Chart

7. Select format number **7** and click the **Next** command button to obtain Step 4 as in Figure 2.15.

8. For Step 4 make sure **Columns** is selected and click on the **Next** button.

Figure 2.15 Chart Wizard Step 4 for Column Chart

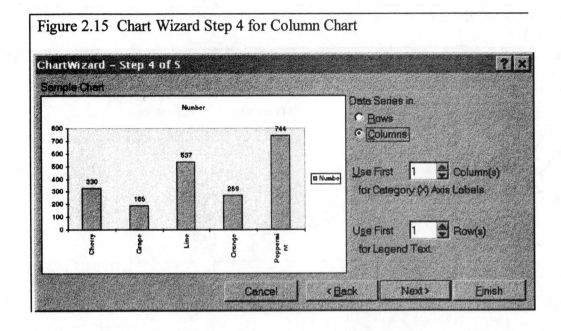

9. As shown in Figure 2.16, select **No** for the Add a Legend option and enter a title for the chart, the x-axis and the y-axis. Click on the **Finish** button to obtain the final results of Figure 2.17.

Figure 2.16 Chart Wizard Step 5 for Column Chart

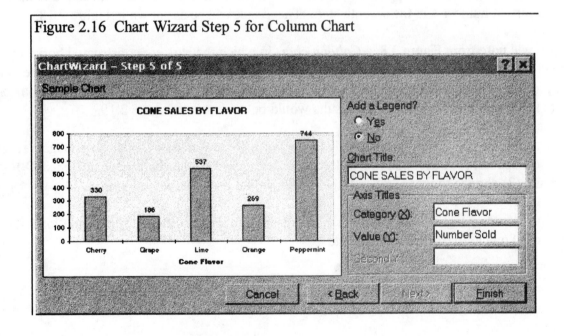

As with previous charts you may wish to enlarge the chart.

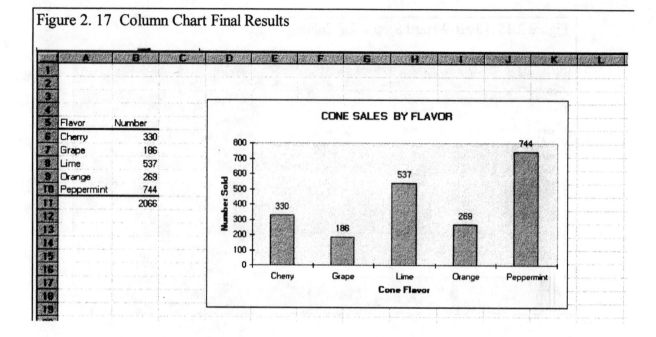

Figure 2. 17 Column Chart Final Results

To obtain a three-dimensional version of the column chart of Figure 2.17, you should repeat the above nine steps with three changes. *First*, select cell L5 instead of D5 in the fourth step as the upper left corner of the chart. *Second*, choose a **3-D Column** chart in the sixth step and *third*, choose format number **4** in the seventh step. The result will be as shown in Figure 2.18.

As you will note from Figure 2.8, a *Column chart* in which the bars are constructed horizontally instead of vertically is called a *Bar chart* in Excel. To obtain such a chart, again repeat the nine-step procedure but (1) select cell D25 as the upper left corner of the chart, (2) choose a **Bar** chart and (3) choose format number **7**, the results would be as shown in Figure 2.19.

Finally, suppose you wished to obtain the three-dimensional version of a Bar chart. Again repeat the nine steps but (1) select cell L25 as the upper left corner of the chart, (2) choose a **3-D Bar** chart and (3) choose format number **4**, the results would be as shown in Figure 2.20.

The four charts of Figures 2.17 through 2.20 provide similar but different representations of the same set of qualitative or categorical data.

Figure 2.18 3-Dimensional Column Chart

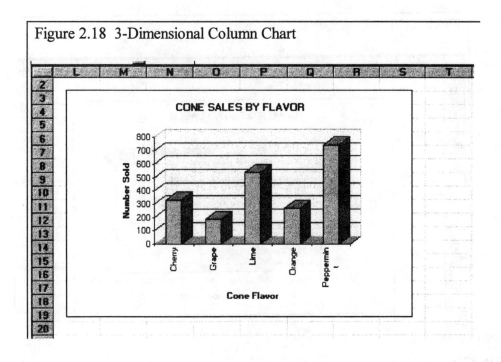

Figure 2.19 Bar Chart

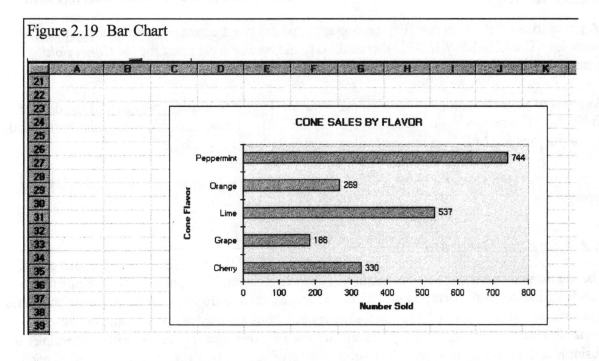

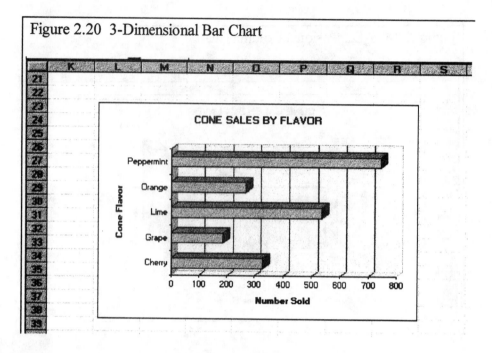

Figure 2.20 3-Dimensional Bar Chart

2.2.3 Pie Chart

A pie chart is used for representing percentages and relative frequencies usually for qualitative variables. The CHART WIZARD can be used to also create a pie chart for the *Cones Sold* example of the prior subsection.

As a test of your knowledge of the CHART WIZARD use it to create a pie chart of the data of Table 2.2. The results should be as given in Figure 2.21.   The specifications for this chart include an output location of **D45**, a range of values of **A5:B10**, and Chart type **7**.

Also construct the chart of Figure 2.22. It presents a 3-D Pie chart in cell L45. It also is Chart type **7**.

2.2.4 Scatter Diagram

The graphs and charts discussed so far in this chapter included histograms, ogives, frequency polygons, bar/column charts and pie charts. These are used to display a frequency distribution for one variable. Histograms, ogives and frequency polygons are used for **one quantitative variable**. Bar/column charts and pie charts are used for **one qualitative variable**. Oftentimes in business and industry problems, it is desired to determine how two variables are related to each other. The graphical method for displaying relationships between **two quantitative variables** is the scatter diagram as presented in this subsection. The relationship between **two qualitative**

variables can be explored with the tabular approach called a cross-tabulation or contingency table as presented in Section 9.2 of Chapter 9.

Figure 2.21 Pie Chart

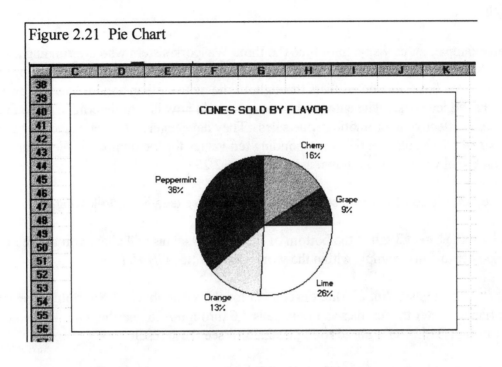

Figure 2.22 3-Dimensional Pie Chart

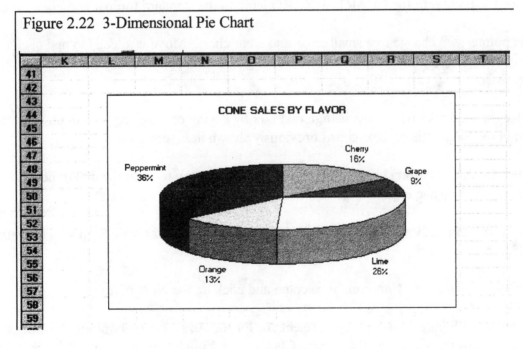

We construct a scatter diagram from the values for two variables. The value for one variable is plotted on the x-axis (the abscissa) and the corresponding value for the second variable on the y-axis (the ordinate). Each pair of values for the x-variable and the y-variable result in one point on the graph.

As an example, let us visit a third time the three Waspork sisters who are running a stand selling shaved ice cones near the shopping mall in their home town of Markay. For the last 10 days, they have distributed fliers throughout the metropolitan area of Markay promoting their shaved ice stand. The enterprising sisters would now like to determine if the fliers have been effective in promoting cone sales. They have entered the ten values for the number of cones sold and the corresponding ten values for the number of fliers distributed into an Excel worksheet as shown in later Figure 2.25.

The procedure for constructing a scatter diagram for these data is the following.

1. Click on the **Sheet 3** tab at the bottom of the window. This will allow you to create a third worksheet for this example within the workbook entitled *CHARTS*.

2. Enter the data labels **No. of Fliers** in cell A5 for the x-variable and **No. Sold** in cell B5 for the y-variable. Enter the ten flier values in cells A6 through A15 and the ten sales values in cells B6 through B15. Refer ahead to Figure 2.25 to see these results.

3. Move the pointer to the CHART WIZARD icon on the standard toolbar and click once.

4. The pointer will change to a small cross and a bar chart. Move it to cell D5 and click the mouse button. The *Chart Wizard Step 1* dialog box will appear as was previously shown in Figure 2.9.

5. Enter the range A5:B10 in the **Range** text box by keying or dragging. Click on **Next** to obtain the Step 2 dialog box as was previously shown in Figure 2.8.

6. Select the **XY (Scatter)** chart and click on the **Next** button to yield the dialog box as previously shown in Figure 2.10.

7. Select format number **3** and click the **Next** command button to obtain Step 4 as in Figure 2.23.

8. For Step 4 make sure **Columns** is selected and click on the **Next** button.

9. As shown in Figure 2.24 for Step 5, select **No** for the Add a Legend option and enter a title for the chart, the x-axis and the y-axis. Click on the **Finish** button to obtain the final results of Figure 2.25.

Figure 2.23 Chart Wizard Step 4 for Scatter Diagram

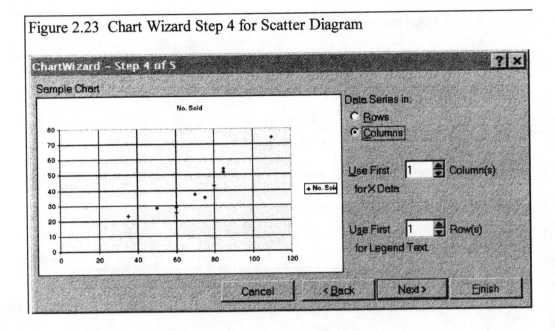

Figure 2.24 Chart Wizard Step 5 for Scatter Diagram

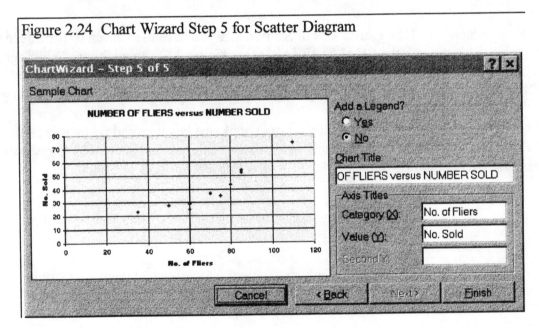

As with previous charts you may wish to enlarge the chart.

The chart of Figure 2.25 suggests there is a positive relationship between the number of fliers distributed and the number of cones sold. Moreover, it suggests the relationship is linear. It isn't a perfect linear relationship since all the points do not lie on a straight line. We will consider further such relationships in Chapter 10 where we will use regression analysis to find the *best* straight line relationship for such data sets.

Figure 2.25 Scatter Diagram Final Results

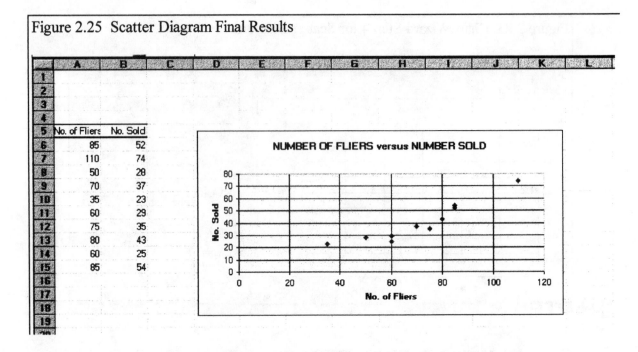

If you have completed all the instructions of Section 2.2, you have used seven of the fifteen types of charts available through the CHART WIZARD (see Figure 2.8). In addition, the histogram-ogive chart of Figure 2.7 in Section 2.1 is an example of an eighth type, a **Combination** chart. The CHART WIZARD will be used also in chapters 4, 10, 11 and 12 for additional charting.

At this time you may wish to save your Excel workbook one last time and perhaps print the results. You will then need to close your workbook and exit Excel. If you need to review the process of these operations, you may wish to review Subsection 1.2.3 of Chapter 1.

CHAPTER 3. DESCRIPTIVE NUMERICAL MEASURES

Excel includes two Data Analysis Tools which compute numerical measures for summarizing a data set for one quantitative variable. The first of these two analysis tools, DESCRIPTIVE STATISTICS, computes and displays most of the usual statistical measures of location, variability and shape for ungrouped data. It is presented in **Section 3.1**. The second tool is RANK AND PERCENTILE as discussed in **Section 3.2**. This tool displays the original data values sorted in ascending order and gives the rank and percentile for each data value.

Section 3.3 discusses four additional descriptive statistics which can be computed by individual statistical functions. **Section 3.4** discusses how to combine two or more individual statistical functions in order to compute four further descriptive statistic values. Finally, **Section 3.5** presents two Data Analysis Tools which compute measures of association between two quantitative variables.

3.1 THE DESCRIPTIVE STATISTICS ANALYSIS TOOL

The easiest way to obtain values for a number of the most common descriptive statistical measures is to use Excel's analysis tool DESCRIPTIVE STATISTICS. To demonstrate the use of this tool we will consider the following example.

The Frozo and Son Trucking Company delivers freight in and about Humid City. The number of tons of freight Frozo and Son has delivered the past 24 days is shown in Table 3.1. Frozo would like to summarize these data using the usual statistical measures for central location, variability and shape.

Table 3.1 Frozo and Son Freight Delivered in Tons

45	39	41	46	44	44	41	43
40	40	43	37	44	46	46	43
44	37	43	35	45	48	46	44

The following steps describe how to use the DESCRIPTIVE STATISTICS analysis tool for this example.

1. Use the **Start-up Procedure** of Section 1.1 of Chapter 1 to start Excel.

2. Open a new Excel worksheet and enter the **Identification Material** as discussed in Section 1.5 of Chapter 1: the worksheet title in cell B1, your name in B2, the date in A3 and the file name you wish to use in D3 such as DESCIBE.xls.

3. Enter the label **FREIGHT** in cell A5 and the values for the 24 freight deliveries in cells A6 through A29 as shown in Figure 3.1.

Figure 3.1 Example Data and Tools Pull-Down Menu

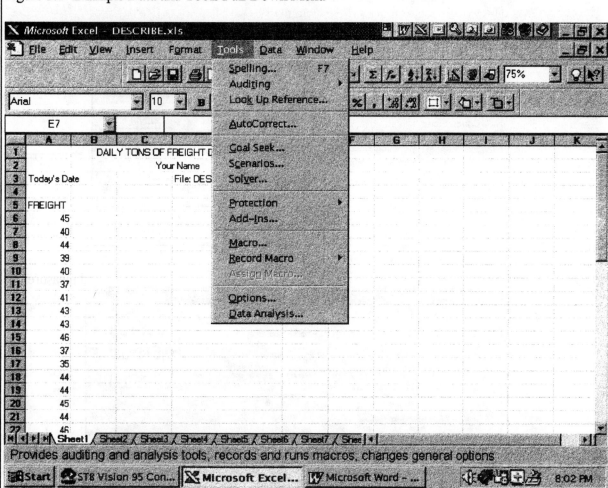

4. Use the **Saving a Workbook** procedure (Step 6 in Subsection 1.2.3 of Chapter 1) to save your worksheet using the file name DESCRIBE.

5. From the menu bar select **Tools** and then **Data Analysis** from the subsequent pull-down menu as shown in Figure 3.1. The Data Analysis dialog box as shown in Figure 3.2 will then appear.

6. Select **Descriptive Statistics** from the scrolling list and then select the command button labeled as **OK.** The Descriptive Statistics dialog box will be displayed as shown in Figure 3.3.

7. Next you will enter the inputs and output options for the Descriptive Statistics analysis tool. Select the first input option by clicking the left mouse button once or twice in the check box to the left of the text **Labels in the First Row** to get a check mark in the box. Do the same for the **Confidence Level of the Mean, the kth largest and kth smallest**. See Figure 3.3.

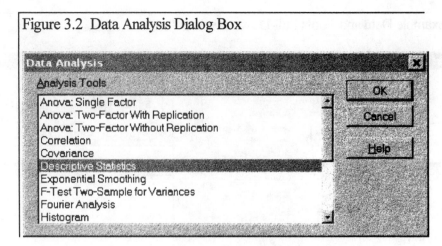

Figure 3.2 Data Analysis Dialog Box

Figure 3.3 Descriptive Statistics Dialog Box

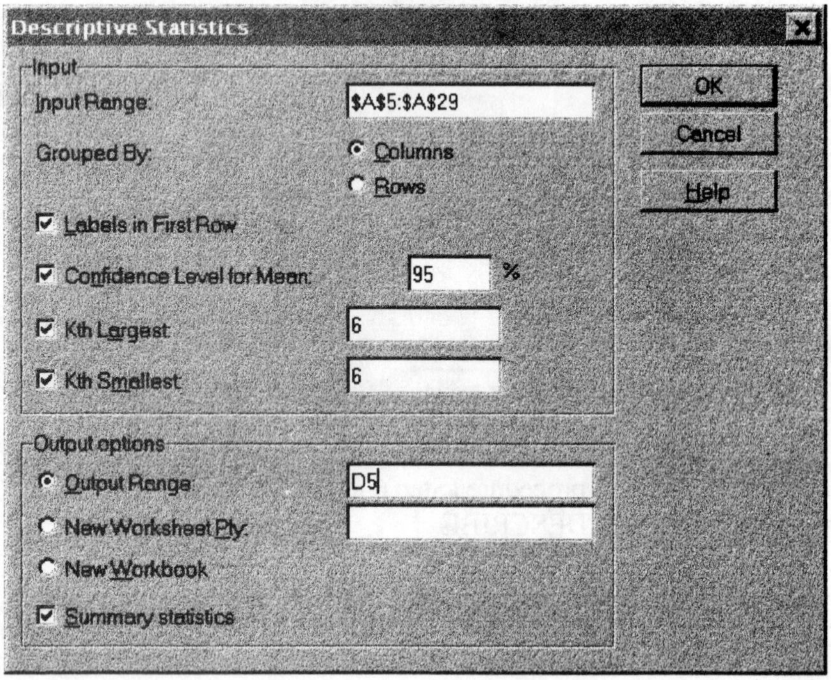

8. Select the output option by first clicking once on the option button to the left of the text **Output Range** in order to place a dot in the button. Also, click once or twice in the **Summary Statistics** check box to get a check mark in the box.

9. Move the pointer to the text box to the right of **Input Range** and click the left mouse button. Enter the range of cells for the data including the label in cell A5. You may either type A5:A29 or click on cell A5 and drag to cell A29. Excel automatically adds $ signs to the cell addresses to

indicate absolute addresses when you use the drag operation.

10. Press the **Tab** key to proceed to the next dialog box field. Select **Column***s* for the **Grouped By** input since the data are in a column.

11. Press the tab key three times to move the cursor to the **Confidence Level for Mean** box. Enter 95 in order to obtain the 95% confidence level (confidence intervals are discussed in Chapter 5).

12. Tab twice to the **Kth Largest** text box and enter **6** in order to obtain the approximate value for the third quartile or 75th percentile (6th largest of 24 data points). Tab twice to **Kth Smallest** text box enter **6** to obtain the approximate value for the first quartile or 25th percentile (6th smallest of 24 data points). (Exact values for the third and first quartiles can be computed using the individual statistical function QUARTILE as discussed in Section 3.4 below.)

13. Tab twice to **Output Range** text box and enter the upper left cell for the output results. For this example enter **D5**.

14. Click on **OK** and Excel will compute and display the values as shown in Figure 3.4. (Note the width of column C has been increased so labels appear in full.)

Figure 3.4 Descriptive Statistics Results

	A	B	C	D	E	F
1			DAILY TONS OF FREIGHT DELIVERED			
2			David L. Eldredge			
3	Date: September 23, 1996			File: Frozo.xls		
4						
5	FREIGHT			*FREIGHT*		
6	45					
7	40			Mean	42.666667	
8	44			Standard Error	0.6720795	
9	39			Median	43.5	
10	40			Mode	44	
11	37			Standard Deviation	3.2925036	
12	41			Sample Variance	10.84058	
13	43			Kurtosis	0.0207696	
14	43			Skewness	-0.762475	
15	46			Range	13	
16	37			Minimum	35	
17	35			Maximum	48	
18	44			Sum	1024	
19	44			Count	24	
20	45			Largest(6)	45	
21	44			Smallest(6)	40	
22	46			Confidence Level(95.0%)	1.3903004	
23	48					

---

15. Use the **Saving a Workbook** procedure (Step 6 in Subsection 1.2.3 of Chapter 1) to save your

worksheet.

The descriptive statistics results given in Figure 3.4 present measures of central location, measures of variability, measures of shape and some additional descriptive measures. These are discussed in the following four subsections.

3.1.1 Measures of Central Location

The measures of central location include values for the **mean** in cell E7, the **median** in cell E9 and the **mode** in cell E10. In addition, cells E20 and E21 show the approximate values for the **third** and **first quartiles**.

3.1.2 Measures of Variability

The most frequently used measures of variability are the **sample standard deviation**, the **sample variance** and the **range** as given respectively in cells E11, E12 and E15 of Figure 3.4.

3.1.3 Measures of Shape

The results of Figure 3.4 also include measures of shape. A value for **skewness** is given in cell E14 and a value for **kurtosis** in cell E13. The value for skewness is based on the differences around the mean raised to the third power. The value for kurtosis is based on the differences around the mean raised to the fourth power. For a further explanation you should access Help for the Excel statistical functions SKEW and KURT. Help for these functions is accessed by selecting the FUNCTION WIZARD (labeled as *fx* on the standard toolbar), then the **Statistical** category of functions, then the function **SKEW** or **KURT** and finally **Help**.

An alternate measure of skewness is Pearson's Coefficient of Skewness which is somewhat simpler to compute and is perhaps a more usual measure of skewness. It is presented in Section 3.4 below.

3.1.4 Other Descriptive Measures

Figure 3.4 includes six additional outputs. Cell E8 contains the value for the **standard error**. It is equal to the sample standard deviation divided by the square root of the sample size. It is used for computing confidence intervals and conducting hypothesis tests as discussed later in Chapter 5. Cells E16 through E19 present the values for the **smallest value** of the sample, the **largest value**, the **sum** of all the values and the **number of values** in the sample. The final output given in cell E22 is the **half-width** for the 95% confidence interval which is discussed in Chapter 5.

3.2 THE RANK AND PERCENTILE ANALYSIS TOOL

The second Data Analysis Tool which computes numerical measures for summarizing a data set of one quantitative variable is named RANK AND PERCENTILE. Again the data of Table 3.1 will be used to demonstrate this analysis tool.

The following steps will result in a new table within the worksheet with the data values given in descending order.

1. From the menu bar select **Tools** and then select **Data Analysis** from the subsequent pull-down menu. The Data Analysis dialog box (Figure 3.2) will then appear. Scroll down the list and select **Rank and Percentile** and then **OK** in order to obtain the Rank and Percentile dialog box as shown in Figure 3.5.

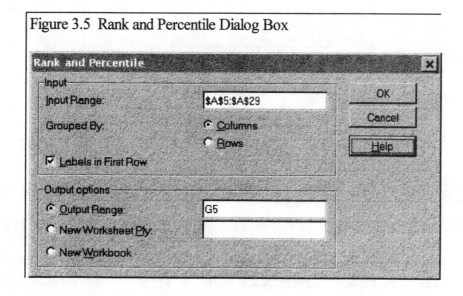

Figure 3.5 Rank and Percentile Dialog Box

2. Next fill in the Inputs and Output options as you did starting with Step 7 of the procedure given in Section 3.1. For the **Output Range** enter **G5**.

3. Click on **OK** and Excel will compute and display the values as shown in Figure 3.6.

The results are given in columns G through J. The original data values, given in column H, are now sorted in descending order. The numbers in column G indicate which data value is in each row. The values in columns I and J present the rank and percentile for each data value.

Figure 3.6 Rank and Percentile Results

	A	B	C	D	E	F	G	H	I	J
	FREIGHT			*FREIGHT*			*Point*	*FREIGHT*	*Rank*	*Percent*
5										
6	45						18	48	1	100.00%
7	40			Mean	42.666667		10	46	2	82.60%
8	44			Standard Error	0.6720795		17	46	2	82.60%
9	39			Median	43.5		20	46	2	82.60%
10	40			Mode	44		21	46	2	82.60%
11	37			Standard Deviation	3.2925036		1	45	6	73.90%
12	41			Sample Variance	10.84058		15	45	6	73.90%
13	43			Kurtosis	0.0207696		3	44	8	52.10%
14	43			Skewness	-0.762475		13	44	8	52.10%
15	46			Range	13		14	44	8	52.10%
16	37			Minimum	35		16	44	8	52.10%
17	35			Maximum	48		24	44	8	52.10%
18	44			Sum	1024		8	43	13	34.70%
19	44			Count	24		9	43	13	34.70%
20	45			Largest(6)	45		22	43	13	34.70%
21	44			Smallest(6)	40		23	43	13	34.70%
22	46			Confidence Level(95.0%)	1.3903004		7	41	17	26.00%
23	48						19	41	17	26.00%
24	41						2	40	19	17.30%
25	46						5	40	19	17.30%
26	46						4	39	21	13.00%
27	43						6	37	22	4.30%
28	43						11	37	22	4.30%
29	44						12	35	24	.00%

3.3 DESCRIPTIVE STATISTICAL FUNCTIONS

In addition to the Data Analysis Tools for performing statistical analysis, Excel has 71 (80 for Excel 8) individual functions for computing statistical values. These functions are listed in Appendix B by the category of analysis each supports. As presented in Appendix B, 27 of the 71 functions are listed in one of the six categories representing descriptive statistics. These 27 functions both duplicate and supplement the analytical capabilities of the three descriptive statistics data analysis tools, HISTOGRAM, DESCRIPTIVE STATISTICS and RANK AND PERCENTILE.

For example, the statistical functions AVERAGE, MEDIAN, MODE, STDEV and VAR compute values for the mean, median, mode, sample standard deviation and sample variance respectively. The DESCRIPTIVE STATISTICS analysis tool also computes values for these five common descriptive numerical measures. However, a number of the descriptive numerical measures provided by the statistical functions are not computed by the DESCRIPTIVE STATISTICS tool. We demonstrate some of these additional measures through the presentation of four individual functions. The first three, the, the population variance, the population standard deviation and the mean absolute deviation provide additional measures of variability. The fourth is z-score which provides a measure of position.

3.3.1 Population Variance

One of the statistical functions is VARP which computes the **population variance (N in the denominator)** as opposed to the **sample variance (n-1 in the denominator)** previously given in Figure 3.4 which also can be computed by the function VAR. To determine the population variance using the Function Wizard, perform the following steps.

1. Enter the label **Population Variance** in cell D24.

2. Move the worksheet pointer to cell E24 and click the Function Wizard icon, *fx*. The result should be Step 1 dialog box as shown in Figure 3.7.

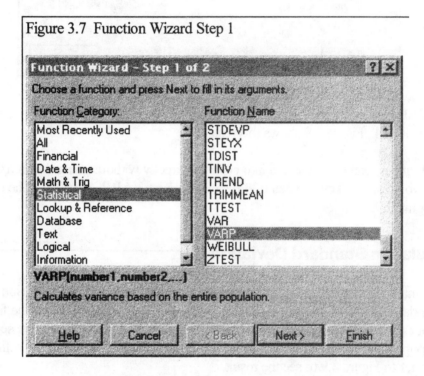

Figure 3.7 Function Wizard Step 1

Function Wizard – Step 1 of 2

Choose a function and press Next to fill in its arguments.

Function Category:

- Most Recently Used
- All
- Financial
- Date & Time
- Math & Trig
- Statistical
- Lookup & Reference
- Database
- Text
- Logical
- Information

Function Name

- STDEVP
- STEYX
- TDIST
- TINV
- TREND
- TRIMMEAN
- TTEST
- VAR
- VARP
- WEIBULL
- ZTEST

VARP(number1,number2,...)

Calculates variance based on the entire population.

Help   Cancel   < Back   Next >   Finish

3. Click on the Function Category **Statistical** in the scrolling list on the left.

4. Scroll to and click on the Function Name **VARP** in the scrolling list on the right.

5. Click on the **Next** command button and the Step 2 dialog box as shown in Figure 3.8 will be presented on the computer screen.

6. Enter the range of values for the input data by either keying in the range or by clicking and dragging through cells A6 through A29. Notice that the value for the population is displayed at the top right of the dialog box after the range is entered.

7.   Click on the **Finish** command button.

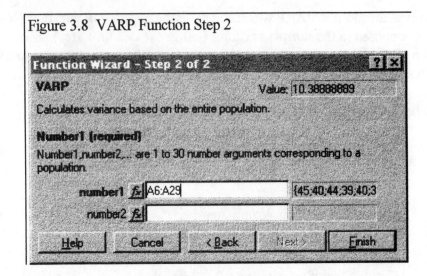

Figure 3.8 VARP Function Step 2

The function VARP with the range A6 through A29 is placed in cell E24 and the value for the function is displayed in cell E24. Figure 3.9 shows this result.

Alternatively, you may enter the function into cell E24 directly without going through the Function Wizard. You would simply key into cell E24 the expression **=VARP(A6:A29)**. The result would be as shown in Figure 3.9.

3.3.2 Population Standard Deviation

Another individual function, STDEVP, computes the **population standard deviation** as opposed to the sample standard deviation given in Figure 3.4 which also can be computed by the function STDEV. As a test of your understanding of the use of the FUNCTION WIZARD, repeat the seven steps given above for the population variance to compute the population standard deviation in cell E25 with a label in cell D25. Refer to Figure 3.9 to see the result.

3.3.3 Mean Absolute Deviation

Another measure of variability which can be obtained through the use of these same seven steps is the **Mean Absolute Deviation (MAD)**. The function which computes it is AVEDEV. Use this function to compute the value for MAD in cell E26 with its label in cell D26. Figure 3.9 also shows this result.

Figure 3.9 VARP, STDEVP and AVEDEV Function Results

	A	B	C	D	E	F	G	H	I	J
5	FREIGHT			*FREIGHT*			*Point*	*FREIGHT*	*Rank*	*Percent*
6	45						18	48	1	100.00%
7	40			Mean	42.666667		10	46	2	82.60%
8	44			Standard Error	0.6720795		17	46	2	82.60%
9	39			Median	43.5		20	46	2	82.60%
10	40			Mode	44		21	46	2	82.60%
11	37			Standard Deviation	3.2925036		1	45	6	73.90%
12	41			Sample Variance	10.84058		15	45	6	73.90%
13	43			Kurtosis	0.0207696		3	44	8	52.10%
14	43			Skewness	-0.762475		13	44	8	52.10%
15	46			Range	13		14	44	8	52.10%
16	37			Minimum	35		16	44	8	52.10%
17	35			Maximum	48		24	44	8	52.10%
18	44			Sum	1024		8	43	13	34.70%
19	44			Count	24		9	43	13	34.70%
20	45			Largest(6)	45		22	43	13	34.70%
21	44			Smallest(6)	40		23	43	13	34.70%
22	46			Confidence Level(95.0%)	1.3903004		7	41	17	26.00%
23	48						19	41	17	26.00%
24	41			Population Variance	10.388889		2	40	19	17.30%
25	46			Population Std. Dev.	3.2231799		5	40	19	17.30%
26	46			Mean Absolute Deviation	2.6111111		4	39	21	13.00%
27	43						6	37	22	4.30%
28	43						11	37	22	4.30%
29	44						12	35	24	.00%

3.3.4 Z-Score

A measure of position for a data value relative to the other values in a data set is provided by its **z-score**. The z-score for a data value is equal to the number of standard deviations it is above or below the mean for the data set. The Excel function which computes a z-score is STANDARDIZE.

To compute the z-score for each data value of the *Frozo and Son* example proceed as follows.

1. Enter the label **Z-Score** in cell B5 and move the cell pointer to cell B6.

2. Click the Function Wizard icon, *fx*, with the left mouse button. The result should be as previously shown in Figure 3.7.

3. Click on the Function Category **Statistical** in the left scrolling list. Scroll to and click on the function **STANDARDIZE** in the right list. Click on the **Next** command button to obtain the result given in Figure 3.10.

4. Click on the value in cell **A6** to enter the cell address for the x value.

Figure 3.10 STANDARDIZE Function Step 2

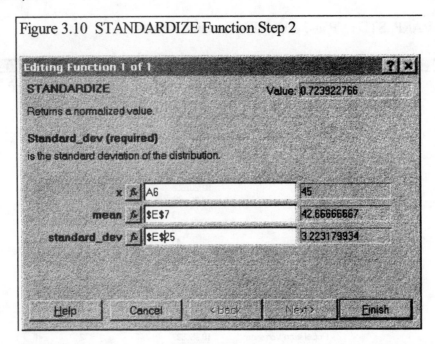

5. Depress the **Tab** key to move to the text box for the mean.   Key the cell address for the mean, **E7**, and press the **F4** key. Depressing the F4 key changes the cell address from a relative address to an absolute address. The $ sign before the column letter and before the row number indicate it is an absolute address. This is done so the cell address will remain the same when it is subsequently copied.

6. Push the **Tab** key to move to the standard deviation text box, labeled as **Standard_Dev**. Key the cell address **E25** and press the **F4** key.

7. Click on the **Finish** button. The result will be the z-score for the data value in cell A6.

8. Click on the **Copy** icon. Click and drag through cells B7 through B29.

9. Click on the **Paste** icon. The result will be the z-scores in column B for each of the values in cells A7 through A29. These results are shown in Figure 3.11.

3.4 COMBINATIONS OF STATISTICAL FUNCTIONS

Two or more individual statistical functions can be combined to compute additional descriptive numerical measures. Four of these commonly presented in business statistics textbooks include the coefficient of variation, the interquartile range, Pearson's coefficient of skewness and the box plot. The first two of these offer additional measures of variability. The third is another measures of shape, and the fourth provides a pictorial summary of the shape of a data set. It also goes by the name a *box and whisker plot*.

Figure 3.11 Z-Score Results

	A	B	C	D	E	F
4						
5	FREIGHT	Z-SCORE		*FREIGHT*		
6	45	0.7239				
7	40	-0.8273		Mean	42.666667	
8	44	0.4137		Standard Error	0.6720795	
9	39	-1.1376		Median	43.5	
10	40	-0.8273		Mode	44	
11	37	-1.7581		Standard Deviation	3.2925036	
12	41	-0.5171		Sample Variance	10.84058	
13	43	0.1034		Kurtosis	0.0207696	
14	43	0.1034		Skewness	-0.762475	
15	46	1.0342		Range	13	
16	37	-1.7581		Minimum	35	
17	35	-2.3786		Maximum	48	
18	44	0.4137		Sum	1024	
19	44	0.4137		Count	24	
20	45	0.7239		Largest(6)	45	
21	44	0.4137		Smallest(6)	40	
22	46	1.0342		Confidence Level(95.0%)	1.3903004	
23	48	1.6547				
24	41	-0.5171		Population Variance	10.388889	
25	46	1.0342		Population Std. Dev.	3.2231799	
26	46	1.0342		Mean Absolute Deviation	2.6111111	
27	43	0.1034				
28	43	0.1034				

3.4.1 Coefficient of Variation

The **coefficient of variation** measures the relative variability in a data set by dividing the population standard deviation by the mean and multiplying the result by 100. This computation can be performed in Excel by using the statistical function STDEVP to obtain the population standard deviation and the function AVERAGE to obtain the mean. Continuing with the worksheet from above, we will proceed as follows.

1. Enter the label **Coefficient Variation** in cell D28. Move the worksheet pointer to cell E28.

2. Click the Function Wizard icon, *fx*, with the left mouse button. The result should be Step 1 for the Function Wizard as previously shown in Figure 3.7.

3. Click on the Function Category **Statistical**. Scroll to and click on the Function Name **STDEVP** and click on the **Next** button to obtain Figure 3.12.

4. Enter or click and drag through cells A6 to A29 and click on the **Finish** button. The population standard deviation will be displayed in cell E28.

5. Press the **F2** key to enter the edit mode.

Figure 3.12 STDEVP Function Step 2

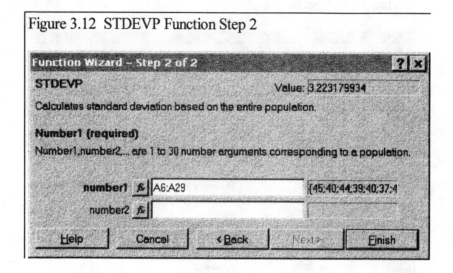

6. Key in a slash after the right-most parenthesis of the STDEVP function shown in cell E28 to indicate the population standard deviation is to be divided by the mean.

7. To compute the mean repeat Steps 2, 3 and 4 above but use the statistical function AVERAGE instead of STDEVP.

8. Key in an * (asterisk) at the end of the AVERAGE function to indicate the result is to be multiplied.

9. Key in the number 100 and press the **Enter** key.

The final results should appear as shown in Figure 13.13.

You may have noted that we could have computed the coefficient of variation more simply by dividing the value in cell E25 by the value in E7 and multiplying by 100. However, we presented the above procedure to demonstrate how to combine two or more statistical functions when they have not been computed separately within the worksheet.

3.3.2 Interquartile Range

 Another measure of variability, the **interquartile range** is found by subtracting the first quartile from the third quartile. The Excel's statistical function QUARTILE can be used to obtain these two quartile values.

Figure 3.13 Results for Coefficient of Variation, Interquartile
Range, Pearson's Coefficient of Skewness and
Five-Number Summary

	A	B	C	D	E	F
23	48	1.6547				
24	41	-0.5171		Population Variance	10.388889	
25	46	1.0342		Population Std. Dev.	3.2231799	
26	46	1.0342		Mean Absolute Deviation	2.6111111	
27	43	0.1034				
28	43	0.1034		Coefficient of Variation	7.554328	
29	44	0.4137		Interquartile Range	4.25	
30				Coefficient of Skewness	-0.775632	
31						
32				FIVE-NUMBER SUMMARY		
33				Smallest Value	35	
34				First Quartile	40.75	
35				Median	43.5	
36				Third Quartile	45	
37				Largest Value	48	
38						

QUARTILE Function Note: There are a number of variations in the conventions used to compute quartiles. The conventions used by Excel may differ from those used in your textbook. If they do differ, the results will oftentimes be the same and sometimes differ by at most one item. For example, textbooks oftentimes define the first quartile as the $[(n + 1) / 4]^{th}$ item in the ordered array of data values. However, Excel defines the first quartile as the $[(n + 3) / 4]^{th}$ item. A little algebraic manipulation shows that Excel's definition is always 0.5 greater than the first definition. Thus, the result after any needed rounding will oftentimes be the same and sometimes differ by at most one item. Similarly, the third quartile is often defined in textbooks as the $[3(n + 1) / 4]^{th}$ item as opposed to Excel's definition of $[(3n + 1) /4]^{th}$. Excel's definition for the third quartile will always be 0.5 less than the first definition. Again after rounding the result will either be the same or will differ by at the most one item. Excel's definition of the second quartile, the median, is $[(n + 1) / 2]^{th}$ as usually presented in statistics textbooks.

The following is the procedure for determining the interquartile range for the *Frozo and Son* example data set using Excel's statistical function QUARTILE.

1. Enter the label **Interquartile Range** in cell D29 and move the worksheet pointer to cell E29.

2. Click the Function Wizard icon, *fx*, with the left mouse button. The result should be Step 1 for the Function Wizard (see previous Figure 3.7).

3. Click on the Function Category **Statistical**. Scroll to and click on the Function Name **QUARTILE** and click on the **Next** button. The result will be as shown in Figure 3.14.

4. Enter or click and drag through cells A6 to A29..

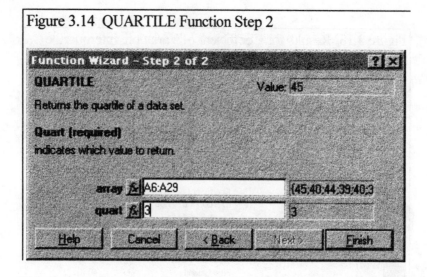

Figure 3.14 QUARTILE Function Step 2

5.   Click on text box to the right of the **quart** label and enter the number **3** to designate the third quartile. Click on the **Finish** command button.

6.   Press the **F2** key to enter the edit mode.

7.   Key in a minus at the end of the QUARTILE function.

8.   Repeat Steps 2 through 5 for the first quartile by using the number **1** in place of the number 3 in step 5.

9.   Press the **Enter** key.

The final results should appear as shown in cell E29 of Figure 13.13 above.

3.4.3 Pearson's Coefficient of Skewness

As mentioned in Section 3.1 above, the DESCRIPTIVE STATISTICS analysis tool computes a measure of skewness as the third power of the deviations about the mean. It provides a measure of the shape of a data set. A simple, and more standard, alternative to this measure of skewness is found by multiplying the difference between the mean and median times 3 and dividing the result by the standard deviation. This is called **Pearson's coefficient of skewness**. The three statistical functions AVERAGE, MEDIAN and STDEVP can be combined to obtain a value for this measure. You should perform the following steps.

1.   Enter the label **Coefficient of Skewness** in cell D30.

2.   In cell E30 enter the following formula. Although you may use the Function Wizard to enter the three functions, it is perhaps easier to simply key the formula into the cell.

$$= 3 * (\text{AVERAGE(A6:A29)} - \text{MEDIAN(A6:A29)}) / \text{STDEVP(A6:A29)}$$

Your results should appear as shown in cell E30 of Figure 3.13.

3.3.4 Box Plot

The **box plot**, also called the box and whisker plot, provides a pictorial representation of the shape of a data set. It graphically shows the two extreme values for a data set, the center of the data set and the variability of the data set. It is constructed using a **five-number summary** for the data set. The five numbers are the median, the first quartile, the third quartile, the smallest value and the largest value. These all can be found with the statistical function QUARTILE (see **QUARTILE Function Note** in Subsection 3.3.2 above). We proceed in the following manner.

1. Key the labels *FIVE-NUMBER SUMMARY, Smallest Value, First Quartile, Median, Third Quartile and Largest Value* in cells D32 through D37 respectively.

2. In cells E33 through E37 key the following five QUARTILE expressions.

$$\text{=QUARTILE(A6:A29,0)}$$
$$\text{=QUARTILE(A6:A29,1)}$$
$$\text{=QUARTILE(A6:A29,2)}$$
$$\text{=QUARTILE(A6:A29,3)}$$
$$\text{=QUARTILE(A6:A29,4)}$$

The resulting five values as shown in Figure 3.13 can be used to draw the Box Plot.

3.5 MEASURES OF ASSOCIATION BETWEEN TWO VARIABLES

In the process of using the Data Analysis Tools and Statistical Functions presented so far in this chapter, you have computed a large number of different statistics. All of these are used to summarize a data set of **one quantitative** variable. Oftentimes for business problems we wish to determine how **two quantitative** variables are related to each other. In Chapter 2 we presented the scatter diagram for graphically displaying such a relationship. In this section of Chapter 3, we will present two data analysis tools, and three statistical functions, for computing two numerical measures of the relationship between two quantitative variables. The first measure is the covariance and the second the coefficient of correlation.

3.5.1 The COVARIANCE Analysis Tool

As an example, let us revisit the *Frozo and Son Trucking Company*. Suppose Frozo feels there is a relationship between the maintenance cost for trucks and the number of delivery stops trucks make. From Frozo's records they have compiled the total maintenance cost and the total number of stops made for 12 trucks. He has entered the 12 values for maintenance cost and the corresponding 12 values for number of delivery stops into cells A6 through B17 of an Excel worksheet as shown in Figure 3.15.

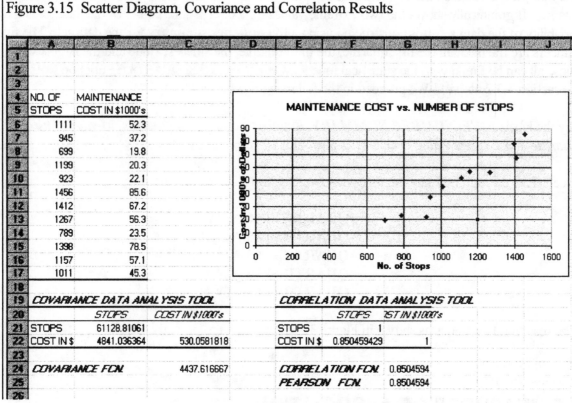

Figure 3.15 Scatter Diagram, Covariance and Correlation Results

The process of analyzing these data should begin with the construction of a scatter diagram to graphically illustrate the relationship between the two variables.   We will use the procedure of Subsection 2.2.4 of Chapter 2 to construct a scatter diagram.

1. Click on the **Sheet 2** tab at the bottom of the window. This will allow you to create a second worksheet for this second example within the workbook entitled DESCRIBE.

2. Enter the data labels **No. of Stops** and **Maintenance Cost in $1000's** as shown in Figure 3.15. Also enter the 12 pairs of data values in cells A6 through B17.

3. Use steps 3 through 9 of Subsection 2.2.4 in Chapter 2 to create the scatter diagram of Figure 3.15.

4. From the menu bar select **Tools** and next select **Data Analysis** for the pull-down menu and then select **Covariance** from the scrolling list. Finally select **OK** to obtain the Covariance dialog box as shown in Figure 3.16.

5. Make the entries given in Figure 3.16. These include (a) the input range, (b) the grouped by column option button, (c) the labels in first row check box, (d) the output range option button and (e) the output range.

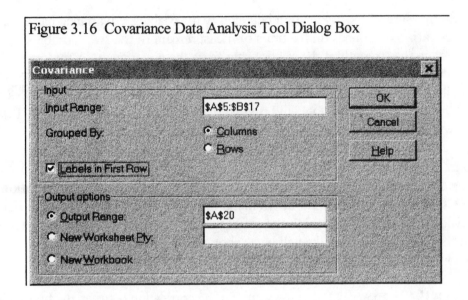

Figure 3.16 Covariance Data Analysis Tool Dialog Box

The results are as displayed in cells A20 through C22 of Figure 3.15. The label directly above these cells has been added for clarification. The value of 4841.036364 is the value of covariance for the two variables *No. of Stops* and *Maintenance Cost*. It is the **sample covariance** (n - 1 in the denominator, not N). The values given in cells B21 and C22 are the sample variance values for the *No. of Stops* and the *Maintenance Cost* respectively.

> **Excel 5 Note:** The Covariance Data Analysis Tool of Excel 5 displays the **population** covariance between the two variables and population variances for each of them. To compute the corresponding **sample** statistics, multiply each of the three results by the value of N / (n - 1).

As we have previously noted, Excel also has built-in statistical functions for computing the statistical results provided by the data analysis tools. (The general differences between the results from functions as opposed to those from tools are discussed beginning on the first page of Appendix B.) Excel's statistical function for computing covariance is COVAR. The value from this function for our example is shown in cell C24 of Figure 3.15 with a corresponding label added in cell A24. The entry in cell C24 may be keyed directly into the cell or the FUNCTION WIZARD may be used to insert it. In either case the entry in the cell is **=COVAR(A6:A17,B6:B17)**.

You will note the value in cell C24 differs from that of cell B22. The reason is the COVAR function computes the **population covariance** but the COVARIANCE tool computes the **sample covariance**. The truth of this statement can be demonstrated by multiplying the population value in cell C24 times N / (n - 1), that is, 12 / 11 = 1.090909. The result of the multiplication is 4841.0359 which equals sample value given in cell B22.

3.5.2 The CORRELATION Analysis Tool

As a numerical measure of the association between two variables, covariance has a weakness. The value of covariance depends on the units of measurement of the two variables. As a result, it is difficult to judge the strength of the relationship from the covariance. A measure of the relationship between two variables which avoids this difficulty is the correlation coefficient, sometimes called the Pearson product moment correlation coefficient. Excel provides a data analysis tool, called CORRELATION, and two statistical functions, called CORREL and PEARSON, which compute this numerical measure.

The procedure for using the CORRELATION data analysis tool is that for the COVARIANCE tool with one change. In particular for Step 4 of the above procedure, the substitution of the selection of **Correlation** from the pull-down menu instead of the selection of Covariance will result in a dialog box almost identical to that of Figure 3.16. If the dialog box entries are made as described in Step 5 above, the results will be as shown in cells E20 through G22 of Figure 3.15. Note the label in cell E19 was added for clarification.

The value 0.8504194 given in cell F22 is the value for the correlation between the two variables *No. of Stops* and *Maintenance Cost*. It is the **sample correlation** (n - 1 in the denominator, not N). The values given in cells F21 and G22 will always have the value 1. They indicate that each variable has perfect positive correlation with itself. Thus, these two values are not particularly useful.

Excel's two statistical functions for computing correlation are CORREL and PEARSON. Values for these two functions are shown in cells G24 and G25 respectively with appropriate labels in cells E24 and E25. The entry in cell G24 may be keyed directly into the cell or the function wizard may be used to insert it. In either case the entry in the cell is **=CORREL(A6:A17,B6:B17)** and that for cell G25 is **=PEARSON(A6:A17,B6:B17)**. These two functions always yield the exact same results.

This then completes are look at descriptive numerical measures. At this point you may wish to save your worksheet one last time and perhaps print out your results. Then you will need to close your worksheet and exit Excel. If you need to review the process of these operations, you may wish to review Subsection 1.2.3 of Chapter 1.

CHAPTER 4. PROBABILITY AND SAMPLING DISTRIBUTIONS

4.1 Discrete Probability Distributions
    4.1.1 Binomial Distribution
    4.1.2 Poisson Distribution
    4.1.3 Hypergeometric Distribution

4.2 Continuous Probability Distributions
    4.2.1 Normal Distribution
    4.2.2 Exponential Distribution
    4.2.3 Uniform Distribution

4.3 Sampling Distributions
    4.3.1 Sample Mean
    4.3.2 Sample Proportion

Twenty-four of the 71 (80 for Excel 8) statistical functions listed in Appendix B compute values for various probability distributions. These include many common probability distributions such as the binomial, Poisson and normal, and some less well known distributions such as the beta, negative binomial and Weibull. **Section 4.1** presents three of the most common discrete probability distributions functions. Those for the binomial, the Poisson and the hypergeometric probability distributions.

Section 4.2 presents three commonly used continuous probability distributions functions: the normal, the exponential and the uniform. Some of the other distribution functions given in Appendix B such as those for the chi-square distribution, the t distribution and the F distribution are discussed in the appropriate later chapters. The final section, **Section 4.3**, of this chapter demonstrates the Central Limit Theorem through the use of analysis tool RANDOM NUMBER GENERATION. In this section we show that the sampling distribution for the two most well-used sample statistics, the sample mean and the sample proportion, become approximately normally distributed as sample size increases.

4.1 DISCRETE PROBABILITY DISTRIBUTIONS

The FUNCTION WIZARD includes functions for four standard discrete probability distributions, the binomial, Poisson, hypergeometric and negative binomial. For the binomial and the Poisson distributions, the Function Wizard can directly compute both an individual probability value (the probability an individual value for the variable will occur) and the cumulative probability (the probability an individual value or less will occur.). For the other two standard discrete distributions, Excel directly computes only individual probability values.

4.1.1 Binomial Distribution

As an example, consider the Small Tomato Café. Its specialty is a pasta dish called the Bean Scene. Over the years, the owner has determined that about 20 per cent of the customers who enter the café purchase a Bean Scene. In other words the probability that an individual customer purchases a Bean Scene is 0.20. Suppose 12 customers enter the store, what is the probability that no one purchases a Bean Scene? That three persons make a purchase? That four or fewer persons make a purchase? Such values can be obtained from the binomial probability distribution.

The following procedure allows you to use Excel to compute all the individual probabilities and cumulative probabilities for this example. In addition, it uses the HISTOGRAM analysis tool to plot both the individual and cumulative probabilities.

1. Use the **Start-up Procedure** of Section 1.1 of Chapter 1 to start Excel.

2. Open a new Excel worksheet and enter the **Identification Material** as discussed in Section 1.5 of Chapter 1: the worksheet title in cell B1, your name in B2, the date in A3 and the file name you wish to use in D3 such as PROBS.xls.

3. Enter the label **No. Purchased** in Cell A5, and the values **0** through **12** in cells A6 through A18. Refer ahead to Figure 4.3 to see the results of these first three steps.

4. Enter the label **Prob.** in Cell B5.

5. Use the **Saving a Workbook** procedure given in Subsection 1.2.3 of Chapter 1 to save your worksheet using the file name PROBS.

6. Move the pointer to cell B6 and click the FUNCTION WIZARD icon, *fx*, with the left mouse button. The result should be as shown in Figure 4.1.

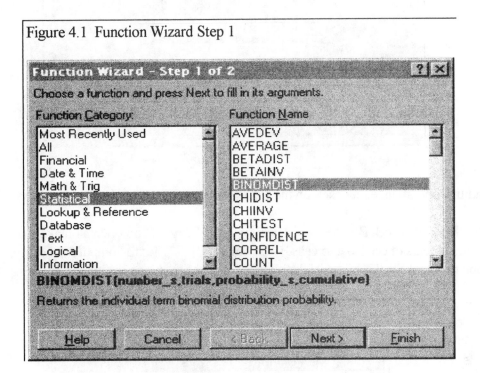

Figure 4.1 Function Wizard Step 1

7. Click on the Function Category **Statistical** in the left scrolling list box.

8. Click on the Function Name **BINOMDIST** in the right scrolling list box and then click on **Next** .

9. In the first field of the subsequent dialog box as shown in Figure 4.2, enter the cell address for the cell containing the first value for No. Purchased. Enter **A6**.

10. Use the Tab key to move to the next field and enter **12** for the number of trials.

11. Tab to the next field and enter **0.2** for the probability value.

12. Tab to the last field and enter the word **FALSE** to indicate that the individual probability values are to be computed. (As a shortcut, you may enter the number **0** instead of the word FALSE.)

Figure 4.2 BINOMDIST Function Step 2

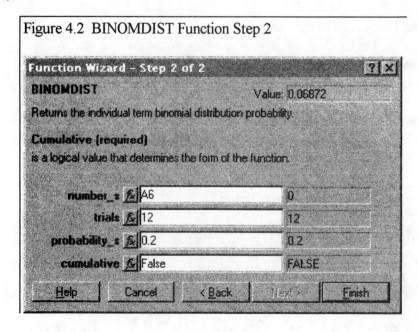

13. To end this operation, either click on the **Finish** command button or press the **Enter** key.

14. **The result** shown in cell B6 of Figure 4.3 is the probability that no one will make a purchase.   Now copy the contents of cell B6 into cells B7 through B18 in order to compute the other 12 individual probability values for this binomial distribution.   These are shown in Column B of Figure 4.3.

Figure 4.3 Binomial Distribution Results

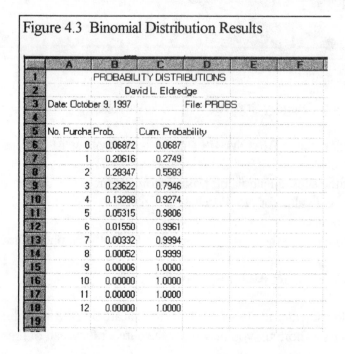

15. To adjust the number of decimal values, click and drag over the 13 probability values. Then move the pointer to the **Decrease Decimal (or Increase Decimal)** icon on the formatting toolbar and click to get the number of decimal values you would like to view.

As a check, you may wish to compare the results you have computed to those values given in the table of binomial probabilities in your textbook.

Continuing with your worksheet, repeat the process above starting with Step 4. For Step 4, enter the label **Cum. Probability** in cell C5. For Step 6 move the pointer to Cell C6. For Step 12 enter **TRUE** (or the number 1 as a shortcut) in the fourth field (cumulative) this time. Copy the equation in cell C6 into cells C7 through C18 to obtain all the values for the cumulative distribution. These values are shown in Column C of Figure 4.3.

Next we will develop a combination chart which graphs both the individual probability values and the cumulative probability values. The procedure is the following. (Note: If you have not used the Chart Wizard before you may wish to refer to Figures 2.8 through 2.12 of Chapter 2 for Excel 7 and 5, or of Appendix C for Excel 8.)

1. Move the pointer to the CHART WIZARD icon on the standard toolbar and click once.

2. The pointer will change to a small cross and bar chart. Move it to cell E5 and click the mouse.

3. Step 1 of the Chart Wizard will ask for the range of the data. Enter the range **B6:C18** either by keying it or dragging through the range. Click on **Next**.

4. For Step 2 of the Chart Wizard select chart type **Combination** and click on **Next**.

5. For Step 3 select format number **2** and click **Next**.

6. For Step 4 make sure **Columns** is selected for the **Data Series in** option and click **Next**.

7. For Step 5 select **Yes** for add a legend. Enter a **Chart Title** such as *BINOMIAL PROBABILITIES FOR N=12 & P=0.2* The **X-axis** title might be *Number Purchased* the **Y-axis** title *Individual Probability* and the **Second Y-axis** title *Cumulative Probability* Click on **Finish**.

The result should be as shown in Figure 4.4. Note the chart in this figure as been increased in size by using its sizing handles.

4.1.2 Poisson Distribution

The procedure for producing Poisson probability distribution values is almost the same as that for the binomial distribution. To demonstrate the process consider the following example.

Figure 4.4 Chart of Binomial Distribution Results

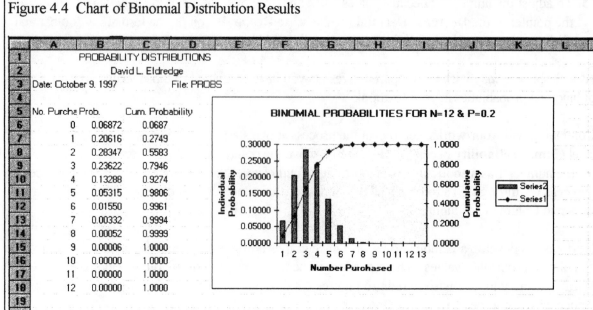

The historical records for the University Branch of Persons Bank indicate that the average number of customers arriving at the bank is four per hour. Suppose the manager wishes to determine the probability that no customers arrive in an hour? That three arrive in an hour? That four or fewer arrive in an hour? Such values can be determined from the Poisson probability distribution.

We may proceed by continuing with the worksheet for the binomial distribution of the prior subsection as follows.

1. Enter the label **No. of Arrivals** in Cell A25 and the values **0** through **16** in cells A26 through A42 as shown later in Figure 4.6.

2. Enter the label **Probability** in Cell B25.

3. Use the **Saving a Workbook** procedure of Chapter 1 to save your worksheet using the file name PROBS.

4. Move the pointer to cell B26 and click the FUNCTION WIZARD icon, *fx*. The result should be as was previously shown in Figure 4.1.

5. Click on the Function Category **Statistical**. Scroll to and click on the Function Name **POISSON** and **Next.**

6. In the first field of the subsequent dialog box as shown in Figure 4.5, enter the cell address for the cell containing the first value for *No. of Arrivals*. Enter **A26**.

Figure 4.5 POISSON Function Step 2

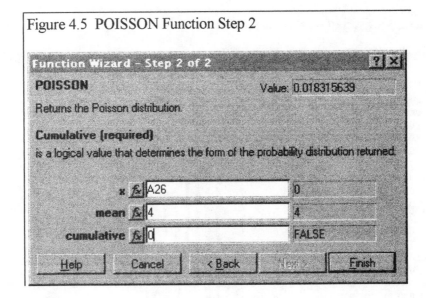

7. Use the Tab key to move to the next field and enter **4** for the mean of the distribution.

8. Tab to the last field and enter the word **FALSE** to indicate the individual probability values are to be computed. (As a shortcut, you may enter the number 0 instead.)

9. To end this operation, either click on **Finish** or press the **Enter** key.

10. The result in cell B26 as shown in Figure 4.6 is the probability that no customers arrive in an hour. Now copy the contents of cell B26 into cells B27 through B42 in order to compute the next 15 individual values for this Poisson probability distribution.

11. You may wish to select cells B26 through B42 and move the pointer to the **Decrease Decimal** icon on the formatting toolbar in order to adjust the number of decimal values.

How do the values given in Column B of Figure 4.6 compare to the probability values in the Poisson distribution table of your textbook?

Continuing with your worksheet, repeat the process above starting with Step 2. For Step 2, enter the label **Cum. Probability** in cell C25. For Step 4 move the pointer to Cell C26. For Step 9 enter **TRUE (**or the number 1 as a shortcut) in the third field (cumulative) this time. Copy the equation in cell C26 into cells C27 through C42 to obtain all the values for the cumulative distribution. These values are shown in Column C of Figure 4.6.

As with binomial distribution, you can develop a chart which shows both the individual probability values and the cumulative probability values. (Note: If you have not used the Chart Wizard before you may wish to refer to Figures 2.8 through 2.12 given in Chapter 2 for Excel 7 and 5, and given in Appendix C for Excel 8.)

Figure 4.6 Poisson Distribution Results with Chart

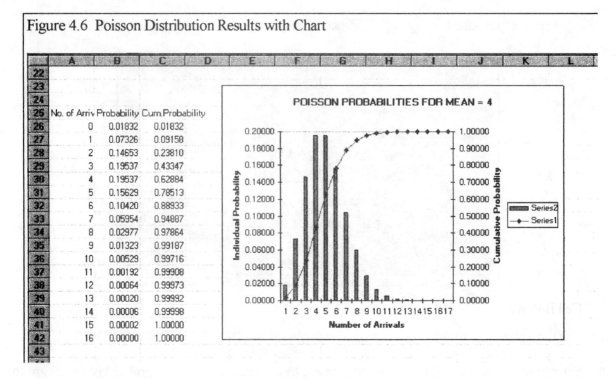

No. of Arriv	Probability	Cum.Probability
0	0.01832	0.01832
1	0.07326	0.09158
2	0.14653	0.23810
3	0.19537	0.43347
4	0.19537	0.62884
5	0.15629	0.78513
6	0.10420	0.88933
7	0.05954	0.94887
8	0.02977	0.97864
9	0.01323	0.99187
10	0.00529	0.99716
11	0.00192	0.99908
12	0.00064	0.99973
13	0.00020	0.99992
14	0.00006	0.99998
15	0.00002	1.00000
16	0.00000	1.00000

The procedure is as before.

1. Move the pointer to the CHART WIZARD icon on the standard toolbar and click once.

2. The pointer will change to a small cross and bar chart. Move it to cell E25 and click the mouse button.

3. Step 1 of the Chart Wizard will ask for the range of the data. Enter the range **B26:C42** either by keying it or dragging through the range. Click on **Next**.

4. For Step 2 of the Chart Wizard select chart type **Combination** and click on **Next**.

5. For Step 3 select format number **2** and click **Next**.

6. For Step 4 make sure **Columns** is selected for the **Data Series in** option and click **Next**.

7. For Step 5 select **Yes** for add a legend. Enter a **Chart Title** such as *POISSON PROBABILITIES FOR MEAN = 4* The **X-axis** title might be *Number of Arrivals* the Y-axis title *Individual Probability* and the **Second Y-axis** title *Cumulative Probability* Click on **Finish**.

The result should be as shown in Figure 4.6.

4.1.3 Hypergeometric Distribution

The FUNCTION WIZARD also includes the function HYPGEOMDIST. It computes individual probability values, but not cumulative probability values, for the hypergeometric distribution.

Consider the following example. Twenty-four people have applied for a position at Merry State University. Eight of the applicants are women. If five of the applicants are randomly selected from the 24, what is the probability that no women are in the sample? That three women are in the sample? That four or fewer are in the sample? The hypergeometric probability distribution can be used to compute such values.

As a demonstration of what you have learned from the two prior examples, use the FUNCTION WIZARD to create the results of Figure 4.7. Two suggestions which may be of help to you are the following.

1. Cell B46 will contain the HYPGEOMDIST function. The four values for its Step 2 dialog box are (a) the value for the random variable (the number of women in the sample), enter the cell address **A46**, (b) the sample size, enter **5**, (c) the number of women in the population, enter **8** and (d) the population size, enter **24**.

2. Since Excel's hypergeometric function does not directly return the cumulative probabilities, you must compute them. In particular, the cumulative probability for cell C46 should be set equal to the value in cell B46, that in cell C47 should be set equal to the value in B47 plus C46, that in C48 is equal to B48 plus C47, that in C49 is equal to B49 plus C48, and so on.

Figure 4.7 Hypergeometric Distribution Results with Chart

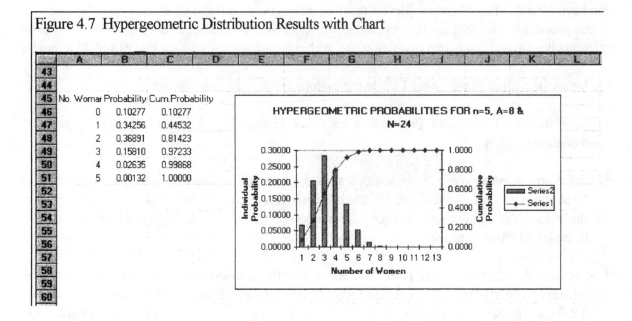

4.2 CONTINUOUS PROBABILITY DISTRIBUTIONS ───────

Excel includes functions for nine standard continuous distributions: the beta, chi-square, exponential, F, gamma, lognormal, normal, t and Weibull. In addition Excel can be used to easily compute values for a tenth continuous distribution, the uniform. We present three of these in this section, the normal, the exponential and the uniform. The t is introduced later in Chapter 5, the F and chi-square in Chapter 7.

4.2.1 Normal Distribution ──────────────────────────

The normal distribution is the most important in business statistics. Excel includes functions for both the standard normal distribution (mean = 0 and standard deviation =1) and a general normal distribution (mean other than 0 and/or standard deviation other than 1). To obtain probability values for a standard normal distribution, the Excel function NORMSDIST is used. On the other hand, to obtain probability values for a general normal distribution the Excel function is named NORMDIST (note there is not an *S* between the *M* and *D*). We will use an example to demonstrate the use of NORMDIST. The use of NORMSDIST is identical except you do not have to specify the mean and standard deviation for the distribution since Excel knows they are zero and one respectively.

> To demonstrate consider the following example. Cones Unlimited, known locally as the CU, sells an ice cream product known as the Schneesturm. They have determined that the number of Schneesturms sold each day can be described by a normal probability distribution with a mean of 485 and a standard deviation of 105.

Suppose you wished to compute and graph both the individual and the cumulative probability values as you have done for the prior three discrete distributions. You would use an approach almost identical to that previously described for the binomial distribution. We will continue with our work of the prior examples but we will begin a second worksheet within the workbook entitled PROBS.

1. Move the pointer to the **Sheet 2** tab at the bottom of the worksheet and click.

2. Enter the three labels **Sales, Probability** and **Cum. Probability** on Sheet 2 in cells A5, B5 and C5 respectively.

3. In Column A enter possible sales values starting with **65** and ending with **905** using increments of 40 between two successive numbers. Excel's command sequence **Edit-Fill-Series** can be used to easily do this or you can merely enter each number individually. Refer to later Figure 4.9 to view the result of these entries.

4. For cell B6, select the FUNCTION WIZARD, then the function category **Statistical** and then the function **NORMDIST** (not NORMSDIST which is for the standard normal distribution). Figure 4.8 shows the Step 2 dialog box for the function. You will note the values have been entered for (a) the cell location for the first Sales value of 65, (b) the mean, (c) the standard deviation and (d)

the word **FALSE** which indicates *the individual probability value* will be computed and displayed.

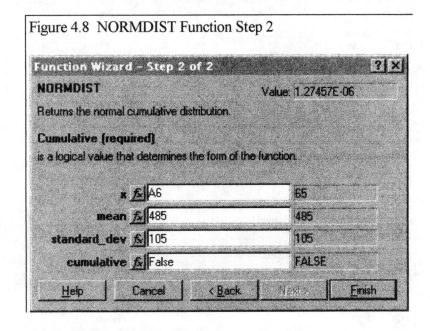

Figure 4.8 NORMDIST Function Step 2

5. Next we will use **NORMDIST** function a second time in cell C6 to compute and display *the cumulative probability value*. The entries for the dialog box are the values of Step 4 above except the word **TRUE** is entered instead of FALSE.

6. Finally, copy the functions in cells B6 and C6 into cells B7 through C27. The results will be as displayed in columns A, B and C of Figure 4.9.

You will also note in Figure 4.9, graphs of both the individual and cumulative probability values. The steps required for you to graph the individual probability values are the following. (Note: If you have not used the Chart Wizard before you may wish to refer to Figures 2.8 through 2.12 given in Chapter 2 for Excel 7 and 5, and given in Appendix C for Excel 8.)

1. Select cells A6 through B27 and click on the CHART WIZARD. Move the chart icon pointer to cell E5 and click the left mouse button.

2. In the Step 1 Chart Wizard dialog box, verify that the range is A6:B27.

3. Select the **Area** chart for the Step 2 dialog box and select format number **4** for Step 3. After clicking on the **Next** command button, the result will be as shown in Figure 4.10 for Step 4 dialog box.

Figure 4.9 Normal Distribution Results

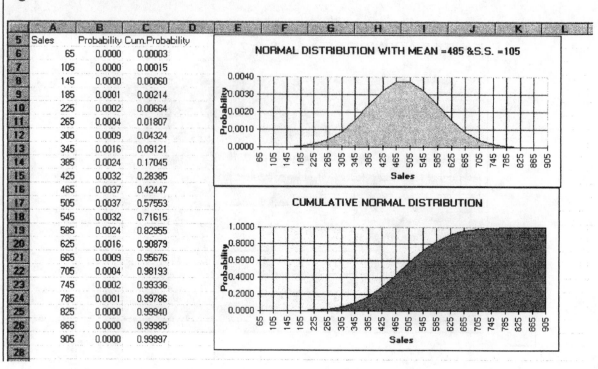

Figure 4.10 Initial Chart Wizard Step 4 for Normal Distribution

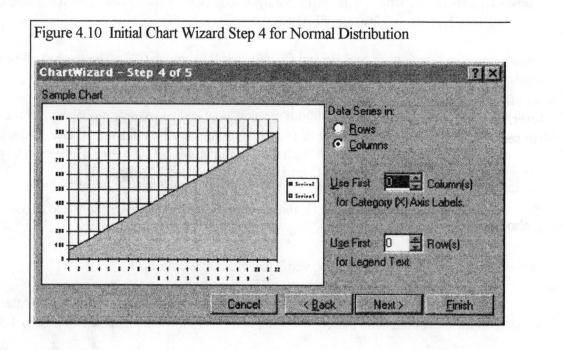

4. For the Step 4 dialog box, select *Data Series in* **Columns** and use the spinner to select **1** for the *Use First   Column(s) for Category (X) Axis Labels.* The result will be as shown in Figure 4.11.

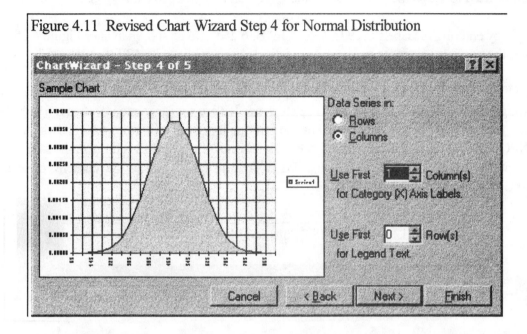

Figure 4.11 Revised Chart Wizard Step 4 for Normal Distribution

5. For the Step 5 dialog box, click **No** for *Add a Legend.* Also, Enter the **Chart Title**, the **X-axis** label and the **Y-axis** label. Click **Finish.** The result should be as shown by the chart in the top right of Figure 4.9.

The cumulative graph shown at the bottom right of Figure 4.9 is developed using the same 5 steps with one change.   The change is that the range selected for Step 1 of the CHART WIZARD is **A6:C27** instead of **A6:B27**. The chart which results actually has graph of both the column B and C values. However, the area graph of the column B values is obscured by that for the column C values. If you wish to see both graphs, select a **Line** chart instead of an **Area** chart in Step 3 of the above procedure.

4.2.2 Exponential Distribution

Excel also has a function which compute values for the exponential distribution. It is EXPONDIST. To demonstrate the use of this function consider the following example.

The average number of customers arriving at Boomes' Cleaners and Laundry is 15 per hour, that is, 0.25 per minute. Thus, the average time between customer arrivals is 4 minutes (=1 / 0.25). Furthermore the distribution of the time between arrivals appears to be exponentially distributed. The probability distribution can be used to answer questions such as, *If a customer has just arrived, what is the probability that the next customer will arrive within 5 minutes or less?*

The EXPONDIST function can be used to compute individual and cumulative probability values as was done above for the normal distribution using the NORMDIST function. The CHART WIZARD can then be used to graph the probability values. You should proceed as follows.

1. Begin by entering the labels in cells A35, A36, B36 and C36 as shown in later Figure 4.15. Also enter the possible values for time between arrivals as shown in cells A37 through A57.

2. The FUNCTION WIZARD provides the appropriate EXPONDIST function terms for cells B37 through B57 and C37 through C57. The steps needed are similar to steps 4, 5 and 6 of Subsection 4.2.1 for the NORMDIST function. For the formula for cell B37, Figure 4.12 shows the EXPONDIST Function Step 2 dialog box. The formula for cell C37 is done in the same manner except the last entry in the Step 2 dialog box is **True** instead of False. The contents of cells B37 and C37 are copied into cells B38 through C57.

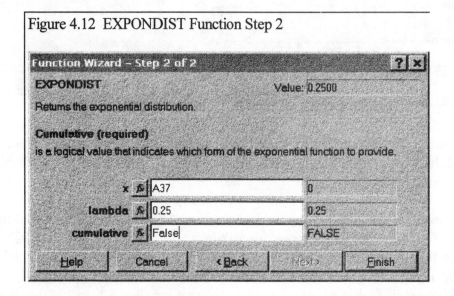

Figure 4.12 EXPONDIST Function Step 2

3. Use the CHART WIZARD to graph the individual and cumulative probability values on one chart. For Step 1 use the range **A36:C57**. For Step 2 select a **Line** chart. For Step 3 select format number **2**. After clicking on the **Next** command button for Step 3, the Step 4 dialog box shown as Figure 4.13 will be displayed on the screen. (Note: If you have not used the Chart Wizard before you may wish to refer to Figures 2.8 through 2.12 given in Chapter 2 for Excel 7 and 5, and given in Appendix C for Excel 8.)

4. For this chart we will use the first column as X-axis label and the first row for the legend. To accomplish this, use the spinner next to the word *Column(s)* to change the first 0 to a **1**, and use the spinner next to the word *Row(s)* to change the second 0 to a **1**. The result is shown in Figure 4.14.

Figure 4.13 Initial Chart Wizard Step 4 for Exponential Distribution

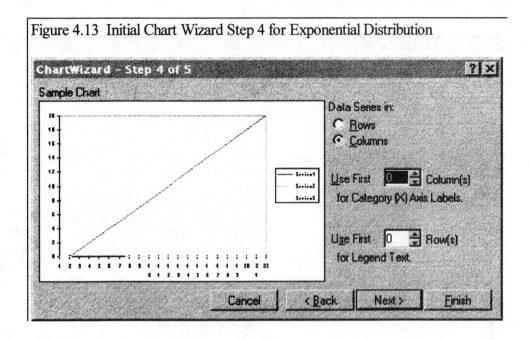

Figure 4.14 Revised Chart Wizard Step 4 for Exponential Distribution

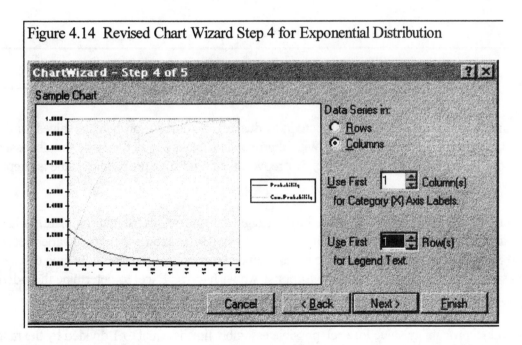

5. For Step 5 enter the **Chart Title**, **X-axis** title and **Y-axis** title and the result will be as shown in Figure 4.15.

Figure 4.15 Exponential Distribution Results

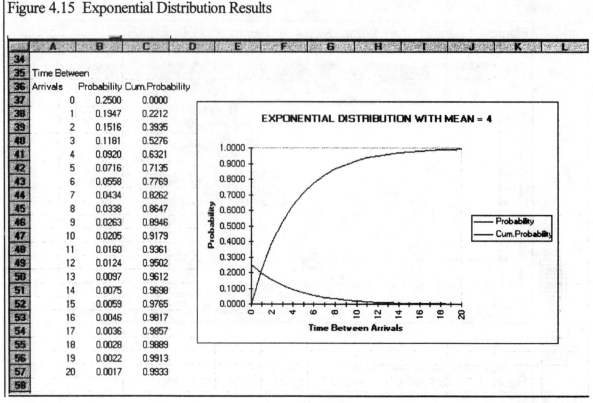

Time Between Arrivals	Probability	Cum.Probability
0	0.2500	0.0000
1	0.1947	0.2212
2	0.1516	0.3935
3	0.1181	0.5276
4	0.0920	0.6321
5	0.0716	0.7135
6	0.0558	0.7769
7	0.0434	0.8262
8	0.0338	0.8647
9	0.0263	0.8946
10	0.0205	0.9179
11	0.0160	0.9361
12	0.0124	0.9502
13	0.0097	0.9612
14	0.0075	0.9698
15	0.0059	0.9765
16	0.0046	0.9817
17	0.0036	0.9857
18	0.0028	0.9889
19	0.0022	0.9913
20	0.0017	0.9933

4.2.3 Uniform Distribution

 A special function is not needed to compute individual and cumulative probability values for the continuous uniform distribution. The individual probability values are all the same for all possible values for a uniformly distributed variable. Moreover, the cumulative probability value is simply equal to the area of a rectangle.

To demonstrate consider the situation for the Riggs and Bratton manufacturing plant. It has been determined that the amount of time it takes to assemble an engine module varies between 29 to 39 seconds. Moreover, suppose it has been determined that the assembly time can be represented by a uniform distribution. Suppose we wish to use Excel to determine the individual and cumulative probability values for assembly times at 1 second increments.

The individual probability value for each possible assembly time is equal to 1 divided by the range of possible values which is 39 - 29 = 10. This division results in the answer 0.10. The cumulative probability for a particular time value is that time value minus 29 times 0.10. For example, the cumulative probability for 32 seconds is (32 - 29) times 0.10 for an answer of 0.30. As a test of your understanding of the prior examples you should compute the probability values and create the chart given in Figure 4.16.

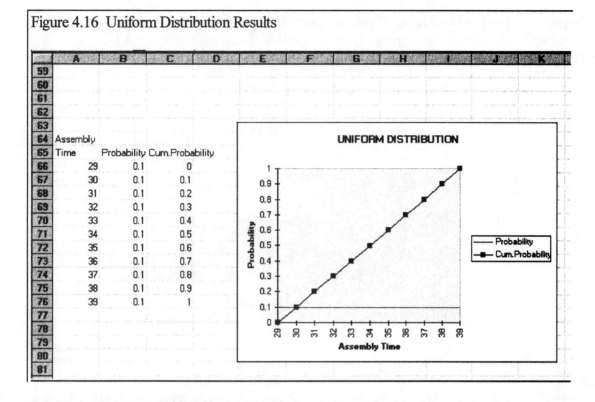

Figure 4.16 Uniform Distribution Results

4.3 SAMPLING DISTRIBUTIONS

A sampling distribution is a probability distribution for a sample statistic such as the sample mean, sample variance, sample standard deviation or sample proportion. In this section we use the data analysis tool RANDOM NUMBER GENERATION to explore the form of the sampling distribution for two sample statistics, the sample mean and the sample proportion.

4.3.1 Sample Mean

The Central Limit Theorem states that the sampling distribution of the sample mean is approximately normally distributed when the mean is computed from the values of a large sample. This is true regardless of the shape of the population distribution from which the sample is taken. This property is easily demonstrated with the use of Excel's RANDOM NUMBER GENERATION analysis tool.

The RANDOM NUMBER GENERATION tool fills a specified number of rows and columns within a worksheet with random values drawn from a selected probability distribution. The six distributions which may be selected include the uniform, normal, Bernoulli, binomial, Poisson and discrete. (It also has a non-random selection called patterned.)

Suppose we wish to draw a sample for a variable which is uniformly distributed between the values of 50 and 150. The population distribution for the variable is as shown in Figure 4.17.

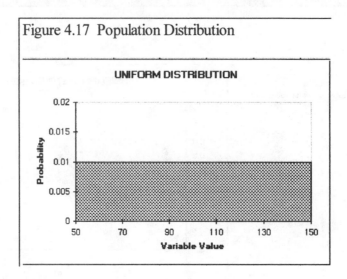

Figure 4.17 Population Distribution

Our procedure would be as follows.

1. First select the **Sheet 3** tab for the PROBS worksheet. From the **Tools** menu select **Data Analysis** and then the **Random Number Generation** analysis tool. The resulting dialog box would be as shown in Figure 4.18.

2. Figure 4.18 indicates you are to enter **2** for the *Number Of Variables* and **60** for the *Number Of Random Samples*. The *Number Of Variables* corresponds to the number of columns to be filled with random values drawn from the uniform distribution of Figure 4.17. The *Number Of Random Samples* corresponds to the number of rows to be filled with random values. Thus, this command will result in 120 random values arranged in 60 rows and 2 columns of random values. For our example, we will use these as 60 samples, one in each row, each with a sample size of 2.

3. The third input to be specified is the population distribution. The drop-down list box labeled with the word *Distribution* is used to specify a **Uniform** distribution. The lower limit of **50** and the upper limit of **150** are entered as the parameters for the distribution.

4. We can ignore the box labeled as **Random Seed** and use the mouse button to select **Output Range** as the Output Option and enter the output range as **A22**.

5. Select the **OK** button and the result will be 60 rows and 2 columns of numbers randomly selected from the specified uniform distribution. See Figure 4.19. (Your random values will not be the same.)

Figure 4.18 Random Number Generation Dialog Box

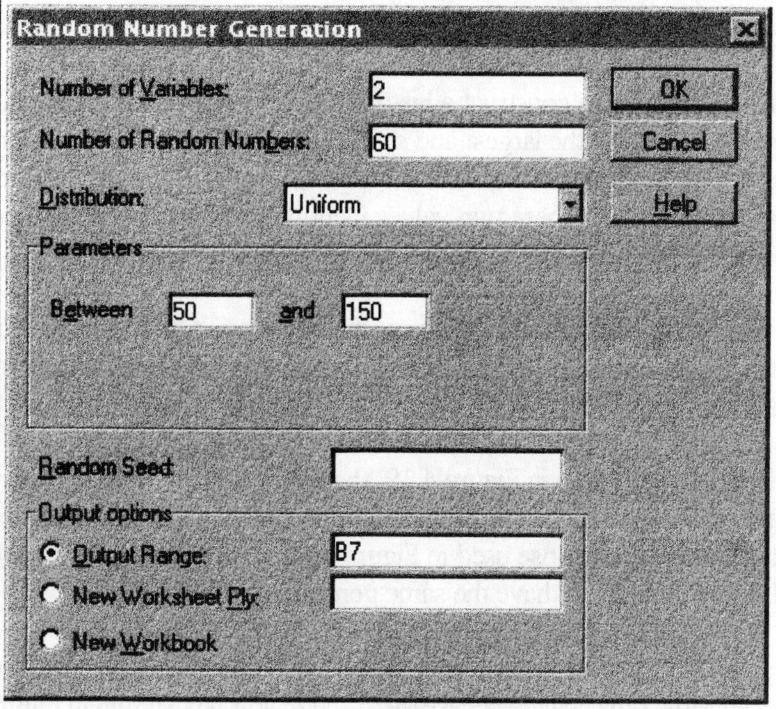

Figure 4.19 Distribution of Sample Mean for n=2

B	C	D	E	F	G	H	I	J	K	L
Observation Number		Sample								
1	2	Mean		Bins						
91.3068	89.9884	90.6476		50						
52.81075	109.7583	81.28452		60						
86.58559	111.2934	98.93948		70						
127.0226	94.03821	110.5304		80						
149.1699	68.89706	109.0335		90						
143.3653	101.9547	122.66		100						
81.34556	124.3187	102.8321		110						
62.06397	68.50948	65.28672		120						
81.08005	124.7368	102.9084		130						
68.38435	107.503	87.94366		140						
148.2635	96.70553	122.4845								
53.98877	79.92035	66.95456	Bin	Frequency						
141.9462	86.95181	114.449	50	0						
57.0864	86.02405	71.55522	60	1						
66.67837	115.8315	91.25492	70	6						
64.5085	71.63457	68.07154	80	3						
116.1061	59.13724	87.62169	90	9						
128.7927	89.34141	109.067	100	13						
51.83721	123.8578	87.84753	110	10						
103.4532	105.1958	104.3245	120	8						
145.8892	133.4651	139.6771	130	6						
149.5514	91.554	120.5527	140	4						

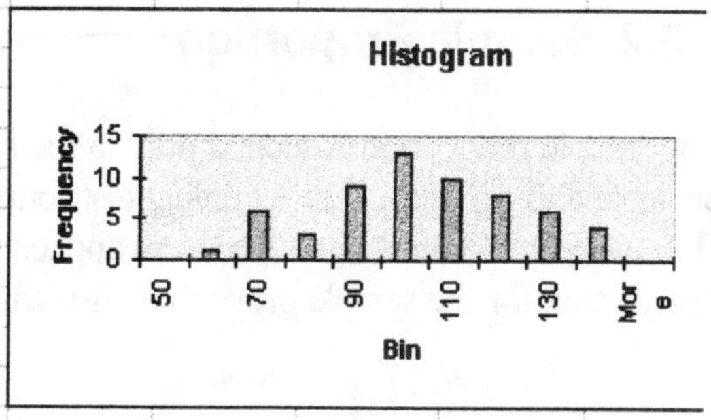

6. In cell D7, enter the formula **=AVERAGE(C7:D7)** in order to compute the mean of the first sample given in row 7. Copy the equation down in order to compute the remaining 59 sample means for rows 8 though 66.

7. Our last step is to use Excel to construct a histogram of the 60 sample means in cells D7 through D66. First we will determine the largest and smallest values for the means by entering at the bottom of Column D the expression **=MAX(D7:D66)** in cell D68, and the expression **=MIN(D7:D66)** in cell D69. These two values identify the range of mean values to be included in the histogram.

8. Based on the range of values and the number of bins to be used, the bin values are selected. As shown in cells F7 through F16 in Figure 4.19, we have selected 9 bins with an increment of 10 and starting with a lower limit of 50. The Histogram output range is specified as E18.

As you will note from the histogram in Figure 4.19, the distribution of these means with a sample size of 2 is peaked or triangular in shape, not shaped as a normal distribution. Since your random sample values in all likelihood differ from those used in Figure 4.19, your histogram will not be exactly like that of Figure 4.19. However, it should have the same general appearance.

This process is repeated in Figure 4.20 except 60 samples of size 30 are generated instead of 60 samples of size 2. Thus the only change necessary to the dialog box shown in Figure 4.18, is to set the number of variables (sample size) to 30 instead of 2. Depending on the performance capability of the computer you are using, the generation of 60 times 30 (= 1800) random observations from the uniform distribution may take a few moments or a few minutes. The resulting 1800 values will be shown in rows 7 through 66 and in columns B through AE. The entries in column AF compute the means for the 60 samples. The histogram of these means is constructed.

The results of Figure 4.20 show two significant changes from those of Figure 4.19. First, the range of values for the sample means is much reduced. Second, the histogram of the sample means is more normal shaped than that of Figure 4.19. Thus, this example demonstrates that the distribution of the means of samples taken from a non-normal population becomes more normal shaped as the sample size is increased. You may wish to repeat the example for a sample size of 100 to make the demonstration more emphatic.

4.3.2 Sample Proportion

The sample proportion is second only to the sample mean as the most well used sample statistic in business and industry. The sampling distribution for the sample proportion is the binomial distribution. However, the Central Limit Theorem applies to it also. That is, for large sample sizes the sampling distribution for the sample proportion also can be approximated by the normal distribution.

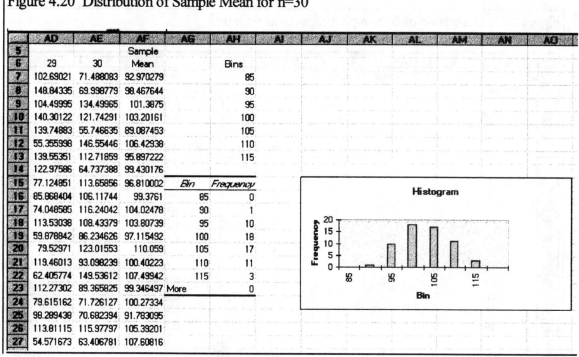

Figure 4.20 Distribution of Sample Mean for n=30

To demonstrate this fact, we can use the RANDOM NUMBER GENERATION analysis tool to generate samples from a **Bernoulli** distribution. The possible values for the Bernoulli distribution are 0 and 1. Accordingly, the proportion of times the value 1 occurs in a sample is equal to the average value for the sample. The histogram of these proportions can than be plotted in order to see the shape of the distribution.

To test your comprehension of the instructions of Subsection 4.3.1, you should set up the dialog box of Figure 4.18 for the sample proportion. As shown in Figure 4.21, the worksheet is to be setup to for generate 60 samples (rows) with a sample size of 5 (columns) from a Bernoulli distribution with a probability of success of 0.20.

The histogram for these 60 sample proportions is shown in Figure 4.22. As you will note, the form of the histogram suggests a binomial distribution as would be expected. Because of the random outcomes your results may differ slightly from those we have presented.

If this process is repeated using 60 samples of size 50 the resulting distribution of the 60 sample proportions is much more normally distributed in its shape as is shown in Figure 4.23. This is what we would expect based on the Central Limit Theorem.

At this time you may wish to save your Excel workbook one last time and perhaps print the results. You will then need close your workbook and exit Excel.

Figure 4.21   Generation of 60 Sample Proportions with n=5

Sample Number	Observation Number					Sample Proportion		Bins
	1	2	3	4	5			
1	0	0	0	1	0	0.2		0
2	1	0	0	0	0	0.2		0.2
3	0	0	0	0	0	0		0.4
4	0	0	1	1	0	0.4		0.6
5	0	0	0	0	1	0.2		0.8
6	0	0	1	1	0	0.4		1
7	0	0	0	0	0	0		
8	1	0	1	0	1	0.6		
9	0	0	0	1	0	0.2		
10	1	1	0	1	1	0.8		
11	0	0	1	1	0	0.4		
12	0	0	0	0	0	0		
13	1	0	0	0	1	0.4		
14	0	0	0	0	1	0.2		
15	0	1	1	0	1	0.6		
16	0	0	1	0	0	0.2		
17	0	0	0	0	0	0		
18	0	0	0	0	0	0		
19	0	1	0	0	0	0.2		
20	1	1	0	0	0	0.4		
21	0	0	0	1	0	0.2		
22	0	0	0	0	0	0		

Figure 4.22   Histogram of 60 Sample Proportions with n=5

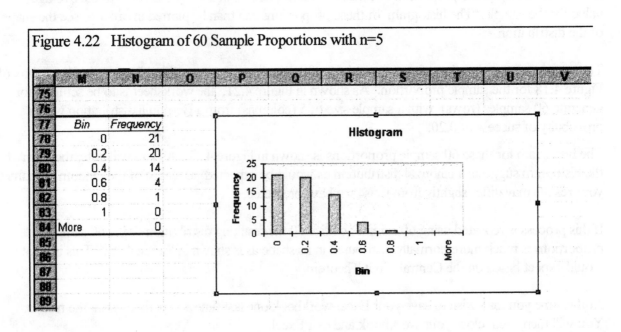

Bin	Frequency
0	21
0.2	20
0.4	14
0.6	4
0.8	1
1	0
More	0

Figure 4.23 Histogram of 60 Sample Proportion with n=50

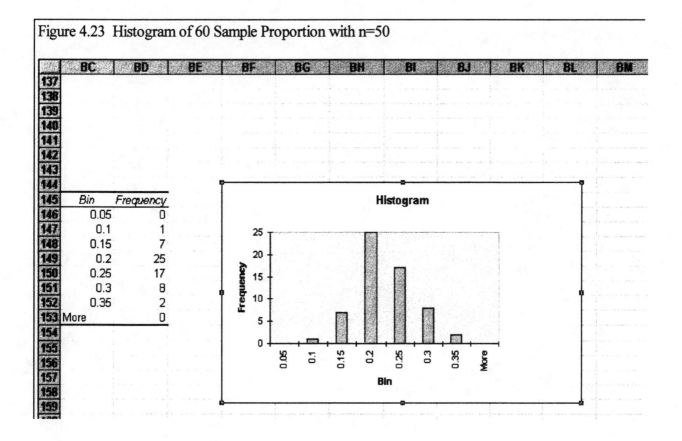

	Bin	Frequency
145	Bin	Frequency
146	0.05	0
147	0.1	1
148	0.15	7
149	0.2	25
150	0.25	17
151	0.3	8
152	0.35	2
153	More	0

CHAPTER 5. STATISTICAL INFERENCE FOR POPULATION MEANS

5.1 One Population Mean
    5.1.1 Point Estimate and Confidence Interval—Normal Distribution
    5.1.2 Hypothesis Test—Normal Distribution
    5.1.3 Point Estimate and Confidence Interval—t Distribution
    5.1.4 Hypothesis Test—t Distribution
    5.1.5 Determining the Necessary Sample Size

5.2 The t-TEST: TWO-SAMPLE ASSUMING UNEQUAL VARIANCE Analysis Tool
    5.2.1 Hypothesis Test for Two Population Means with Independent Samples
    5.2.2 Point Estimate and Confidence Interval for Two Population Means
    5.2.3 Statistical Inference for One Population Mean

5.3 Two Additional Analysis Tools for Two Independent Samples
    5.3.1 The t-TEST: TWO-SAMPLE ASSUMING EQUAL VARIANCE Tool
    5.3.2 The z-TEST: TWO SAMPLE FOR MEANS Analysis Tool

5.4 The t-TEST: PAIRED TWO SAMPLE FOR MEANS Analysis Tool
    5.4.1 Hypothesis Test for Two Population Means with dependent samples
    5.4.2 Point Estimate and Confidence Interval for Two Population Means
    5.4.3 Statistical Inference for One Population Mean

At this point in this manual we have used Excel to support our study of the **descriptive use of sample statistics**, commonly called **descriptive statistics**. In Chapter 2 we constructed descriptive graphs and charts and in Chapter 3 we computed descriptive numerical measures. In Chapter 4 we computed values for probability and sampling distributions. The study of these distributions provide background needed for understanding the material of the current chapter. In this chapter we use Excel to support our study of the **inferential use of sample statistics**, commonly called **inferential statistics** or **statistical inference**.

The term statistical inference refers to the process of acquiring information and drawing conclusions about **populations** based on **samples** taken from the populations. The two main thrusts of statistical inference are the statistical estimation and the statistical testing of an unknown **population parameter** through the use of a value for the corresponding **sample statistic**.

In business and industry, three of the most important population parameters are the population mean, the population proportion and the population variance (or standard deviation). For each one of these three, we can use the capability of Excel to (1) compute a **point estimate** with its corresponding **confidence interval** (also called **interval estimate**), and (2) conduct a **hypothesis test** for a single population. Moreover many times, it is necessary to estimate and/or test a comparison of parameters for two populations, that is a comparison of two population means, two population proportions or two population variances. Again for these situations Excel provides the capability to easily compute a point estimate with its corresponding confidence interval and to conduct a hypothesis test.

This current chapter presents statistical inference for population means. The chapter treats both statistical estimation and testing for one population mean and also for two population means. Chapter 6 provides similar coverage of statistical inference for population proportions and Chapter 7 for population variances.

Section 5.1 covers statistical inference for one population mean. In it we demonstrate the use of formulas and statistical functions to compute values for the point estimate with its corresponding confidence interval and values for the hypothesis test. (Alternate approaches using two Excel data analysis tools designed for the two population situation are presented in subsections 5.2.3 and 5.4.3.)

Sections 5.2 and 5.3 cover statistical inference for two population means using independent samples. These two sections present the three approaches commonly given in statistics textbooks for estimating and testing the difference between two population means using independent samples. Usually the first approach given in a textbook is that based on the normal (or z) distribution. This approach is valid if the population variances are known. It is also used when the sample sizes of the two samples are large so the normal distribution can be used to approximate the t distribution. The second and third approaches given in most statistics textbooks are based on the t distribution (*note some textbooks only present one or the other of these two*). These two approaches are applicable if the population variances are not known and if the z distribution is not to be used to approximate the t distribution. One of these two approaches requires the condition that the unknown variances of the two populations are known to be equal to each other. The other does not require this condition.

Some statisticians feel the most general of these three approaches is that which uses the t distribution and does not require the condition that the population variances are known to be equal. Accordingly, **Section 5.2** presents this approach in detail. Using Excel's t-TEST: TWO-SAMPLE ASSUMING UNEQUAL VARIANCE analysis tool, we compute values for the point estimate with its corresponding confidence interval and values for the hypothesis test for two population means using independent samples. Also in this section we show how to use this two population analysis tool to compute the same values for the one population situation. **Section 5.3** then discusses the other two approaches. These are based on the t-TEST: TWO-SAMPLE ASSUMING EQUAL VARIANCE analysis tool and z-TEST: TWO SAMPLE FOR MEANS analysis tool. Section 5.3 highlights the differences between the use of these two analysis tools and the tool presented in Section 5.2.

Finally **Section 5.4** covers statistical inference for two population means using dependent samples. Your textbook may call dependent samples paired samples, matched samples, related samples or matched pairs. The approach of this section uses the t distribution and is based on the t-TEST: PAIRED TWO SAMPLE FOR MEANS analysis tool. Section 5.4 also indicates how to use this two population analysis tools to compute the same values for the one population situation.

5.1 ONE POPULATION MEAN

As previously mentioned, the two main thrusts of statistical inference is the estimation and testing. **Estimation** involves using the value for a sample statistic, such as the sample mean, to provide a **point estimate** for an unknown corresponding population parameter, such as the population mean. In order to quantify the precision or accuracy of the point estimate, a corresponding **confidence interval** (or interval estimate) is computed. The confidence interval is of the form

Point Estimate ± (Confidence Level Critical Value) * (Standard Error for the Point Estimate).

The confidence level critical value is found from an appropriate probability distribution such as the normal, the t, the F and so on.

On the other hand, **testing** involves using the value for a sample statistic, such as the sample mean, to test a tentative assumption regarding an unknown value for a corresponding population parameter. The results of the **hypothesis test** is either the rejection or not of the tentative hypothesis which is called the null hypothesis. The test is conducted using a test statistic which generally is of the form

Test Statistic = (Point Estimate-Null Hypothesis Value) / (Standard Error for the Point Estimate).

The value computed by this equation is compared to critical value from an appropriate probability distribution such as the normal, the t, the F and so on. Based on this comparison, the null hypothesis is either rejected or not.

In order to demonstrate the use of the above formulas in Excel we will consider the following example in this section.

Ms. Lizabert Humperdinck, the general manager of the Read and Feed chain of restaurants, is investigating promotional ideas for the *Country Basket* dinners. She has proposed using spot advertisements on local TV to promote the product. Furthermore, she feels the spot ads will increase average sales to 215 per store. The advertising program is pursued in the service area of eight randomly selected restaurants and the resulting sales from the eight are as given in Table 5.1.

Table 5.1 Number of Country Basket Dinners Sold after TV Promotion								
Number Sold	240	220	190	175	220	215	219	195

We will use this example to demonstrate the computations for both (1) the point estimate and confidence interval, and (2) the hypothesis test for one population mean. If you wish to compute these using the **normal (or z) distribution** proceed through subsections **5.1.1** and **5.1.2**. If you wish to use the **t distribution** you should proceed through subsections **5.1.3** and **5.1.4**. These parts of the manual are written assuming you will be studying either 5.1.1 and 5.1.2, or 5.1.3 and 5.1.4. In particular, 5.1.3 and 5.1.4 do not refer to any material in 5.1.1 and 5.1.2. Instead they repeat some material from these prior subsections. If you proceed through all four sections, there will be some repeated material in subsections 5.1.3 and 5.1.4. We use *Sheet1* of our workbook for the normal distribution computations and *Sheet2* for the t distribution. The last subsection, 5.1.5, shows how to compute the sample size required to attain a specified width and confidence level for a confidence interval. These computations are included on *Sheet3* of the workbook. They follow either the normal distribution computations of Sheet1 or the t distribution computations of Sheet2.

5.1.1 Point Estimate and Confidence Interval—Normal Distribution

The point estimate and confidence interval can be computed easily for the data set of Table 5.1. For example, we can proceed in the following manner in order to compute the point estimate and 95% confidence interval.

1. Start Excel, enter the **Identification Material** shown in rows 1 and 2 of later Figure 5.2. Then enter the labels of rows 3 through 17. (Note some of the column widths have been adjusted for readability. You may also wish to do this.) Enter the data values in cells A5 through A12 and the input value in cell E4. (Note the labels in rows 18 through 25 and the input values given in cells E6 and E7 will be entered later when the hypothesis test computations are entered.) Save the workbook with the name MEANS-1.

2. Compute the value for the sample mean, sample standard deviation and sample size by entering the functions **AVERAGE**, **STDEV** and **COUNT** in cells L5, L6 and L7 as shown in Figure 5.1. As you will note from the figure, we have set the range for these functions as A5 through A104. Thus, the worksheet will compute these sample statistics for data sets with up to 100 data values.

3. To compute the point estimate for the population mean, enter the formula **=L5** in cell L9.

4. Cell L13 uses the Excel function NORMSINV to find the critical z-value for the specified confidence level given in cell E4. The confidence level is converted from percentage to decimal form by first dividing by 100, and then it is converted to the two-tailed value by dividing by 2. Finally 0.5 is added to the result in order to find the z-value on the right-hand of the distribution. The resulting formula for cell L13 is **=NORMSINV(E4/100/2+0.5)** as shown in Figure 5.1.

Figure 5.1 Statistical Inference Formulas for One Population Mean—Normal Distribution

	H	I	J K	L
1				
2			File:	
3				
4	Sample Statistics			
5		Sample Mean		=AVERAGE(A5:A104)
6		Sample Standard Deviation		=STDEV(A5:A104)
7		Sample Size		=COUNT(A5:A104)
8				
9	Point Estimate			=L5
10				
11	Confidence Interval			
12				
13		Confidence Level Critical z-value		=NORMSINV(E4/100/2+0.5)
14		Standard Error of the Point Estimate		=L6/SQRT(L7)
15		Confidence Interval--Half Width		=L13*L14
16		--Lower Limit		=L9-L15
17		--Upper Limit		=L9+L15
18	Hypothesis Test			
19		Test Statistic		=(L9-E6)/L14
20		z critical value--Form I		=-1*NORMSINV($E$7/2)
21		--Form II		=-1*NORMSINV($E$7)
22		--Form III		=NORMSINV($E$7)
23		p-value--Form I		=IF($L$19<0,2*NORMSDIST($L$19),2*(1-NORMSDIST($L$19)))
24		--Form II		=1-NORMSDIST($L$19)
25		--Form III		=NORMSDIST($L$19)

5. The formula in cell L14 computes the standard error of the point estimate from the values for the sample standard deviation and the sample size computed in cells L6 and L7 respectively. The formula in cell L14 is **=L6/SQRT(L7)**.

6. Half the width of the confidence interval is found by multiplying the critical z-value times the standard error of the point estimate as shown in cell L15.

7. The half width is subtracted from the point estimate to compute the confidence interval lower limit as shown in cell L16. It is added to the point estimate to compute the upper limit in L17.

Figure 5.2 shows the results of these computations. Cell L9 presents the best estimate of Read and Feed's sales after the spot advertisement campaign to be 209.25. The precision of this estimate is quantified by the 95% confidence interval given in cells L16 and L17. It is from 194.782 to 223.718. Since this 95% confidence interval includes Lizabert's postulated sales value of 215, she can conclude her sales expectations have been attained.

Figure 5.2 Statistical Inference for One Population Mean—Normal Distribution

	A	B	C	D	E	F	G	H	I	J	K	L	M
1	STATISTICAL INFERENCE FOR ONE MEAN WITH NORMAL DISTRIBUTION												
2	Date: November 17, 1997				David L. Eldredge						File: MEANS-1.xls		
3	INPUT DATA							STATISTICAL OUTPUTS					
4	Data Values		Confidence Level =		95 %			Sample Statistics					
5	240								Sample Mean			209.250	
6	220		Hypothesized Mean =		215				Sample Standard Deviation			20.879	
7	190		Significance Level of Test=		0.05				Sample Size			8	
8	175												
9	220							Point Estimate				209.250	
10	215												
11	219							Confidence Interval					
12	195												
13									Confidence Level Critical z-value			1.95996	
14									Standard Error of the Point Estimate			7.382	
15									Confidence Interval--Half Width			14.468	
16									--Lower Limit			194.782	
17									--Upper Limit			223.718	
18								Hypothesis Test					
19									Test Statistic			-0.779	
20									z critical value--Form I			1.960	
21									--Form II			1.645	
22									--Form III			-1.645	
23									p-value--Form I			0.436	
24									--Form II			0.782	
25									--Form III			0.218	

5.1.2 Hypothesis Test—Normal Distribution

The values needed for conducting a hypothesis test can also be computed easily with Excel. To demonstrate we will use the data set of Table 5.1 to compute the values needed to conduct a hypothesis test both for the **critical z-value approach** and for the **p-value approach**. We will compute the values needed for these two testing approaches for all three of the possible forms for the hypothesis test as shown in Table 5.2. We will refer to the three forms as I, II and III.

Table 5.2 Possible Hypothesis Forms for Testing One Population Mean

Form I	Form II	Form III
$H_0: \mu = 215$	$H_0: \mu \leq 215$	$H_0: \mu \geq 215$
$H_a: \mu \neq 215$	$H_a: \mu > 215$	$H_a: \mu < 215$

We can proceed in the following manner in order to conduct a hypothesis test to determine if the sales level is 215 after the advertising campaign. We will conduct the test using a significance level of 0.05 and continue with the worksheet presented in Figure 5.2.

1. Enter the labels in rows 18 through 25 and the input values in cells E6 and E7 as shown in Figure 5.2..

2. Enter the formula **=(L6-E6)/L14** into cell L19 to compute the z-statistic value for the sample (Figure 5.1 shows the formula in the worksheet.)

3. In cell L20 the function NORMSINV is used to determine the critical value for the z-statistic for a two-tailed test, **Form I** of Table 5.2. The function is multiplied by a minus one to obtain the needed a positive value. Thus, the entry for cell L20 is **= - 1*NORMSINV($E$7/2)**. (Note it is not necessary for E7 to have the absolute address, $E$7.)

4. The NORMSINV function is also used in cells L21 and L22 to determine the critical value for the z-statistic for the two possible one-tailed tests, **Form II** and **Form III** of Table 5.2. For cell L21 the formula is **= -1*NORMSINV($E$7)** and for cell L22 **=NORMSINV($E$7)**.

5. Move the cell pointer to cell L25 and enter the formula **=NORMSDIST($L$19)** to compute the p value for the **Form III** hypotheses.

6. Cell L24 computes the p value for the **Form II** hypotheses by the formula **=1-NORMSDIST($L$19)**.

7. Finally in cell L23 an IF function is used to determine the p value for a two-tailed test, **Form I**. If the value for the test statistic, cell L19, is less than zero, the p value is computed as two times the computation of cell L25. Otherwise it is computed as two times the computation of L24. You may feel the resulting formula appears somewhat intimidating. However, it is merely made up of three parts separated by commas: (1) a test for negativity, (2) a

computation similar to cell L25 and (3) a computation similar to cell L24. The resulting formula is =IF($L$19<0,2*NORMSDIST($L$19),2*(1-NORMSDIST($L$19))).

The results of these steps are as shown in previous Figure 5.2. Your worksheet provides the statistics necessary to conduct the single sample hypothesis test for both the critical z-value and the p-value approaches. For both of these two approaches, it provides for testing all three of the possible forms of the hypotheses as given in Table 5.2.

For the **CRITICAL z-VALUE APPROACH,** the value for the test statistic in cell L19 of Figure 5.2 is -0.779. For the **Form I** two tailed test, cell L20 indicates the critical values for the test statistic are -1.960 and +1.960. Since the value of -0.779 does not fall outside these limits the null hypothesis is not rejected. The sample evidence does not support rejecting the hypothesis that Read and Feed sales level is 215 after the advertising campaign. In other words, in light of the sample evidence the assumption of a sales level of 215 seems reasonable.

For the **Form II** hypotheses, the test value of -0.779 is not greater than the critical value of +1.645 given in cell L21 of Figure 5.2. Thus, we can not reject the null hypothesis. The sample data supports the contention that the market share is less than or equal to 215.

Finally for the **Form III** hypotheses, the test value of -0.779 is not less than the critical value of -1.645 given in cell L22 so the hypothesis of a sales level of greater than or equal to 215 is not rejected. Thus, all three forms of the test indicate an acceptance of the null hypothesis which includes the possibility of equality to 215 for the sales level. We conclude that Lizabert's hypothesis (conjecture, hunch, estimate, guess, etc.) that the spot TV advertisements would boost sales of the Country Dinners to 215 per store is supported by the sample evidence.

The results of Figure 5.2 also let us consider the **p-VALUE APPROACH** to this test. Conventional usage of p-values classifies test results according to the categories given in Table 5.3 (see for example Siegel, *Practical Business Statistics*, Irwin, 1997, p.328).

Table 5.3 p-Value Classification Categories

If the P-Value is	Then the Difference is
Greater than 0.05	Not Significant
Greater than 0.01 but less than or equal to 0.05	Significant
Greater than 0.001 but less than or equal to 0.01	Highly Significant
Less than or equal to 0.001	Very Highly Significant

Utilizing the classification categories of this table, we would classify the results as *not significant* for all three forms of the hypotheses. That is, the p values of 0.436, 0.782 and 0.218 are all greater than 0.05. The conclusion is not to reject the null hypothesis regardless of what hypotheses form we were testing. This is the same conclusions drawn using the critical z-value approach.

You should save your completed worksheet of Figure 5.2 for future use. Although you developed it for a particular test situation, it is completely general. Thus, you can use it for estimating and testing a population mean based on a sample from that population. To use the worksheet, you only need to enter

1. The data values for the sample beginning in cell A5. As previously indicated the formulas you entered allow for up to 100 data values. This limit could be increased by simply expanding the range used in cells L5, L6 and L7,

2. The confidence level you desire for the confidence interval in cell E4, and

3. The hypothesized value for the mean in cell E6 and the significance level for the test in cell E7.

After entering these input values, your worksheet will provide you with the point estimate and its confidence interval based on the normal distribution. In addition, it will return all the necessary values for conducting all three forms of the hypothesis test for both the critical z-value and the p-value approaches.

5.1.3 Point Estimate and Confidence Interval—t Distribution ─────────

The point estimate and confidence interval can be computed easily for the data set of Table 5.1. For example, we can proceed in the following manner in order to compute the point estimate and 95% confidence interval. To begin click on **Sheet2** at the bottom of the worksheet window.

1. Start Excel, enter the **Identification Material** shown in rows 1 and 2 of later Figure 5.4. Then enter the labels of rows 3 through 17. (Note some of the column widths have been adjusted for readability. You may also wish to do this.) Enter the data values in cells A5 through A12 and the input value in cell E4. (Note the labels in rows 18 through 25 and the input values given in cells E6 and E7 will be entered later when the hypothesis test computations are entered.) Save the workbook with the name MEANS-1.

2. Compute the value for the sample mean, sample standard deviation and sample size by entering the functions **AVERAGE, STDEV** and **COUNT** in cells L5, L6 and L7 as shown in Figure 5.3. As you will note from the figure, we have set the range for these functions as A5 through A104. Thus, the worksheet will compute these sample statistics for data sets with up to 100 data values.

3. To compute the point estimate for the population mean, enter the formula =**L5** in cell L9.

4. Cell L12 computes the degrees of freedom as equal to the sample size minus one, and cell L13 uses the Excel function TINV to find the critical t value for the specified confidence level given in cell E4. The confidence level is converted from percentage to decimal form by first dividing by 100, and the resulting values is subtracted from one to obtain the probability in the tail of the distribution. It is not necessary to divide by 2 because the TINV function returns a two-tailed value. The resulting formula for cell L13 is =**TINV(1-E4/100,L12)** where cell L12 refers to the degrees of freedom.

5. The formula in cell L14 computes the standard error of the point estimate from the values for the sample standard deviation and the sample size computed in cells L6 and L7 respectively. The formula in cell L14 is =**L6/SQRT(L7)**.

Figure 5.3 Statistical Inference Formulas for One Population Mean—t Distribution

	H	I	J K	L
4	Sample Statistics			
5		Sample Mean		=AVERAGE(A5:A104)
6		Sample Standard Deviation		=STDEV(A5:A104)
7		Sample Size		=COUNT(A5:A104)
8				
9	Point Estimate			=L5
10				
11	Confidence Interval			
12		Degrees of Freedom		=L7-1
13		Confidence Level Critical t-value		=TINV(1-E4/100,L12)
14		Standard Error of the Point Estimate		=L6/SQRT(L7)
15		Confidence Interval--Half Width		=L13*L14
16		--Lower Limit		=L9-L15
17		--Upper Limit		=L9+L15
18	Hypothesis Test			
19		Test Statistic		=(L9-E6)/L14
20		t critical value--Form I		=TINV($E$7,L12)
21		--Form II		=TINV(2*$E$7,L12)
22		--Form III		=-1*TINV(2*$E$7,L12)
23		p-value--Form I		=TDIST(ABS(L19),L12,2)
24		--Form II		=IF(L19<0,1-TDIST(ABS(L19),L12,1),TDIST(ABS(L19),L12,1))
25		--Form III		=1-L24
26				

6. Half the width of the confidence interval is found by multiplying the critical t value times the standard error of the point estimate as shown in cell L15.

7. The half width is subtracted from the point estimate to compute the confidence interval lower limit as shown in cell L16. It is added to the point estimate to compute the upper limit in cell L17.

Figure 5.4 shows the results of these computations. As given in cell L9 the best estimate of Read and Feed's sales after the spot advertisement campaign is 209.25. The precision of this estimate is quantified by the 95% confidence interval given in cells L16 and L17. Based on the t distribution it is 191.795 to 226.705. Since this 95% confidence interval includes Lizabert's postulated sales value of 215, she can conclude her sales expectations have been attained.

Figure 5.4 Statistical Inference for One Population Mean—t Distribution

	A	B	C	D	E	F	G	H	I	J	K	L	M
1	STATISTICAL INFERENCE FOR ONE MEAN WITH t DISTRIBUTION												
2	Date: November 18, 1997				David L. Eldredge						File: MEANS-1.xls		
3	INPUT DATA						STATISTICAL OUTPUTS						
4	Data Values		Confidence Level =		95 %		Sample Statistics						
5	240							Sample Mean				209.250	
6	220		Hypothesized Mean =		215			Sample Standard Deviation				20.879	
7	190		Significance Level of Test=		0.05			Sample Size				8	
8	175												
9	220							Point Estimate				209.250	
10	215												
11	219							Confidence Interval					
12	195							Degrees of Freedom				7	
13								Confidence Level Critical t-value				2.365	
14								Standard Error of the Point Estimate				7.382	
15								Confidence Interval--Half Width				17.455	
16									--Lower Limit			191.795	
17									--Upper Limit			226.705	
18								Hypothesis Test					
19								Test Statistic				-0.779	
20								t critical value--Form I				2.365	
21									--Form II			1.895	
22									--Form III			-1.895	
23								p-value--Form I				0.462	
24									--Form II			0.769	
25									--Form III			0.231	

5.1.4 Hypothesis Test—t Distribution

The values needed for conducting a hypothesis test can also be computed easily with Excel. To demonstrate we will use the data set of Table 5.1 to compute the values needed to conduct a hypothesis test both for the **critical t-value approach** and for the **p-value approach**. We will compute the values needed for these two testing approaches for all three of the possible forms for the hypothesis test as shown in Table 5.4. We will refer to the three forms as I, II and III.

We can proceed in the following manner in order to conduct a hypothesis test to determine if the sales level is 215 after the advertising campaign. We will conduct the test using a significance level of 0.05 and continue with the worksheet presented in Figure 5.4.

Table 5.4 Possible Hypothesis Forms for Testing One Population Mean

Form I	Form II	Form III
$H_0: \mu = 215$	$H_0: \mu \leq 215$	$H_0: \mu \geq 215$
$H_a: \mu \neq 215$	$H_a: \mu > 215$	$H_a: \mu < 215$

1. Enter the labels in rows 18 through 25 and the input values in cells E6 and E7 as shown in Figure 5.4.

2. Enter the formula **=(L6-E6)/L14** into cell L19 to compute the t-statistic value for the sample (Figure 5.3 shows the formula in the worksheet.)

3. In cell L20 the function TINV is used to determine the critical value for the t-statistic for a two-tailed test, **Form I** of Table 5.4. The function refers to the significance level of the test and to the degrees of freedom. Thus, the entry for cell L20 is **=TINV($E$7,L12)**. (Note it is not necessary that the E7 address be the absolute form $E$7.)

4. The TINV function is also used in cells L21 and L22 to determine the critical value for the t-statistic for the two possible one-tailed tests, **Form II** and **Form III** of Table 5.4. For cell L21 the formula is **=TINV(2*$E$7,L12)** and for cell L22 it is **= -1*TINV(2*$E$7,l12)**.

5. Move the cell pointer to cell L23 and enter the formula   **=TDIST(ABS(L19),L12,2)** to compute the p value for the **Form I** hypotheses.

6. In cell L24 the p value is computed for the **Form II** hypotheses. This computation is performed by one of two ways depending on the value of the t-statistic value computed in cell L19. We use an IF function to determine the value of L19 and then compute the p-value using one of two formulas. The entry for cell L24 is **=IF(L19<0,1-TDIST(ABS(L19),L12,1),TDIST(ABS(L19),L12,1))**.

7. Finally in cell L25 the p value for **Form III** hypothesis is computed. The entry for this cell is **=1-L24**.

The results of these steps are as shown in previous Figure 5.4. Your worksheet provides the statistics necessary to conduct the single sample hypothesis test for both the critical t-value and the p-value approaches. For both of these two approaches, it provides for testing all three of the possible forms of the hypotheses as given in Table 5.4.

For the **CRITICAL t-VALUE APPROACH,** the value for the test statistic in cell L19 of Figure 5.4 is -0.779. For the **Form I** two tailed test, cell L20 indicates the critical values for the test statistic are -2.365 and +2.365. Since the value of -0.779 does not fall outside these limits, the null hypothesis is not rejected. The sample evidence does not support rejecting the hypothesis that Read and Feed sales level is 215 after the advertising campaign. Thus, Lizabert's hypothesis (conjecture, hunch, estimate, guess, etc.) that the spot TV advertisements would boost sales of the Country Dinners to 215 per store is supported by the sample evidence.

For the **Form II** hypotheses, the test value of -0.779 is not greater than the critical value of +1.895 given in cell L21 of Figure 5.4. Thus, we can not reject the null hypothesis. The sample data supports the contention that the market share is less than or equal to 215.

Finally for the **Form III** hypotheses, the test value of -0.779 is not less than the critical value of -1.895 given in cell L22 so the hypothesis of a sales level of greater than or equal to 215 is not rejected. Thus, all three forms of the test indicate an acceptance of the null hypothesis which includes the possibility of equality to 215 for the sales level.

The results of Figure 5.4 also let us consider the **p-VALUE APPROACH** to this test. Conventional usage of p-values classifies test results according to the categories given in Table 5.5 (see for example Siegel, *Practical Business Statistics*, Irwin1997, p.328).

Table 5.5 p-Value Classification Categories

If the P-Value is	Then the Difference is
Greater than 0.05	Not Significant
Greater than 0.01 but less than or equal to 0.05	Significant
Greater than 0.001 but less than or equal to 0.01	Highly Significant
Less than or equal to 0.001	Very Highly Significant

Utilizing the classification categories of this table, we would classify the results as *not significant* for all three forms of the hypotheses. That is, the p values of 0.462, 0.769 and 0.231 are all greater than 0.05. The conclusion is not to reject the null hypothesis regardless of what hypotheses form we were testing. This is the same conclusions drawn using the critical t-value approach.

You should save your completed worksheet of Figure 5.4 for future use. Although you developed it for a particular test situation, it is completely general. Thus, you can use it for estimating and testing a population mean based on a sample from that population. To use the worksheet, you only need to enter

1. The data values for the sample beginning in cell A5. As previously indicated the formulas you entered allow for up to 100 data values. This limit could be increased by

simply expanding the range used in cells L5, L6 and L7.

2. The confidence level you desire for the confidence interval in cell E4, and

3. The hypothesized value for the mean in cell E6 and the significance level in cell E7.

After entering these input values, your worksheet will provide you with the point estimate and its confidence interval. In addition, it will return all the necessary values for conducting any three forms of the hypothesis test for both the critical t-value and the p-value approaches.

5.1.5 Determining the Necessary Sample Size

The precision of a point estimate is measured by the width of the corresponding confidence interval. The confidence interval width is inversely related to the sample size. If the sample size is increased, the width of the confidence interval is decreased, and vice versa. Consequently, if sample size is increased sufficiently, we can obtain a confidence interval small enough to satisfy any desired level of precision for the point estimate of a population mean. In this subsection, we use Excel to compute the sample size which is necessary for a specified width and specified confidence level for a confidence interval. We will continue with the workbook of this chapter but we will use the worksheet *Sheet3*.

Let us continue with the example of this section. As you will recall we began with the Read and Feed sales data of Table 5.1. The confidence interval was computed for these data in Figure 5.2 using the normal distribution and in Figure 5.4 using the t distribution. The 95% confidence interval width was ±14.468 with the normal distribution and ±17.455 with the t distribution. Suppose we wish to have a 95% confidence interval width of ±10. How many additional observations would be required to attain this specified confidence interval?

We can proceed in the following manner

1. Enter the **Identification Material** shown in rows 1, 2 and 3 of later Figure 5.6. Then enter the labels of rows 5 through 20. Enter the desired confidence level in cell D8 and the desired half width in cell D9. Also enter the sample standard deviation and the sample size for our initial sample in cells D12 and D13.

2. Cell E18 uses the Excel function NORMSINV to find the critical z-value for the specified confidence level given in cell D8. The confidence level is converted from percentage to decimal form by first dividing by 100, and then it is converted to the two-tailed value by dividing by 2. Finally 0.5 is added to the result in order to find the z-value on the right-hand of the distribution. The resulting formula for cell E18 is **=NORMSINV(D8/100/2+0.5)** as shown in Figure 5.5.

Figure 5.5 Formulas for Necessary Sample Size

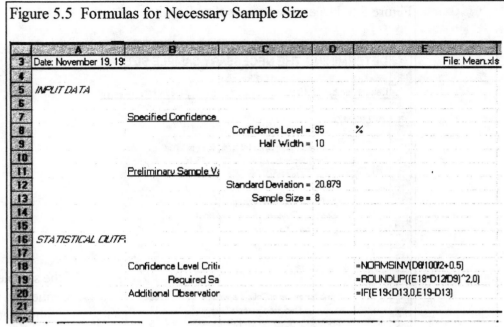

3. The formula in cell E19 computes the number of observations required to attain the specified confidence interval. Then the function ROUNDUP is used to always round the result up to the next integer. The formula in cell E19 is **=ROUNDUP((E18*D12/D9)^2,0)**.

4. Finally, an IF function is used to determine how many additional observations are required. If the initial sample was sufficient, the result will be zero. The formula in cell E20 is **=IF(E19<D13,0,E19-D13)**.

Figure 5.6 shows the results of these computations. As indicated in cell E19, approximately 17 observations are required to attain the specified confidence interval. Accordingly, cell E20 shows that nine additional observations are required.

After obtaining nine additional observations, these nine sales values would be combined with the original eight sales values of Table 5.1. This combined data set of 17 observations would be entered into the worksheet of Figure 5.2 (for the normal distribution) or of Figure 5.4 (for the t distribution). The worksheet would compute the new confidence interval. The width of the confidence interval should be near ±10. Since the process of Figure 5.6 is an approximation, it is possible the width may be larger than ±10. For that situation, the new sample standard deviation computed for sample of size 17 should be entered into cell D12 and the sample size of 17 entered into cell D13 of Figure 5.6. The worksheet will then provide an estimate of the number of observations needed in a third sample in order to attain the specified confidence interval.

You should close this workbook after saving it. The next section will start a new workbook.

Figure 5.6 Necessary Sample Size Results

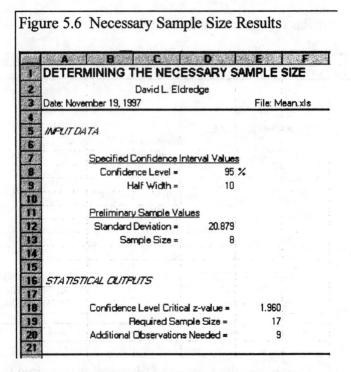

5.2 THE t-TEST: TWO-SAMPLE ASSUMING UNEQUAL VARIANCE ANALYSIS TOOL

This section presents hypothesis tests, point estimates and confidence intervals for population means utilizing Excel's data analysis Tool t-TEST: TWO-SAMPLE ASSUMING UNEQUAL VARIANCES. This tool is designed to test the difference between two population means under the following conditions.

1. The samples from the two populations are independent
2. The appropriate sampling distribution is the t distribution
3. The unknown variances of the two populations are not known to be equal

Subsection 5.2.1 presents the hypothesis test and **Subsection 5.2.2** presents the point estimate and confidence interval for comparing two population means. **Subsection 5.2.3** shows how this tool can also be used for the one population situation. We will see that the one population results obtained from this two-population tool duplicate those of subsections 5.1.3 and 5.1.4.

In order to demonstrate the two independent sample, unequal variance t-test tool consider the following.

Ms. Lizabert Humperdinck, the general manager of the Read and Feed chain of restaurants, is continuing her investigation of promotional ideas for the *Country Basket* dinners. One of her ideas is to hang posters that picture the item in the restaurant. To test effectiveness of this idea she randomly selected eight restaurants to feature the poster and she randomly selected another eight which did not use the poster. Table 5.1 shows the number of Country Basket dinners which were sold in these 16 restaurants.

Table 5.6 Number of Country Basket Dinners Sold

With Posters	Without Posters
215	240
180	220
150	190
180	175
201	220
207	215
195	219
180	195

We will use this example to demonstrate both (1) the hypothesis test, and (2) the point estimate and confidence interval for the comparison of the two population means using independent samples. We will begin a new workbook entitled *MEANS-2.xls* for these computations.

5.2.1 Hypothesis Test for Two Population Means
with Independent Samples

Suppose we wish to use the data of the two samples to see if the difference in the two population means appears to be significantly different from zero. Furthermore, suppose we wish to use a significance level of 0.05 for the test. We would proceed as follows after opening a new workbook.

1. Enter the **Identification Material** shown in rows 1, 2 and 3 of later Figure 5.8. Then enter the labels and data in columns B and C. Save the workbook with the title MEANS-2.

2. From the menu bar select **Tools, Data Analysis** and **t-Test: Two-Sample Assuming Unequal Variances** and the dialog box shown in Figure 5.7 will appear.

3. Enter the ranges for the two variables either by keying the cell locations or by dragging the mouse pointer over the data (Excel will show the cell locations as absolute addresses if you drag).

Figure 5.7 t-Test Two-Sample, Unequal Variances Dialog Box

4. The hypothesized difference between the two means is entered as **0**, the alpha or significance level of the test as **0.05** and the upper left cell of the output range as **E5**. Click on **OK** and the result will be the screen shown in Figure 5.8. Note that the width of column E has been increased.

Figure 5.8 t-Test: Two-Sample Assuming Unequal Variances Results

As you will note Excel has computed values for sample statistics for the two individual samples: the means, variances and sample sizes. In addition, the bottom of the results table displays values for conducting a t-test to determine if the two population means are equal or not. These values allow you to conduct the test in the two most well-used methods, the critical t-value approach and the p-value approach. For both of these approaches the null and the alternative hypothesis can be one of the three forms shown in Table 5.7.

Table 5.7 Possible Hypothesis Forms for Test of Two Population Means

Form I	Form II	Form III
H_0: $\mu_1 - \mu_2 = 0$	H_0: $\mu_1 - \mu_2 \leq 0$	H_0: $\mu_1 - \mu_2 \geq 0$
H_a: $\mu_1 - \mu_2 \neq 0$	H_a: $\mu_1 - \mu_2 > 0$	H_a: $\mu_1 - \mu_2 < 0$

Let us first consider the **CRITICAL t-VALUE APPROACH**. If the hypotheses have **Form I**, the testing rule is that the null hypothesis is rejected when the absolute value of the number labeled *t Stat* is greater than the value of the number labeled *t Critical two-tail*. Otherwise the null hypothesis is not rejected. For the example of Figure 5.8, we note the *absolute value* of t Stat is 2.00573 and the value for t Critical two-tail is 2.144789. Thus, we would not reject the null hypothesis. We would conclude that from a statistical standpoint the difference between the two means is not significantly different from zero.

Suppose the hypotheses are **Form II** of Table 5.7. For these hypotheses the testing rule is that the null hypothesis is rejected if *t Stat* is greater than *t Critical one-tail* and otherwise it is not rejected. From Figure 5.8 we note the t Stat value of -2.00573 is less than the t Critical one-tail value of 1.761309. Thus, we would not reject the null hypothesis and would conclude the difference between the mean of the first population and the second population is less than or equal to zero.

Finally, suppose the hypotheses are **Form III** of Table 5.7. For this situation, the testing rule is that the null hypothesis is rejected if *t Stat* is less than minus one times the value for *t Critical one-tail*. From Figure 5.8 we note the t Stat value of -2.00573 is less than -1.761309, minus one times t Critical one-tail value. Thus for this form of the hypotheses, we would reject the null hypothesis but again conclude the difference in the two means is not greater than or equal to zero.

In order to clarify the decision rules presented in the three preceding paragraphs, Table 5.8 summarizes the critical t-value approach for hypothesis testing using the results from the t-TEST: TWO-SAMPLE ASSUMING UNEQUAL VARIANCES analysis tool. It shows the conditions under which the null hypothesis is rejected for each of the three possible forms of the hypotheses. To interpret the results of this data analysis tool, **first** refer to Table 5.7 and identify the form of your hypotheses. **Second** select the appropriate decision rule from Table 5.8. **Third**, use the value for t Stat and the appropriate t Critical value to determine if the null hypothesis is rejected or not.

Table 5.8 Conditions for Rejecting the Null Hypothesis

Hypotheses	Reject Null Hypothesis If
Form I	$\lvert t\ Stat \rvert$ > t Critical two-tail
Form II	t Stat > t Critical one-tail
Form III	t Stat < - t Critical one-tail

The results of Figure 5.8 also let us consider the **p-VALUE APPROACH** to this test. If our hypotheses have **Form I** of Table 5.7, the p-value for the test is equal to the value given for *P(T<=t) two tail*. For the example of Figure 5.8, this value is 0.06461. Using the p-value categories of Table 5.3 (or 5.5), we would conclude that the difference in the population means is not statistically significant.

For the **Form II** and **Form III** hypotheses, the p-value depends upon two items from the results of Figure 5.8 One is the *P(T<=t) one tail* and other is the algebraic sign of *t Stat*. The p-value is either equal to (P(T<=t) one tail) or equal to (1 - P(T<=t) one tail). There are four possibilities. Table 5.9 summarizes these.

Table 5.9 Computation of p-Values for Form II and Form III Hypotheses

	FORM OF HYPOTHESES	
Sign of *t Stat*	Form II	Form III
Negative	1 - *P(T<=t) one tail*	*P(T<=t) one tail*
Positive	*P(T<=t) one tail*	1 - *P(T<=t) one tail*

To demonstrate the use of this table, suppose we are testing the **Form II** hypotheses for the example of Figure 5.8. We note that the sign of *t Stat* is negative so the p-value for this test is equal to *1 - P(T<=t) one tail* or 0.96795. Referring to the p-value categories of Tables 5.3 (or 5.5), we would classify the results as not significant. As with the critical t-value approach we would conclude the difference between the mean of the first population and the second population is less than or equal to zero.

On the other hand, suppose we were conducting the test with the **Form III** hypotheses. For this situation Table 5.9 indicates the p-value is equal to *P(T<=t) one tail,* that is, 0.0323205. Table

5.3 (or 5.5) suggests these results are *significant*. Thus for this form of the hypotheses, we would reject the null hypothesis but again conclude the difference in the two means is not greater than or equal to zero.

5.2.2 Point Estimate and Confidence Interval for
Two Population Means ————

As shown in your textbook, the point estimate of the difference between the two population means is equal to the difference in the two corresponding sample means. The precision of this estimate is measured by a confidence interval. The computation of both of these statistics, the point estimate and the confidence interval, can continue from the results we have obtained above for the hypothesis test.

Continuing with the worksheet represented in Figure 5.8, we can proceed as follows.

1. Enter the labels in cells I8 through I17 as shown in Figure 5.9.

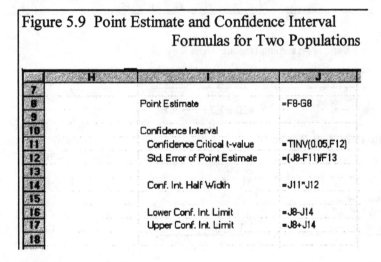

Figure 5.9 Point Estimate and Confidence Interval
Formulas for Two Populations

	H	I	J
7			
8		Point Estimate	=F8-G8
9			
10		Confidence Interval	
11		Confidence Critical t-value	=TINV(0.05,F12)
12		Std. Error of Point Estimate	=(J8-F11)/F13
13			
14		Conf. Int. Half Width	=J11*J12
15			
16		Lower Conf. Int. Limit	=J8-J14
17		Upper Conf. Int. Limit	=J8+J14
18			

2. Enter the formula **=F8-G8** in cell J8 to compute the point estimate of the difference between the two population means.

3. Cell J11 uses the Excel function TINV to find the critical t-value for a specified confidence level. For a confidence level of 95%, enter the value 0.05 for the first argument of the function as shown in Figure 5.9. In general the first argument equals 100 minus the confidence level with this result divided by 100. The second argument for TINV is equal to the degrees of freedom as given in cell F12 from the prior hypothesis test results. Thus, the

entry for cell J11 is =TINV(0.05,F12).

4. The standard error of the point estimate can be found through the use of the value for t Stat given with the hypothesis test results. The computation involves subtracting the hypothesized test difference from the point estimate and then dividing the t Stat value into the result. This computation is shown in cell J12 as =(J8-F11)/F13.

5. The half width of the confidence interval is found by multiplying the critical t-value times the standard error of the point estimate as shown in cell J14. Cell J14 contains the formula =J11*J12.

6. The half width is subtracted from the point estimate to yield the lower confidence limit in cell J16, and the half width is added to the point estimate to yield the upper limit in cell J17. Thus, cell J16 contains the formula =J8-J14 and cell J17 contains =J8+J14. Figure 5.10 shows the numerical results for this example.

Figure 5.10 Point Estimate and Confidence Interval Results for Two Populations

	D	E	F	G	H	I	J
3	File: STATINF						
4							
5		t-Test: Two-Sample Assuming Unequal Variances					
6							
7			Variable 1	Variable 2			
8		Mean	188.5	209.25		Point Estimate	-20.75
9		Variance	420.2857	435.9286			
10		Observations	8	8		Confidence Interval	
11		Hypothesized Mean Difference	0			Confidence Critical t-value	2.144789
12		df	14			Std. Error of Point Estimate	10.34538
13		t Stat	-2.00573				
14		P(T<=t) one-tail	0.032305			Conf. Int. Half Width	22.18864
15		t Critical one-tail	1.761309				
16		P(T<=t) two-tail	0.06461			Lower Conf. Int. Limit	-42.9386
17		t Critical two-tail	2.144789			Upper Conf. Int. Limit	1.438643
18							

In conclusion the point estimate of the difference between mean number of sales for stores without the posters minus mean number of sales for stores with the posters is -20.75. That is those with posters are estimated to have a greater number of sales. In addition, the precision of this estimate is provided by the 95% confidence interval which is -42.9386 to 1.438643.

5.2.3 Statistical Inference for One Population Mean

The hypothesis tests, point estimates and confidence intervals presented in subsections 5.2.1 and 5.2.2 are for comparing two populations. Such a comparison is oftentimes of interest in the use of statistics for business and industry. However at other times, interest may be in only one population. As discussed in subsections 5.1.2 and 5.1.4, the test of concern might be to determine if a population mean is equal to some specific value or not . Thus, you would proceed by drawing a sample from the population and using the sample mean to determine if there is sufficient evidence to conclude that the population mean is equal to the specified value. The test often used in this situation is a one population t-test as previously presented in Subsection 5.1.4. However, it is possible to use Excel's data analysis tool for a t-test for two populations to perform our computations for the one population situation also.

The validity of this approach is based on the fact that the equations for the two population t-test and those for the one population t-test are equivalent under one condition. The condition is that the second sample is not a sample at all but instead all the values are some constant value. Thus, the mean for this second sample is equal to the constant value and the variance of this second sample is zero. If these values are put into the two population t-statistic equation and the corresponding degrees of freedom equation, these two equations reduce to that for the one population test. Although we spare you the details of this proof here, you may wish to explore it on your own. The conclusion is that the test Excel calls the t-TEST: TWO SAMPLE ASSUMING UNEQUAL VARIANCES as represented by the dialog box of Figure 5.7 can also be used for single sample hypothesis tests, point estimates and confidence intervals.

Let us pursue this approach by again visiting the Read and Feed chain of restaurant example given in Section 5.1. For this example, Lizabert the manager had obtained the data in Table 5.1 and wished to determine if the average sales was 215 per store.

So that you may more easily compare the one population results to those of the prior two population example, these sample values have been made the same as the second column in Table 5.6. We will use this example to demonstrate both (1) the hypothesis test, and (2) the point estimate and confidence interval for one population mean.

A one population **HYPOTHESIS TEST** using the two population data analysis tool can be done in one of two ways. Referring to The dialog box of Figure 5.11, the most obvious approach would be to set the *Hypothesized Mean Difference* equal to specified value for the mean. That is for this example, equal to 215. In addition, the *Variable 2 Range* could be set equal to an empty column. However, this approach results in an error in the data analysis tool. It will not perform the computations if one of the two ranges refers to an empty column. Consequently, a second approach is used. This second approach enters values for the second sample equal to the specified value, that is 215. The number of values entered for this second example can be two or more. However, we feel it might be clearer if the number of values for this second sample is equal to the number of values for the first sample. This is not necessary but perhaps more appealing from the standpoint of understanding.

Our approach for this example is the following.

1. Begin by entering the values shown in Table 5.1 into column B starting with cell B28. Enter the number 215 in column C beginning in cell C28. As you will note in later Figure 5.12, labels for these columns have also been entered.

2. Select **Tools/Data Analysis/t-Test: Two-Sample Unequal Variances** to obtain the dialog box of Figure 5.11.

3. Make the appropriate entries as shown in Figure 5.11 and the results of Figure 5.12 will be obtained.

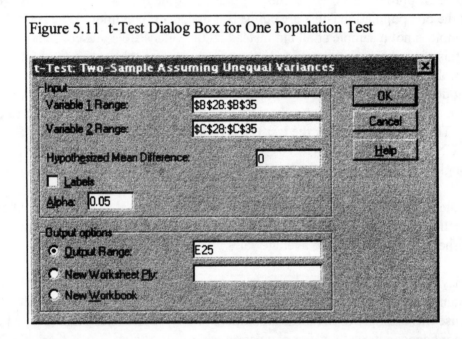

Figure 5.11 t-Test Dialog Box for One Population Test

The results given in Figure 5.12 are quite similar to the two-sample results of Figure 5.8. You will note that the values for the sample mean, sample variance and number observations for Variable 1 are the same as those given for Variable 2 in Figure 5.8. This is as it should be since the sample observations are the same for these two variables. The mean for Variable 2 in Figure 5.12 is 215, that is, the specified value for the test, and the variance is zero. Both of these values are those we had planned.   The remaining values in Figure 5.12 differ from those of Figure 5.8, as they should. These values are used for conducting the hypothesis tests for both the both the critical t-value and the p-value approaches. Also as before there are three possible forms to the hypotheses. These are shown in Table 5.2 (or 5.4).

For the **Critical t-Value Approach,** Table 5.8 summarizes the conditions under which the null hypothesis is rejected.   For the example represented in Figure 5.12, we would not reject the null hypothesis for any of the three forms of the hypotheses. For **Form I,** 0.77894 is not greater than 2.364623, for **Form II,** -0.77894 is not greater than 1.894578 and for **Form III,** -0.77894 is not less than -1.894578. Thus, the manager's hypothesis (conjecture, hunch, estimate, guess, etc.) that the spot TV advertisements would boost sales of the Country Dinners to 215 per store is supported by the sample evidence as it was in Subsection 5.1.3.

Figure 5.12 t-Test Results for One Population Test

	Sales After TV Promotion	Expected Average Sales	t-Test: Two-Sample Assuming Unequal Variances	Variable 1	Variable 2
28	240	215	Mean	209.25	215
29	220	215	Variance	435.9286	0
30	190	215	Observations	8	8
31	175	215	Hypothesized Mean Difference	0	
32	220	215	df	7	
33	215	215	t Stat	-0.77894	
34	219	215	P(T<=t) one-tail	0.230765	
35	195	215	t Critical one-tail	1.894578	
36			P(T<=t) two-tail	0.46153	
37			t Critical two-tail	2.364623	

The data of Figure 5.12 can be used to establish the p-value for the **p-Value Approach.** If the hypotheses are **Form I**, the p-value is equal to $P(T<=t)$ *two tail*, 0.46153. Using the categories from Table 5.3 (or 5.5), we would conclude the results are *not significant*. That is we would not reject the null hypothesis.   For the other two forms of the hypotheses, Table 5.9 can be used to determine the p-values. Since the sign of t-stat as given in Figure 5.12 is negative, the p-value is equal to 1 - 0.230765 = 0.769235 for the **Form II** hypotheses. In this instance we would not reject the null hypothesis. For the **Form III** hypotheses the p-value is equal to 0.230765 and again we would not reject the null hypothesis. Our final conclusion is that the sales of 215 Country Dinners per store is supported by the sample evidence.

A one population **POINT ESTIMATE AND CONFIDENCE INTERVAL** can also be obtained from the data of this two population data analysis tool The point estimate of the sales level with the spot TV advertisements is equal to the sample mean for the eight stores. From the results of Figure 5.12 we note it is equal to 209.25. The precision of this estimate is measured by a confidence interval and the computation of it can continue from the results we have already obtained for the hypothesis test. We proceed as follows.

1. Enter the labels in cells I27 through I37 as shown in Figure 5.13.

2. Enter the formula **=F28** in cell J27 to compute the point estimate.

Figure 5.13 Point Estimate and Confidence Interval Formulas for One Population

	I	J	K
26			
27	Point Estimate	=F28	
28	Point Estimate-Null Hyp. Value	=F28-G28	
29			
30	Confidence Interval		
31	Confidence Critical t-value	=TINV(0.05,F32)	
32	Std. Error of Point Estimate	=J28/F33	
33			
34	Conf. Int. Half Width	=J31*J32	
35			
36	Lower Conf. Int. Limit	=J27-J34	
37	Upper Conf. Int. Limit	=J27+J34	

3. Enter the formula **=F28-G28** in cell J28 to compute the difference between the point estimate and the value from the null hypothesis.

4. Cell J31 uses the Excel function TINV to find the critical t-value for a specified confidence level. For a confidence level of 95%, enter the value 0.05 for the first argument of the function as shown in Figure 5.13. In general the first argument equals 100 minus the confidence level with this result divided by 100. The second argument for TINV is equal to the degrees of freedom as given in cell F32 from the prior hypothesis test results. Thus, the entry for cell J31 is **=TINV(0.05,F32)**.

5. The standard error of the point estimate can be found through the use of the value for t Stat given with the hypothesis test results. Dividing the difference between the point estimate and the value from the null hypothesis (computed in cell J28) by the value for t Stat value (in cell F33) provides this result. This computation is shown in cell J32 as **=J28/F33**.

6. Half the width of the confidence interval is found by multiplying the critical t-value times the standard error of the point estimate as shown in cell J34. Cell J34 contains the formula **=J31*J32**.

7. The half width is subtracted from the point estimate to yield the lower confidence limit in cell J36, and the half width is added to the point estimate to yield the upper limit in cell J37. Thus, J36 contains the formula **=J27-J34**, and cell J37 contains **=J27+J34**. Figure 5.14 shows the results for this example.

In conclusion the point estimate of the number of sales for stores after the TV promotions is 209.25. The accuracy of this estimate is provided by the 95% confidence interval which is 191.7948 to 226.7052. These results are the same as those of Table 5.4 as they should be.

Figure 5.14 Point Estimate and Confidence Interval Results for One Population

	E	F	G	H	I	J	K
24							
25	t-Test: Two-Sample Assuming Unequal Variances						
26							
27		Variable 1	Variable 2		Point Estimate	209.25	
28	Mean	209.25	215		Point Estimate-Null Hyp. Value	-5.75	
29	Variance	435.9286	0				
30	Observations	8	8		Confidence Interval		
31	Hypothesized Mean Difference	0			Confidence Critical t-value	2.364623	
32	df	7			Std. Error of Point Estimate	7.381807	
33	t Stat	-0.77894					
34	P(T<=t) one-tail	0.230765			Conf. Int. Half Width	17.45519	
35	t Critical one-tail	1.894578					
36	P(T<=t) two-tail	0.46153			Lower Conf. Int. Limit	191.7948	
37	t Critical two-tail	2.364623			Upper Conf. Int. Limit	226.7052	
38							

5.3 TWO ADDITIONAL ANALYSIS TOOLS
FOR TWO INDEPENDENT SAMPLES

Excel includes three data analysis tools which compute statistics for testing or estimating two population means based on data from two independent samples. Section 5.2 presented the t-TEST: TWO-SAMPLE ASSUMING UNEQUAL VARIANCE analysis tool in great detail. It applies when the following conditions exist.

1. The from the two populations are independent
2. The appropriate sampling distribution is the t distribution
3. The unknown variances of the two populations are not known to be equal

On the other hand, a second tool, the t-TEST: TWO-SAMPLE ASSUMING EQUAL VARIANCE, discussed in Subsection 5.3.1 below is applicable for the following situation.

1. The samples from the two populations are independent
2. The appropriate sampling distribution is the t distribution
3. The unknown variances of the two populations are known to be equal

Third, the z-TEST: TWO SAMPLE FOR MEANS analysis tool of subsection 5.3.2 applies to the following situation.

1. The samples from the two populations are independent
2. The appropriate sampling distribution is the normal (z) distribution

As you will note from these conditions, the last two analysis tools can be used in special situations, whereas that given in Section 5.2 is more generally applicable. The inputs and outputs for these two special purpose analysis tools are almost identical to analysis tool of Section 5.2. Thus, the detailed instructions of that section are equally applicable to these two additional tools. The following highlight the small differences that do exist.

5.3.1 The t-TEST: TWO-SAMPLE ASSUMING EQUAL VARIANCE Analysis Tool

The t-TEST: TWO-SAMPLE ASSUMING EQUAL VARIANCES analysis tool is appropriate if it is known, or if a hypothesis test has shown, the variance for the first population and that for the second population to be equal. The use of this test is quite similar to that assuming unequal variances. For example, its dialog box is exactly as given in Figure 5.7 except for the box's title. Moreover, the output for this test is the same as that given in Figure 5.8 except it presents one additional output. The extra output is the value for the **Pooled Variance**. Under the condition of equal variances for the two populations, it is appropriate to combine the two samples in order to estimate the common population variance value. The interpretation of the test results for both the critical t-value approach and the p-value approach is exactly as has been explained is Section 5.2.

5.3.2 The z-TEST: TWO SAMPLE FOR MEANS Analysis Tool

The z-TEST: TWO-SAMPLE FOR MEANS analysis tool is appropriate if the variances of the two populations are known. They do not have to be equal but the values must be known. This approach is also used for test situations when both of the samples are large (usually specified to be greater than 30). For such a situation the two sample variances are used as estimates for the two corresponding population variances. The dialog box for the two sample z-test is again as given in Figure 5.7 with the addition of input space for each of the known values for the two population variances. The output is as given in Figure 5.8 except there is no degrees of freedom output and the statistical values are based on the normal distribution not the t distribution.

5.4 THE t-TEST: PAIRED TWO SAMPLE FOR MEANS ANALYSIS TOOL

This final section of the chapter considers the situation in which two samples are not independent. This situation occurs when each individual observation within a sample is related (matched or paired) to an individual observation in the second sample. The relatedness may be the result of the individual observations in the two samples

1. Representing before and after results,

2. Having matching characteristics,
3. Being matched by location or
4. Being matched by time.

If there are definite reasons for pairing (or matching) the individual observations in the two samples, the two samples are dependent not independent samples. Generally, the precision from an analysis of dependent samples is greater than that from the analysis of independent samples. Thus, if a paired analysis is appropriate, it is the preferred approach.

In the first two subsections below we utilize Excel's t-TEST: PAIRED TWO-SAMPLE FOR MEANS analysis tool to conduct a hypothesis test and to make a point estimate with a confidence interval. The final subsection shows how to also use the tool for the one population situation.

The Read and Feed restaurant example will again be used.

Lizabert is continuing her investigation of hanging posters in the restaurants as a means of promoting the sales of their *Country Basket* dinners. To test the idea, this time she randomly selects eight restaurants. First, she gathers sales values for the eight restaurants without the posters. Then the posters are placed in the restaurants and she again gathers comparable sales values. The data are as given in Table 5.10. The two samples are related since the same stores are used for both samples. Recall that for the prior Read and Feed two sample example, eight randomly selected restaurants did not have the posters and a second randomly selected sample of eight restaurants did have the posters.

Table 5.10 Number of Dinners Sold Before and After Posters

Store Number	Sales Before	Sales After
218	215	240
224	180	220
236	150	190
252	180	175
270	201	220
282	207	215
292	195	219
304	180	195

5.4.1 Hypothesis Test for Two Population Means with Dependent Samples

Suppose we wish to use the data of the two samples to determine if the population mean of the differences in sales is significantly different from zero using a significance level of 0.05.

Continuing with the MEANS-2 worksheet of Section 5.2, we would proceed in the following manner.

1. Enter the data in cells A48 through C55 and labels in cells A45 through C47 as shown in later Figure 5.16.

2. From the menu bar select **Tools/Data Analysis/t-Test: Paired Two-Sample for Means** and the dialog box shown in Figure 5.15 will appear.

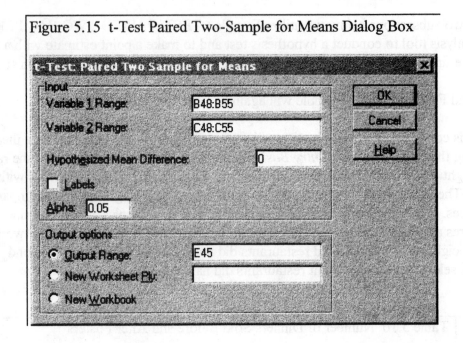

Figure 5.15 t-Test Paired Two-Sample for Means Dialog Box

3. Enter the ranges for the two variables.

4. The hypothesized mean of the differences is entered as **0**, the alpha significance level of the test as **0.05** and the upper left cell of the output range as **E45**. The result is the outputs given in Figure 5.16.

As you will note the sample statistic values for the individual samples, the means, variances and number of observations, are the same as for the independent sample results of Figure 5.8. The next output item in Figure 5.16 is the Pearson Correlation coefficient value. This value is a measure of how well two variables vary together as was discussed earlier in Subsection 3.5.2. The remaining output values given in Figure 5.16 are used for conducting the hypothesis tests. As with the two prior hypothesis test examples, statistical values are provided for conducting both a critical t-value approach and the p-value approach.

Figure 5.16 t-Test: Paired Two-Sample for Means Results

	A	B	C	D	E	F	G	H
45		Sales	Sales		t-Test: Paired Two Sample for Means			
46	Store	without	with					
47	Number	Promotion	Promotion			Variable 1	Variable 2	
48	218	215	240		Mean	188.5	209.25	
49	224	180	220		Variance	420.286	435.929	
50	236	150	190		Observations	8	8	
51	252	180	175		Pearson Correlation	0.72791		
52	270	201	220		Hypothesized Mean Difference	0		
53	282	207	215		df	7		
54	292	195	219		t Stat	-3.84431		
55	304	180	195		P(T<=t) one-tail	0.00317		
56					t Critical one-tail	1.89458		
57					P(T<=t) two-tail	0.00634		
58					t Critical two-tail	2.36462		
59								

Again there are three possible forms for the hypotheses. Those for this test are shown in Table 5.11.

Table 5.11 Possible Hypothesis Forms for Test of Two Paired Population Means

Form I	Form II	Form III
$H_0: \mu_d = 0$	$H_0: \mu_d \leq 0$	$H_0: \mu_d \geq 0$
$H_a: \mu_d \neq 0$	$H_a: \mu_d > 0$	$H_a: \mu_d < 0$

For the **CRITICAL t-VALUE APPROACH,** previously presented Table 5.8 summarizes the conditions under which the null hypothesis is rejected. For the example represented in Figure 5.16, we would reject the null hypothesis for **Form I** since 3.84431 is greater than 2.364623. For **Form II** -3.84431 is not greater than 1.894578 so we would not reject the null hypothesis, and for **Form III** -3.84431 is less than -1.894578 so we would again reject the null hypothesis. Thus, the manager's hypothesis that the poster advertisements boost the sales of the Country Dinners is supported by the sample evidence.

For the **p-VALUE APPROACH** the data of Figure 5.16 can be used to establish the p-value. If the hypotheses are of **Form I**, the p-value is equal to *P(T<=t) two tail*, 0.006339. Using the categories from Table 5.3 (or 5.5), we would conclude the results are *highly significant*. That is, we would strongly reject the null hypothesis. For the other two forms of the hypotheses, Table 5.9 can be used to convert the value from Figure 5.16 for *P(T<=t) one tail* to the corresponding p-value. Since t-stat has a negative sign, the p-value is equal to $1 - 0.00317 = 0.99683$ for the **Form II** hypotheses. For it, we would not reject the null hypothesis. For the **Form III** hypotheses, the p-value is 0.00317 and again we would reject the null hypothesis. Thus the p-value approach also leads to the conclusion that the sales after the posters were used is significantly higher than the sales before the posters were used.

5.4.2 Point Estimate and Confidence Interval
for Two Population Means ——————

The point estimate of the difference in the sales level before and after the poster campaign is equal to the difference in the two sample means. From the results of Figure 5.16 we note the point estimate is -20.75 (= 188.5 - 209.25). The precision of this estimate is measured by a confidence interval. The computation of the confidence interval can continue from the results we have already obtained for the hypothesis test.

Continuing with the worksheet represented in Figure 5.16, we can proceed as follows.

1. Enter the labels in cells I48 through I57 as shown in Figure 5.17.

Figure 5.17 Paired Samples Point Estimate and Confidence Interval Formulas

	I	J
47		
48	Point Estimate	=F48-G48
49		
50	Confidence Interval	
51	Confidence Critical t-value	=TINV(0.05,F53)
52	Std. Error of Point Estimate	=(J48-F52)/F54
53		
54	Conf. Int. Half Width	=J51*J52
55		
56	Lower Conf. Int. Limit	=J48-J54
57	Upper Conf. Int. Limit	=J48+J54
58		

---

2. Enter the formula **=F28-G48** in cell J48 to compute the point estimate of the mean of differences in the number sold.

3. Cell J51 uses the Excel function TINV to find the critical t-value for a specified confidence level of 95%. The second argument is equal to the degrees of freedom as given in cell F53 of Figure 5.16. The entry for cell J51 is **=TINV(0.05,F53)**.

4. The standard error of the point estimate is found by subtracting the hypothesized difference from the point estimate and then dividing the t Stat value into the result. This computation is shown in cell J52 as **=(J48-F52)/F54**.

5. Half the width of the confidence interval is found by multiplying the critical t-value times the standard error of the point estimate as shown in cell J54. Cell J54 contains the formula **=J51*J52**.

6. The half width is subtracted from the point estimate to yield the lower confidence limit in cell J56, and the half width is added to the point estimate to yield the upper limit in cell J57. Thus, the cell J56 contains the formula **=J48-J54**, and the cell J57 contains **=J48+J54**. Figure 5.18 shows the results for this example.

Figure 5.18 Paired Samples Point Estimate and Confidence Interval Results

	E	F	G	H	I	J
46						
47		Variable 1	Variable 2			
48	Mean	188.5	209.25		Point Estimate	-20.75
49	Variance	420.286	435.929			
50	Observations	8	8		Confidence Interval	
51	Pearson Correlation	0.72791			Confidence Critical t-value	2.36462
52	Hypothesized Mean Difference	0			Std. Error of Point Estimate	5.39759
53	df	7				
54	t Stat	-3.84431			Conf. Int. Half Width	12.7633
55	P(T<=t) one-tail	0.00317				
56	t Critical one-tail	1.89458			Lower Conf. Int. Limit	-33.5133
57	P(T<=t) two-tail	0.00634			Upper Conf. Int. Limit	-7.98675
58	t Critical two-tail	2.36462				
59						

In conclusion the point estimate of the difference in the sales before and after the poster campaign is -20.75. The accuracy of this estimate is provided by the 95% confidence interval which is from -33.5133 to -7.98675. We could also note that since the confidence interval does not contain zero, we would conclude there is significant difference in sales after the posters were used.

5.4.3 Statistical Inference for One Population Mean

The hypothesis tests, point estimates and confidence intervals presented above are for comparing two populations using paired samples. The data analysis tool t-TEST: PAIRED TWO-SAMPLE MEANS also can be used to provide hypothesis test statistics, point estimates and confidence intervals for the one population situation. This is just as the data analysis tool t-TEST: TWO-

SAMPLE UNEQUAL VARIANCES was used in subsection 5.2.3 for the one population situation. In fact, both these tools for a one population situation provide the same results.

The validity of this approach is based on the fact that the equations for the two population t-test and those for the one population t-test are equivalent under the condition the second sample is not a sample but instead all the values are some constant value. Again we spare you the details of this proof here but demonstrate it with the previous one population Read and Feed example of Subsection 5.1.3.

As previously stated, the manager of the chain is investigating the use of spot TV advertisements to promote *Country Basket* dinners and believes average sales will increase to 215 per store. The resulting sales were presented in Table 5.1.

Figure 5.19 presents the dialog box and Figure 5.20 the results for the data analysis tool.

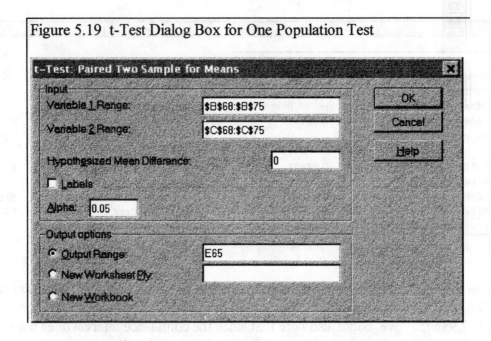

Figure 5.19 t-Test Dialog Box for One Population Test

A comparison of these values in Figure 5.20 to those of the prior one population results of Figure 5.12 show that all are the same. Figure 5.20 has one addition entry that for the Pearson's Correlation coefficient which has no meaning for the one-population situation. Accordingly, there is no need to continue this example any further since the rest of this subsection would be a repeat of Subsection 5.2.3 following Figure 5.12.

The conclusion is that either of the two data analysis tools t-TEST: PAIRED TWO-SAMPLE MEANS or t-TEST: TWO-SAMPLE UNEQUAL VARIANCES may be used to provide the hypothesis test statistics, point estimate and confidence intervals for the one population situation.

This completes our discussion of statistical estimation and hypothesis testing for population means. In the next chapter, we will consider estimation and testing for population proportions.

Figure 5.20 t-Test Results for One Population Test

	B	C	D	E	F	G
64	Sales					
65	After	Expected		t-Test: Paired Two Sample for Means		
66	TV	Average				
67	Promotion	Sales			Variable 1	Variable 2
68	240	215		Mean	209.25	215
69	220	215		Variance	435.929	0
70	190	215		Observations	8	8
71	175	215		Pearson Correlation	#DIV/0!	
72	220	215		Hypothesized Mean Difference	0	
73	215	215		df	7	
74	219	215		t Stat	-0.77894	
75	195	215		P(T<=t) one-tail	0.23076	
76				t Critical one-tail	1.89458	
77				P(T<=t) two-tail	0.46153	
78				t Critical two-tail	2.36462	
79						

CHAPTER 6. STATISTICAL INFERENCE FOR POPULATION PROPORTIONS

```
6.1  One Population Proportion
        6.1.1 Point Estimate and Confidence Interval
        6.1.2 Hypothesis Test
        6.1.3 Determining the Necessary Sample Size

6.2  Two Population Proportions
        6.2.1 Point Estimate and Confidence Interval
        6.2.2 Hypothesis Test
```

Many times for business and industry there is a need to estimate or test the proportion of a population which have a specified attribute. For example, the proportion of the output of a production process which meets quality control specifications, the proportion of income tax returns which have a computation error, or the proportion of potential customers who prefer a particular product. In order to estimate or test proportions, a sample(s) is taken, and the proportion of the sample(s) which have the specified attribute provides the measure for making the estimate or performing the hypothesis test.

This chapter presents statistical estimation and testing for population proportions. As we stated in Chapter 5, estimation involves using the value of a sample statistic, such as the sample proportion, to provide a **point estimate** for the unknown corresponding population parameter, such as the population proportion. As before, we can quantify the precision or accuracy of the point estimate by computing the **confidence interval** (also called **interval estimate**). As in the last chapter, a **hypothesis test** uses the value for a **sample statistic**, such as the sample proportion, to test a tentative assumption regarding the unknown value for a corresponding **population parameter**.

The computations for the confidence interval and hypothesis test are based on the sampling distribution for the sample proportion.   The form of its sampling distribution is the binomial. However, most statistics textbooks use the normal approximation to the binomial distribution for these computations. They take this approach for a number of reasons. First, discrete distributions such as the binomial are awkward to use for statistical inference. Second, a relatively large sample size is usually required to attain a reasonable amount of precision in the estimate or test of a proportion. Third, the binomial distribution can be approximated by the normal distribution for large sample sizes. Accordingly, the normal approximation to the binomial distribution provides the basis for the statistical inference of proportions presented in this chapter.

Section 6.1 presents statistical inference for one population proportion. In it we use formulas and statistical functions to compute values for the point estimate with its corresponding confidence interval and values for the hypothesis test. This section closes with a demonstration of the computations for determining the sample size which is necessary to attain a specified width and confidence level for a confidence interval.

Point estimates, confidence intervals and hypothesis tests for the two population proportion situation are presented in **Section 6.2**.

6.1 ONE POPULATION PROPORTION ⸻⸻⸻⸻

We will consider the following example to demonstrate both the point estimate with confidence interval and the hypothesis test for a single proportion.

Ms. Lizabert Humperdinck, the general manager of the Read and Feed chain of restaurants, wishes to estimate Read and Feed's share of the Sunday morning breakfast market in Buffalo City. She engages Numbers Unlimited, Inc., a marketing research company, to conduct a survey to determine the proportion of Sunday morning breakfast customers who prefer to dine at a Read and Feed restaurant. After a period of time and a few thousand dollars, Numbers Unlimited reports that out of a survey of 1215 Sunday morning breakfast customers 373 preferred Read and Feed.

The tabulation of the number who prefer Read and Feed can be done by hand. However, if the customer responses are within an Excel worksheet, Excel has a feature which can determine the number easily. The feature is the PIVOT TABLE WIZARD. The use of it is presented in Subsection 9.3.1 of Chapter 9.

6.1.1 Point Estimate and Confidence Interval ————————

The point estimate and confidence interval for these sample results can be easily computed with Excel. For example, we may proceed in the following manner in order to compute the point estimate and 95% confidence interval.

1. Start Excel, enter the **Identification Material** shown in rows 1, and 2 of later Figure 6.2. Then enter the labels of rows 3 through 7 and rows 11 through 19. (Note the labels in rows 9, 10 and 20 through 27 will be entered later.) Also, enter the data in cells F4, F5 and F7. (Note the other numerical values given in column F will be entered later.) Save the workbook with the file name PROPOR-1.

2. To compute the point estimate for the population proportion, move the cell pointer to cell F12 and enter the formula **=F5/F4** as shown in Figure 6.1.

Figure 6.1   Statistical Inference Formulas for One Population Proportion

	D	E	F
8			
9	Hypothesized Proporti¦		0.333
10	Significance Level of ¨		0.05
11			
12			=F5/F4
13			
14			
15			=NORMSINV(F7/100/2+0.5)
16			=SQRT(F12*(1-F12)/F4)
17			=F15*F16
18			=IF(F12-F17<0,0,F12-F17)
19			=IF(F12+F17>1,1,F12+F17)
20			
21			=(F12-F9)/F16
22			=-1*NORMSINV($F$10/2)
23			=-1*NORMSINV($F$10)
24			=NORMSINV($F$10)
25			=IF($F$21<0,2*NORMSDIST($F$21),2*(1-NORMSDIST($F$21)))
26			=1-NORMSDIST($F$21)
27			=NORMSDIST($F$21)
28			

---

3. Cell F15 uses the Excel function NORMSINV to find the critical z-value for the specified confidence level given in cell F7. The confidence level is converted to the form necessary for the function by first dividing by 100, then by 2 and finally by adding 0.5 to the result. The resulting formula for cell F15 is **=NORMSINV(F7/100/2+0.5)** as shown in Figure 6.1.

4. The formula in cell F16 computes the standard error of the point estimate from the value of the point estimate in cell F12. The formula **=SQRT(F12*(1-F12)/F4)**.

5. Half the width of the confidence interval is found by multiplying the critical z-value times the standard error of the point estimate. Cell F17 contains the formula **=F15*F16**.

6. The half width is subtracted from the point estimate to compute the lower confidence limit. However, the lower limit can not be less than zero for a proportion. Consequently, an IF function is used to set the value equal to zero when the computation results in a negative number. The formula for cell F18 is **=IF(F12-F17<0,0,F12-F17)**.

7. The half width is added to the point estimate to compute the upper limit. However here, the upper limit can not be more than 1.0 for a proportion. Consequently, an IF function is used to set the value equal to 1.0 when the computation results in a value greater than 1.0. The formula for cell F18 is **=IF(F12+F17>1,1,F12+F17)**.

Figure 6.2 presents the results of these computations. As shown in cell F12 the best estimate of Read and Feed's share of the Sunday morning breakfast market is 0.307. The precision of this estimate is quantified by the 95% confidence interval in cells F18 and F19 as 0.281 to 0.333.

Figure 6.2 Point Estimate and Confidence Interval
for One Population Proportion

	A	B	C	D	E	F	G	H
1		STATISTICAL INFERENCE FOR ONE PROPORTION						
2	Date: December 9, 1997			David L. Eldredge		File: PROPOR-1.xls		
3	INPUT DATA							
4					Sample Size =	1215		
5				Number of Successes in Sample =		373		
6								
7					Confidence Level =	95 %		
8								
9				Hypothesized Proportion =		0.333		
10				Significance Level of Test=		0.05		
11	STATISTICAL OUTPUTS							
12		Point Estimate				0.307		
13								
14		Confidence Interval						
15			Confidence Level Crititcal z-value			1.960		
16			Standard Error of the Point Estimate			0.013		
17			Confidence Interval--Half Width			0.026		
18				--Lower Limit		0.281		
19				--Upper Limit		0.333		

6.1.2 Hypothesis Test

Continuing with our example above, suppose Lizabert wishes to use the sample data to test her feeling that they have a one-third share of the Sunday morning breakfast market. We will enhance our current worksheet to compute the necessary values to perform a hypothesis test using either the critical z-value approach or the p-value approach. In addition, our worksheet will allow the test to be conducted for all three possible forms of the null and alternative hypotheses as shown in Table 6.1.

Table 6.1 Hypothesis Forms for the Test of One Population Proportion		
Form I	**Form II**	**Form III**
H_0: p = 0.333	H_0: p ≤ 0.333	H_0: p ≥ 0.333
H_a: p ≠ 0.333	H_a: p > 0.333	H_a: p < 0.333

We will continue with the current worksheet to develop the necessary critical values and p values for all three hypotheses forms in the following manner.

1. Enter the labels in rows 9, 10 and 20 through 27 as shown in Figure 6.3. Enter the data in cells F9 and F10.

2. Move the cell pointer to cell F21 and enter the formula **=(F12-F9)/F16** to compute the z-statistic value for the sample (Figure 6.1 shows the formula in the worksheet).

3. In cell F22 the function NORMSINV is used to determine the critical value for the z-statistic for a two-tailed test, **Form I** of Table 6.1. The function is multiplied by a minus one in order to obtain a positive value as is needed. The entry **= - 1*NORMSINV($F$10/2)**. (Note it is not necessary that the F10 address be the absolute form, $F$10.)

4. The NORMSINV function is also used in cells F23 and F24 to determine the critical value for the z-statistic for the two possible one-tailed tests, **Forms II** and **Form III**. For cell F23 the formula is **= -1*NORMSINV($F$10)** and for cell F24 **=NORMSINV($F$10)**.

5. Move the cell pointer to cell F27 and enter the formula **=NORMSDIST($F$21)** to compute the p value for the **Form III** hypotheses.

6. Cell F26 computes the p value for **Form II** through the formula **=1-NORMSDIST($F$21)**.

7. Finally in cell F25 an IF function is used to determine the p value for a **Form I** two-tailed test. If the value for the z-statistic, cell F21, is less than zero, the p value is computed as two times the computation of cell F27. Otherwise it is computed as two times the computation of F26. The resulting somewhat intimidating formula is
=IF($F$21<0,2*NORMSDIST($F$21),2*(1-NORMSDIST($F$21))).

The results of these steps are as shown in Figure 6.3. Your worksheet provides the statistics necessary to conduct the single sample hypothesis test for both the critical z-value and the p-value approaches. For both of these two approaches, it provides for testing all three of the possible forms of the hypotheses as given in Table 6.1.

Figure 6.3 Hypothesis Test for One Population Proportion

For the **CRITICAL z-VALUE APPROACH,** the value for the test statistic in cell F21 of Figure 6.3 is -1.965. For the **Form I** two tailed test, cell F22 shows the critical values for the test statistic are -1.960 and +1.960. Since the value of -1.965 just falls outside these limits the null hypothesis is rejected. The sample evidence does support rejecting the hypothesis that Read and Feed has a one-third share of the Sunday morning breakfast market. In other words, in light of the sample evidence the assumption of a one-third share does not seem reasonable.

For the **Form II** hypotheses, the test value of -1.965 is not greater than the critical value of +1.645 given in cell F23 of Figure 6.3. Thus, we can not reject the null hypothesis. The sample supports the contention that the market share is less than or equal to 0.333.

Finally for the **Form III** hypotheses, the test value of -1.965 is less than the critical value of -1.645 given in cell F24. Thus, the hypothesis of a market share of greater than or equal to 0.333 is rejected. The results of the three forms of the test would seem to indicate the market share is not 0.333.

The results of Figure 6.3 also let us consider the **p-VALUE APPROACH** for this test. Utilizing the p-value classification categories previously given in Table 5.3 (or 5.5), we would classify the results as *significant* if the hypotheses are **Form I** or **Form III**, and *not significant* for **Form II**. As for the critical z-value approach, the conclusion is that the results of the three forms of the test would seem to indicate the market share is not 0.333.

You should save your completed worksheet for future use. Although you developed it for a particular test situation, it is completely general. Thus, you can use it for estimating and testing for any one proportion situation in which the normal approximation to the binomial distribution is reasonable. To use the worksheet, you only need to enter values for

1. The two inputs from the sample, the sample size and number of successes, in cells F4 and F5,

2. The confidence level you desire for the confidence interval in cell F7, and

3. The hypothesized value for the proportion in cell F9 and the significance level for the test in cell F10.

After entering these five input values, your worksheet will provide you with the point estimate and its confidence interval. In addition, it will return all the necessary values for conducting any three forms of the hypothesis test by the critical z-value approach and by the p-value approach.

6.1.3 Determining the Necessary Sample Size

The precision of a point estimate is measured by the width of the corresponding confidence interval. The confidence interval width is inversely related to the sample size. If the sample size is increased, the width of the confidence interval is decreased, and vice versa. Consequently, if sample size is increased sufficiently, we can obtain a confidence interval small enough to satisfy any desired level of precision for the point estimate of a population proportion. In this subsection, we use Excel to compute the sample size which is necessary for a specified width and specified confidence level for a confidence interval. We will continue with the prior workbook of this chapter but we will use the worksheet *Sheet2*.

Let us continue with the example of this section. As you will recall 373 respondents out of a sample of 1215 persons preferred the Read and Feed restaurants for Sunday morning breakfast. The confidence interval was computed for these data in Figure 6.2. The 95% confidence interval width was ±0.026. Suppose we wish to have a 95% confidence interval width of ±0.020. How many additional observations would be required to attain this specified confidence interval?

We can proceed in the following manner

1. Enter the **Identification Material** shown in rows 1, 2 and 3 of later Figure 6.5. Then enter the labels of rows 5 through 20. Enter the desired confidence level in cell D8 and the desired

half width in cell D9. Also enter the sample proportion and the sample size for our initial sample in cells D12 and D13.

2. Cell E18 uses the Excel function NORMSINV to find the critical z-value for the specified confidence level given in cell D8. The confidence level is converted from percentage to decimal form by first dividing by 100, and then it is converted to the two-tailed value by dividing by 2. Finally 0.5 is added to the result in order to find the z-value on the right-hand of the distribution. The resulting formula for cell E18 is **=NORMSINV(D8/100/2+0.5)** as shown in Figure 6.4.

3. The formula in cell E19 computes the number of observations required to attain the specified confidence interval. Then the function ROUNDUP is used to round the result up to the next higher integer. The formula in cell E19 is **=ROUNDUP(E18^2*D12*(1-D12)/D9^2,0)**.

4. Finally, an IF function is used to determine how many additional observations are required. If the initial sample was sufficient, the result will be zero. The formula in cell E20 is **=IF(E19<D13,0,E19-D13)**.

Figure 6.5 shows the results of these computations. As indicated in cell E19, approximately 2044 observations are required to attain the specified confidence interval. Accordingly, cell E20 shows that 829 additional observations are required.

Figure 6.4 Formulas for Necessary Sample Size

	A	B	C	D	E
1	DETERMINING 1				
2			David L. Eldredge		
3	Date: December 9, 199				File: PROPOR-1.xls
4					
5	INPUT DATA				
6					
7			Specified Confidence		
8			Confidence Level =	95	%
9			Half Width =	0.02	
10					
11			Preliminary Sample Va		
12			Sample Proportion =	0.307	
13			Sample Size =	1215	
14					
15					
16	STATISTICAL OUTP				
17					
18			Confidence Level Criti		=NORMSINV(D8/100/2+0.5)
19			Required Sa		=ROUNDUP(E18^2*D12*(1-D12)/D9^2,0)
20			Additional Observatior		=IF(E19<D13,0,E19-D13)
21					

Figure 6.5 Necessary Sample Size Results

	A	B	C	D	E	F	G
1	DETERMINING THE NECESSARY SAMPLE SIZE						
2		David L. Eldredge					
3	Date: December 9, 1997			File: PROPOR-1.xls			
4							
5	INPUT DATA						
6							
7		Specified Confidence Interval Values					
8		Confidence Level =		95 %			
9		Half Width =		0.02			
10							
11		Preliminary Sample Values					
12		Sample Proportion =		0.307			
13		Sample Size =		1215			
14							
15							
16	STATISTICAL OUTPUTS						
17							
18		Confidence Level Critical z-value =		1.960			
19		Required Sample Size =		2044			
20		Additional Observations Needed =		829			
21							

After obtaining 829 additional observations, those results would be combined with the original 1215 results. This combined data set of 2044 observations would be entered into the worksheet of Figure 6.2. The worksheet would compute the new confidence interval. The width of the confidence interval should be near ±0.020. Since the process of Figure 6.5 is an approximation, it is possible the width may be larger than ±0.020. For that situation, the new sample proportion computed for sample of size 2044 should be entered into cell D12 and the sample size of 2044 entered into cell D13 of Figure 6.5. The worksheet will then provide an estimate of the number of observations needed in a third sample in order to attain the specified confidence interval.

6.2 TWO POPULATION PROPORTIONS

Frequently for business and industry an analyst wishes to compare two population proportions. In this section we show how to compute point estimates with confidence intervals, and the values needed to conduct a hypothesis test for the difference between two population proportions. Consider the following example.

Lizabert's next project for the Read and Feed restaurant chain is concerned with customers' complaints. Two months ago the number of complaints were 137, and last month there were 196. She is concerned about this drastic increase in the number of complaints. She feels somewhat better when she learns that the estimated number of total customers for the two months increased from 1401 and to 2313, but she still feels the firm has a problem with increasing customer complaints. To investigate the problem further, she first computes a point estimate with a confidence interval for the difference in the proportion of complaints for the two months. Next she conducts a hypothesis test to determine if there is an increase in the proportion of customer complaints from the first month to the second.

6.2.1 Point Estimate and Confidence Interval

We will again develop an Excel worksheet to perform the statistical computations required by Lizabert. The worksheet will be completely general so you may keep it to perform such computations for any situation involving the difference between two population proportions. This worksheet will be an enhanced version of that you did for one population proportion. Whereas Figure 6.6 provides the formulas for this new worksheet, Figure 6.7 shows the computational results. Proceed as follows with a new workbook.

1. Start Excel, enter the **Identification Material** shown in rows 1 and 2 of Figure 6.7, enter the labels of rows 3 through 8 and rows 12 through 21. Also, enter the data of cells F4 through F8. Save the workbook with the title PROPOR-2. (The additional information shown in Figure 6.7 will be entered for the hypothesis test later.)

2. To compute the point estimates for the two population proportions and their difference, successively move the cell pointer to cells F13, F14 and F15, and enter the formulas shown in Figure 6.6 for those cells.

Figure 6.6 Statistical Inference Formulas for Two Population Proportions

	E	F	G
12			
13		=F5/F4	
14		=F7/F6	
15		=F13-F14	
16			
17		=NORMSINV(F8/100/2+0.5)	
18		=SQRT(F13*(1-F13)/F4+F14*(1-F14)/F6)	
19		=F17*F18	
20		=IF(F15-F19<0,0,F15-F19)	
21		=IF(F15+F19>1,1,F15+F19)	
22			
23		=(F5+F7)/(F4+F6)	
24		=SQRT(F23*(1-F23)*(1/F4+1/F6))	
25		=(F15-F10)/F24	
26		=-1*NORMSINV($F$11/2)	
27		=-1*NORMSINV($F$11)	
28		=NORMSINV($F$11)	
29		=IF($F$25<0,2*NORMSDIST($F$25),2*(1-NORMSDIST($F$25)))	
30		=1-NORMSDIST($F$25)	
31		=NORMSDIST($F$25)	

3. Cell F17 uses the Excel function NORMSINV to find the critical z-value for the specified confidence level given in cell F8. The confidence level is converted to the form necessary for the function by first dividing by 100, then by 2 and finally by adding 0.5 to the result. The formula is **=NORMSINV(F8/100/2=0.5)**.

4. The formula in cell F18 computes the standard error of the point estimate of the difference in the two population proportions using the individual point estimates of cells F13 and F14. The formula for the standard error is **=SQRT(F13*(1-F13)/F4+F14*(1-F14)/F6)**.

5. Half the width of the confidence interval is found in cell F19 as **=F17*F18**.

6. The half width is subtracted from the point estimate to compute the lower confidence limit. However, the lower limit can not be less than zero for a proportion. Consequently, the IF function is used in cell F20 to set the value equal to zero when the computation results in a negative number. The formula is **=IF(F15-F19<0,0,F15-F19)**.

7. The half width is added to the point estimate to compute the upper limit. However here, the upper limit can not be more than one for a proportion. Consequently, an IF function is used to set the value equal to one when the computation results in a value greater than one. The formula is **=IF(F15+F19>1,1,F15+F19)**.

Figure 6.7 Point Estimate and Confidence Interval
                    for Two Population Proportions

	A	B	C	D	E	F	G
1	STATISTICAL INFERENCE FOR TWO PROPORTIONS						
2	Date: December 9, 1997			David L. Eldredge		File: PROPOR-2.xls	
3	INPUT DATA						
4		First Sample			Sample Size =	1401	
5				Number of Successes in Sample =		137	
6		Second Sample			Sample Size =	2313	
7				Number of Successes in Sample =		196	
8					Confidence Level =	95	%
9							
10				Hypothesized Proportion Difference =		0	
11				Significance Level of Test=		0.05	
12	STATISTICAL OUTPUTS						
13		Point Estimates			First Population	0.098	
14					Second Population	0.085	
15				Difference Between 2 Populations		0.013	
16		Confidence Interval					
17				Confidence Level Crititcal z-value		1.960	
18				Standard Error of the Point Estimate		0.010	
19				Confidence Interval--Half Width		0.019	
20					--Lower Limit	0.000	
21					--Upper Limit	0.032	

As shown in Figure 6.7, the best estimate of the difference in the two proportions (first month minus the second month) is 0.013 with a confidence interval of 0.000 to 0.032. Accordingly, the proportion of complaints is actually less for the second month so Lizabert should not be concerned there has been an increase.

6.2.2 Hypothesis Test

Suppose Lizabert wishes to use the sample complaint data for the two prior months to test whether there is a statistically significant difference in the two population proportions. As for the previous one population situation, we can enhance our current worksheet to compute the necessary values to perform the hypothesis test for both the critical z-value and the p-value approaches. We will compute the statistics for all three of the possible forms of the null and alternative hypotheses as specified in Table 6.2.

Table 6.2 Hypothesis Forms for the Test of Two Population Proportions

Form I	Form II	Form III
$H_0: p_1-p_2 = 0$	$H_0: p_1-p_2 \leq 0$	$H_0: p_1-p_2 \geq 0$
$H_a: p_1-p_2 \neq 0$	$H_a: p_1-p_2 > 0$	$H_a: p_1-p_2 < 0$

We will proceed with the following steps.

1. Enter the labels in rows 10, 11 and 22 through 31 as shown in Figure 6.6. Enter the data shown in cells F10 and F11.

2. Move the cell pointer to cell F23 and enter the formula **=(F6+F9)/(F5+F8)** to compute the pooled sample proportion.

3. In cell F24 the square root function is used to compute the standard error for the point estimate based on the pooled sample proportion. The formula for it is **=SQRT(F23*(1-F23)*(1/F4+1/F6))**.

4. Move the cell pointer to cell F25 and enter the formula **=(F15-F10)/F24** to compute the z-statistic value for the sample.

5. In cell F26 the function NORMSINV is used to determine the critical value for the z-statistic for a two-tailed test. The function is multiplied by minus one in order to obtain a positive

value. The formula is = -1*NORMSINV($F$11/2).

6. The NORMSINV function is also used in cells F27 and F28 to determine the critical value for the z-statistic for the two possible one-tailed tests. For F27 enter = -1*NORMSINV($F$11) and for F28 enter =NORMSINV($F$11).

7. Move the cell pointer to cell F31 and enter the function =NORMSDIST($F$25) to compute the p value for the **Form III** hypotheses.

8. Cell F30 determines the p value for the **Form II** hypotheses as = -1*NORMSDIST($F$25).

9. Finally in cell F29 an IF function is used to determine the p value for the **Form I** two-tailed test. If the value for the z-statistic, cell F25, is less than zero, the p value is computed as two times the computation of cell F31. Otherwise it is computed as two times the computation of F30. The formula for cell F29 is
    =IF($F$25<0,2*NORMSDIST($F$25),2*(1-NORMSDIST($F$25))).

The results of these steps are shown in Figure 6.8. Your worksheet provides the statistics necessary to conduct the two-sample hypothesis test for both the critical z-value and the p-value approaches. For both of these two approaches, it provides for testing all three of the possible forms of the hypotheses as given in Table 6.2.

Figure 6.8 Hypothesis Test
for Two Population Proportions

	A	B	C	D	E	F	G
12	STATISTICAL OUTPUTS						
13		Point Estimates			First Population	0.098	
14					Second Population	0.085	
15				Difference Between 2 Populations		0.013	
16		Confidence Interval					
17			Confidence Level Crititcal z-value			1.960	
18			Standard Error of the Point Estimate			0.010	
19			Confidence Interval--Half Width			0.019	
20				--Lower Limit		0.000	
21				--Upper Limit		0.032	
22		Hypothesis Test					
23			Proportion--Combined Samples			0.090	
24			Pooled Standard Error of the Point Est.			0.010	
25			Test Statistic			1.349	
26			z critical value--Form I			1.960	
27				--Form II		1.645	
28				--Form III		-1.645	
29			p-value--Form I			0.177	
30				--Form II		0.089	
31				--Form III		0.911	

For the **CRITICAL z-VALUE APPROACH,** Figure 6.8 shows the value for the test statistic in cell F25 as 1.349. For a two tailed test of **Form I,** cell F26 indicates the critical values for the test statistic are -1.960 and +1.960. Since the value of 1.349 does not fall outside these limits the null hypothesis is not rejected. The sample evidence does not support rejecting the hypothesis that the two proportions of customer complaints differ significantly. Similarly, the test statistic value is not greater than the **Form II** critical value. It is less than the **Form III** critical value. Thus for all three forms of the hypotheses result in the acceptance of the null hypothesis which include the possibility of the equality of the two population proportions.

The results of Figure 6.8 also support the **p-VALUE APPROACH** for this test. Utilizing the p-value classification categories previously given in Table 5.3 (or 5.5), we would classify the results as *not significant* for all three forms of the hypotheses. That is, the p values of 0.177, 0.089 and 0.911 are all greater than 0.05. As for the critical z-value approach, the conclusion is not to reject the null hypothesis regardless of what form of the hypotheses we are testing.

You should save your completed worksheet for future use. Although you developed it for a particular test situation, it is completely general. Thus, you can use it for estimating and testing for any two proportions situation in which the normal approximation to the binomial distribution is reasonable. To use the worksheet, you only need to enter values for

1. The four inputs from the two samples, the sample sizes and numbers of successes, in cells F4 through F7.

2. The confidence level you desire for the confidence interval in cell F8, and

3. The hypothesized value for the difference in the two proportions in cell F10 and the significance level for the test in cell F11.

After entering these seven input values, your worksheet will provide you with the point estimate and its confidence interval, and the necessary values for conducting any three forms of the hypothesis test by both the critical z-value and the p-value approaches.

This completes our discussion of statistical estimation and hypothesis testing for population proportions. In the next chapter, we will consider estimation and testing for population variances.

CHAPTER 7. STATISTICAL INFERENCE FOR POPULATION VARIANCES

```
7.1  One Population Variance
        7.1.1  Point Estimate and Confidence Interval
        7.1.2  Hypothesis Test

7.2 The F-TEST: TWO-SAMPLE VARIANCES Analysis Tool
        7.2.1  Hypothesis Test for Two Population Variances
        7.2.2  Point Estimate and Confidence Interval
```

In the preceding two chapters we presented statistical inference methods for population means and population proportions. In this chapter we extend our discussion to statistical inference for variances (and standard deviations). Statistical inference for variances can be used to make decisions in a number of problems in business and industry. This is particularly true for the area of quality control for which the central issue is to control the variability of a production or service process. It is also true for the area of finance for which the variability of an investment or portfolio of investments is used as a measure of risk.

The statistical inference procedures of this chapter utilize either the chi-square distribution or the F distribution. In both instances, it is assumed that the samples are taken from normally distributed populations. This was also assumed for the t distribution statistical inference procedures for means of Chapter 5. Unlike the t distribution procedures, however, the chi-square and F distribution procedures are highly sensitive to departures from the normal population.

Section 7.1 uses Excel for the statistical inference computations for the one population situation. In it we demonstrate the use of formulas and statistical functions to determine the values for the point estimate with its corresponding confidence interval, and values for the hypothesis test. In **Section 7.2**, we demonstrate the use of the F-TEST: TWO-SAMPLE FOR VARIANCES analysis tool for determining the same values for the two population situation.

7.1 ONE POPULATION VARIANCE

Statistical inference for the variance of one population is governed by the chi-square distribution. Although Excel does not provide an analysis tool for this situation, it does have two statistical functions, CHIDIST and CHIINV, for developing confidence intervals and conducting hypothesis tests. We will use the following example to demonstrate the use of these functions.

Suppose Ms. Lizabert Humperdinck, the general manager of the Read and Feed chain of restaurants, needs an estimate of the variance in daily sales of the menu specialty item, *Liver and Biscuit Dinner*. She has gathered sales for eight randomly selected restaurants as given in Table 7.1.

Table 7.1 Number of Liver and Biscuit Dinners Sold								
Number Sold	240	220	190	175	220	215	219	195

7.1.1 Point Estimate and Confidence Interval

The point estimate and confidence interval for these sample results can be computed very easily with Excel. For example, we may proceed in the following manner in order to compute the point estimate and 90% confidence interval.

1. Start Excel, enter the **Identification Material** shown in rows 1, and 2 of later Figure 7.2, enter the labels of rows 3 and 4 on the left-hand side of the worksheet and in rows 3 through 16 on the right-hand side of the worksheet.   Also, enter the data of cells A5 through A12 and cell E4. Save the workbook with the name VARIAN-1.   (The information given in rows 6 and 7 on the left and rows 17 through 26 on the right will be entered later. Also note the width of some columns and the number of decimal places shown have been changed to

accommodate the presentation of the worksheet here.)

2. The sample statistics are computed in cells L5, L6 and L7 using the functions **AVERAGE, VAR** and **COUNT** as shown in Figure 7.1. The ranges shown allow for the inclusion of samples of size up to 100.

Figure 7.1 Formulas for the Statistical Inference
for One Population Variance

	I	J	K	L
5	Sample Mean			=AVERAGE(A5:A104)
6	Sample Variance			=VAR(A5:A104)
7	Sample Size			=COUNT(A5:A104)
8				
9				=L6
10				
11				
12	Degrees of Freedom			=L7-1
13	Chi-square--Lower Val			=CHIINV((1+E4/100)/2,L12)
14	--Upper Va			=CHIINV((1-E4/100)/2,L12)
15	Confidence Interval--L			=L6*$L$12/L14
16	--U			=L6*$L$12/L13
17				
18	Test Statistic			=L12*L6/E6
19	Chi-square critical valu			
20	--Form I (low			=CHIINV(1-E7/2,$L$12)
21	--Form I (upp			=CHIINV(E7/2,$L$12)
22	--Form II			=CHIINV(E7,$L$12)
23	--Form III			=CHIINV(1-E7,$L$12)
24	p-value--Form I			=IF(L25<0.5,2*L25,2*L26)
25	--Form II			=CHIDIST($L$18,$L$12)
26	--Form III			=1-CHIDIST($L$18,$L$12)
27				

3. The point estimate computed in cell L9 is equal to the sample variance and the degrees of freedom in cell L12 is equal to the sample size minus 1.

4. Cell L13 uses the Excel function CHINV to find the lower chi-square value for the specified confidence level given in cell E4. The confidence level is converted to the form necessary for the function by first dividing by 100, then adding 1 and finally by dividing the result by 2. As shown in Figure 7.1, the formula in cell L13 is **=CHIINV((1+E4/100)/2,L12)**.

5. The upper chi-square value is found in cell L14 in the same manner except the plus sign is changed to a negative sign.

6. As shown in Figure 7.1, the formula in cell L15 computes the lower confidence limit and that in cell L16 the upper confidence limit.

Figure 7.2 presents the results for the Liver and Biscuit Dinner example. As shown, the best estimate of the variance in the sales of the dinners is 435.9 with a 90% confidence interval from 216.9 to 1407.9. The range of the confidence interval is quite large. It suggests the need for a larger sample size to provide a more precise estimate.

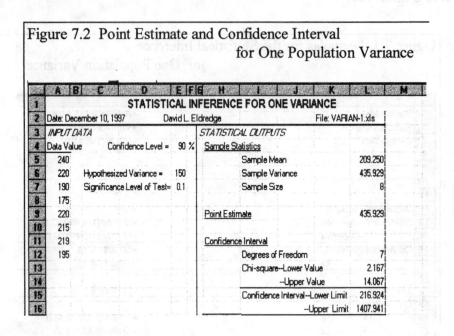

Figure 7.2 Point Estimate and Confidence Interval
for One Population Variance

	STATISTICAL INFERENCE FOR ONE VARIANCE		
Date: December 10, 1997	David L. Eldredge		File: VARIAN-1.xls
INPUT DATA		STATISTICAL OUTPUTS	
Data Value	Confidence Level = 90 %	Sample Statistics	
240		Sample Mean	209.250
220	Hypothesized Variance = 150	Sample Variance	435.929
190	Significance Level of Test= 0.1	Sample Size	8
175			
220		Point Estimate	435.929
215			
219		Confidence Interval	
195		Degrees of Freedom	7
		Chi-square--Lower Value	2.167
		--Upper Value	14.067
		Confidence Interval--Lower Limit	216.924
		--Upper Limit	1407.941

7.1.2 Hypothesis Test

Suppose Lizabert wishes to use the sample data to test her feeling that the variance in sales is equal to 150. We will enhance our current worksheet to compute the necessary values to perform a hypothesis test either using the critical χ^2-value approach or the p-value approach. In addition, our worksheet will allow the test to be conducted for all three of the possible forms of the null and alternative hypotheses shown in Table 7.2.

Table 7.2 Possible Hypothesis Forms for Test of One Population Variance

Form I	Form II	Form III
H_0: $\sigma^2 = 150$	H_0: $\sigma^2 \leq 150$	H_0: $\sigma^2 \geq 150$
H_a: $\sigma^2 \neq 150$	H_a: $\sigma^2 > 150$	H_a: $\sigma^2 < 150$

We will continue with the current worksheet to develop the necessary critical values and p values.

1. Enter the labels in rows 6 and 7 on the left-hand side of the worksheet and rows 17 through 26 of the right-hand side as shown in Figure 7.3. Enter the data in cells E6 and E7.

2. Move the cell pointer to cell L18 and enter the formula **=L12*L6/E6** to compute the chi-square test statistic value for the sample (see Figure 7.1).

Figure 7.3 Hypothesis Test for One Population Variance

	A	B	C	D	E	F	G	H	I	J	K	L	M
6	220		Hypothesized Variance =		150			Sample Variance				435.929	
7	190		Significance Level of Test=		0.1			Sample Size				8	
8	175												
9	220							Point Estimate				435.929	
10	215												
11	219							Confidence Interval					
12	195								Degrees of Freedom			7	
13									Chi-square--Lower Value			2.167	
14									--Upper Value			14.067	
15									Confidence Interval--Lower Limit			216.924	
16									--Upper Limit			1407.941	
17								Hypothesis Test					
18									Test Statistic			20.343	
19									Chi-square critical values				
20									--Form I (lower)			1.690	
21									--Form I (upper)			16.013	
22									--Form II			14.067	
23									--Form III			2.167	
24								p-value--Form I				0.010	
25									--Form II			0.005	
26									--Form III			0.995	

3. In cell L20 the function CHIINV is used to determine the lower critical value for the chi-square statistic for the **Form I** two-tailed test of Table 7.2. The formula for cell L20 is **=CHIINV(1-E7/2,$L$12)**.

4. The upper value is computed in cell L21 as **=CHIINV(E7/2,$L$12)**.

5. As shown in Figure 7.1, the CHIINV function is also used in cells L22 and L23 to determine the critical value for the chi-square statistic for the two possible one-tailed tests, **Form II** and **Form III**. The formulas are **=CHIINV(E7,$L$12)** and **=CHIINV(1-E7,$L$12)**.

6. Next move the cell pointer to cell L25 and enter the function **=CHIIDIST($L$18,$L$12)** to compute the p value for the **Form II** hypotheses.

7. Cell L26 determines the p value the **Form III** hypotheses as **=1-CHIIDIST($L$18,$L$12)**.

8. Finally in cell L24 an IF function is used to determine the p value for the **Form I** two-tailed test. If the value as computed in cell L25 is less than 0.5, the p value is computed as two times the computation of cell L25. Otherwise it is computed as two times the computation of

cell L26. The formula is =IF(L25<0.5,2*L25, 2*L26).

The results allow us to test all three forms of the hypotheses for both the critical χ^2-value and the p-value approaches.

For the **CRITICAL χ^2-VALUE APPROACH,** the value for the test statistic in cell L18 of Figure 7.3 is 20.343. For a two tailed **Form I** test, cells L20 and L21 show the critical values for the test statistic are 1.690 and 16.013. Since the value of 20.343 falls outside these limits, the null hypothesis is rejected. The sample evidence does support rejecting the hypothesis that the population variance is 150. For the **Form II** hypotheses, the test value of 20.343 is greater than the critical value of 14.067 given in cell L22 of Figure 7.3. Thus, we can reject the null hypothesis. The sample does not support the contention that the variance is less than or equal to 150. Finally for the **Form III** hypotheses, the test value of 20.343 is not less than the critical value of 2.167 given in cell L23 so the hypothesis of a variance greater than or equal to 150 is not rejected. All three forms of the test would lead us to believe the population variance is greater than 150.

The results of Figure 7.3 also let us consider the **p-VALUE APPROACH** for this test.   Utilizing the p-value classification categories previously given in Table 5.3 (or 5.5), we would classify the results as *highly significant* for **Form I** and **Form II** and *not significant* for **Form III**. As for the critical value approach, the conclusion for all three forms of the hypotheses is that the variance is greater than 150.

You should save your completed worksheet for future use. Although you developed it for a particular test situation, it is completely general. Thus, you can use it for estimating and testing for a population variance based on a sample from that population. To use the worksheet, you only need to enter

1. The data values for the sample beginning in cell A5. As previously indicated the formulas you entered allow for up to 100 data values. This limit could be increased by simply expanding the range used in the formulas of cells L5, L6 and L7,

2. The confidence level you desire for the confidence interval in cell E4, and

3. The hypothesized value for the variance in cell E6 and the significance level for the test in cell E7.

Your worksheet will provide you with the point estimate and its confidence interval, and the necessary values for conducting any three forms of the hypothesis test by both the critical χ^2-value and the p-value approaches.

7.2 The F-TEST: TWO-SAMPLE
FOR VARIANCES ANALYSIS TOOL ————

Excel provides a data analysis tool for testing the equivalence of the variances of two populations. It is the F-TEST: TWO-SAMPLE FOR VARIANCES tool. We will first demonstrate its use for the equivalence of variances test. We will then extend the results from the data analysis tool to provide a point estimate and confidence interval for the ratio of the two population variances.

In order to demonstrate it consider the following example.

Lizabert Humperdinck, the manager of the Read and Feed chain of restaurants, wishes to investigate promotional ideas for the *Liver and Biscuit* dinners. One of her ideas is to hang posters that picture the item in the restaurant. To test the effectiveness of this idea she randomly selected eight restaurants to feature the poster and she randomly selected another eight which did not use the poster. Table 7.3 shows the number of Liver and Biscuit dinners which were sold in these 16 restaurants.

Table 7.3 Number of Liver and Biscuit Dinners Sold

With Posters	Without Posters
215	240
180	220
150	190
180	175
201	220
207	215
195	219
180	195

7.2.1 Hypothesis Test for Two Population Variances ————

Suppose we wish to use the data of Table 7.3 to determine if the variances of populations are equal or at a significance level of 0.05. We would proceed as follows with a new workbook.

1. Start Excel , enter the **Identification Information** in rows 1 and 2 of later Figure 7.5. Also enter the labels and data in columns B and C. Save the workbook with an appropriate title, we have used VARIAN-2.

2. From the menu bar select **Tools/Data Analysis/F-test: Two-Sample for Variances**. The dialog box of Figure 7.4 will appear on the screen.

Figure 7.4 F-test: Two-Sample for Variances Dialog Box

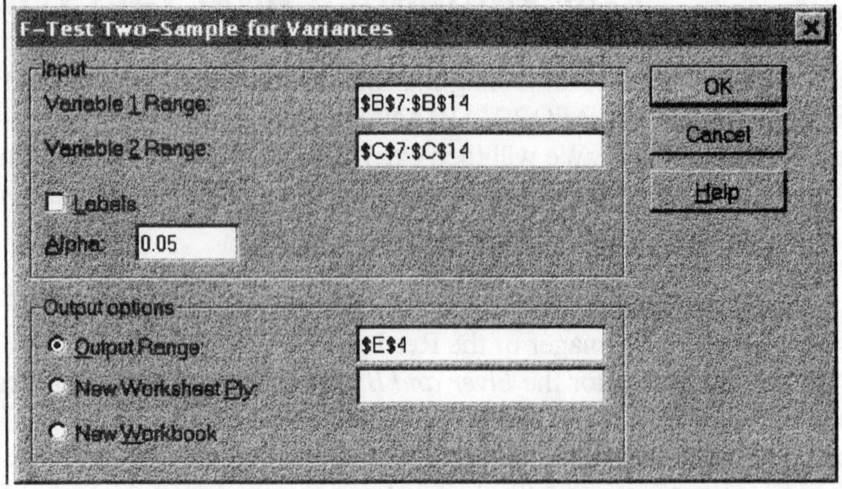

3. Within the dialog box enter, (a) the two ranges for the sample values, (b) the significance level for alpha *(for a Form I two-tailed test, enter one-half the significance level for alpha--see Table 7.5 for further explanation)*, and (c) the upper right hand cell for the output range as shown in the Figure 7.4.

4. Click **OK** and the output as shown in Figure 7.5 will be displayed on your screen.

Figure 7.5 F-test: Two-Sample for Variances Results

	A	B	C	D	E	F	G	H
2	Date: December 10, 1997				David L. Eldredge	File: VARIAN-2.xls		
3								
4		Stores	Stores		F-Test Two-Sample for Variances			
5		without	with					
6		Poster	Poster			Variable 1	Variable 2	
7		215	240		Mean	188.5	209.25	
8		180	220		Variance	420.286	435.92857	
9		150	190		Observations	8	8	
10		180	175		df	7	7	
11		201	220		F	0.96412		
12		207	215		P(F<=f) one-tail	0.5186		
13		195	219		F Critical one-tail	0.26406		
14		180	195					
15								

You will note the results are similar to those of the hypothesis testing data analysis tools discussed in Chapter 5. For example, the values for the means, standard deviations and number of observations are just as they were given in the first three rows of results in Figure 5.8 for a similar example. The fourth row of output in Figure 7.5 presents the two values for the degrees of freedom associated with the F statistic. These are followed in the next three rows by (1) the computed value of the F statistic, (2) the value for conducting the test using p-values and (3) and the critical value for the F-statistic.

As with the previous tests of this chapter, the necessary information is provided for conducting the hypothesis test for either the critical F-value or the p-value approach. All three forms of the null and alternative hypotheses given in Table 7.4 can be pursued for both approaches.

Table 7.4 Possible Hypothesis Forms for Test of Two Population Variances

Form I	**Form II**	**Form III**
$H_0: \sigma_1^2 = \sigma_2^2$	$H_0: \sigma_1^2 \leq \sigma_2^2$	$H_0: \sigma_1^2 \geq \sigma_2$
$H_a: \sigma_1^2 \neq \sigma_2^2$	$H_a: \sigma_1^2 > \sigma_2^2$	$H_a: \sigma_1^2 < \sigma_2^2$

Consider the **CRITICAL F-VALUE APPROACH** first. This approach for the test can be made both when the sample variance of the first sample is greater than that for the second sample, and when it is less than that for the second sample. In other words, both when value for F is greater than 1.0, and vice versa.

Some Excel statistical analysis books suggest the test is valid only if variance of the first sample is greater than the variance for the second sample. However the results of the tool can be used for both situations. The key is that the tool only provides results for the relevant critical value for the F-test. If the value for the F-statistic is greater than 1.0, it provides only the right-hand critical value. If the value for the F-statistic is less than 1.0, it provides only the left-hand critical value.

In order to clarify the interpretation of the results of this tool we present Table 7.5. It provides the interpretation for the six possible combinations of the three forms of the hypotheses and the two ranges of the value for F.

To demonstrate the interpretation provided by Table 7.5, consider our example given in Figure 7.5. For it we note the value for F is less than 1.0. Thus, if we were conducting a two-tail test (**Form I** of Table 7.4) the F value of 0.96412 is not less than the *F Critical one-tail* value of 0.26406 so we would not reject the null hypothesis. We would conclude the variances of the two populations are equal at a significance level of 0.10 (two times the alpha specified in Figure 7.4).

On the other hand, if we were conducting the test using the **Form II** hypotheses, we would note from Table 7.5 that we always fail to reject the null hypothesis. Thus, we would conclude the variance of the first population is less than or equal to that of the second population.

Table 7.5 Interpretation of Variance Test: Critical F-Value Approach

VALUE for F	FORM OF HYPOTHESES		
	Form I	Form II	Form III
≥ 1.0	Reject null if F > F Critical one-tail Sig. Level = 2*Alpha	Reject null if F > F Critical one-tail Sig. Level = Alpha	Always fail to reject null since F ≥ 1.0 Sig. Level = Alpha
< 1.0	Reject null if F < F Critical one-tail Sig. Level = 2*Alpha	Always fail to reject null since F < 1.0 Sig. Level = Alpha	Reject null if F < F Critical one-tail Sig. Level = Alpha

Finally, if we were conducting the test using the **Form III** hypotheses, we also would not reject the null hypothesis. Since the F value of 0.96412 is not less than the *F Critical one-tail* value of 0.26406 , we would conclude the variance for population one is greater than or equal to that for the second population. The significance level in this situation would be 0.05, that is, the alpha value specified in Figure 7.4.

The results of Figure 7.5 also provide the means for conducting the **p-VALUE APPROACH** to this test. The interpretation of the results again depend on the form of the hypotheses and whether the sample value for the F-statistic is greater than 1.0 or not. Table 7.6 presents the formulas for computing the p value for the six possible situations.

Table 7.6 Computation of p-Values for F-Test

VALUE for F	FORM OF HYPOTHESES		
	Form I	Form II	Form III
≥ 1.0	2 * P(F<=f) one-tail	P(F<=f) one-tail	1 - P(F<=f) one tail
< 1.0	2 * (1 - P(F<=f) one-tail)	P(F<=f) one-tail	1 - P(F<=f) one tail

For our example results of Figure 7.5, the F-statistic is less than 1.0. Thus the p value for the three forms of the hypotheses would be computed for **Form I** as 0.9628 [=2*(1-0.5186)], for **Form II** as 0.5186, and **Form III** as 0.4814 (=1-0.5186).

Utilizing the p-value categories of Table 5.3 (or 5.5) from chapter 5, we would classify the results as *not significant* for all three forms of the hypotheses. So as for the critical value approach to this test, we would not reject the null hypothesis for all three forms.

7.2.2 Point Estimate and Confidence Interval

As shown in your textbook, the point estimate of the ratio of two population variances is equal to the ratio of the two corresponding sample variances. The precision of this estimate is measured by a confidence interval. The computations required can continue from the results we have obtained in Figure 7.5 for the hypothesis test. We can proceed as follows.

1. Enter the labels in cells I4 through I15 as shown in Figure 7.6.

2. Enter the confidence level in cell J5. We are using 95%.

3. Enter the formula **=F11** in cell J7 to obtain the value for the point estimate of the ratio of the two population variances.

Table 7.6 Point Estimate and Confidence Interval Formulas for Two Variances

	I	J	K
1			
2			
3			
4	Confidence Interval for a		
5	Confidence Level of	95	%
6			
7	Point Estimate	=F11	
8			
9	F Distribution Values		
10	Left-tailed Value	=1/FINV((100-J5)/100/2,G10,F10)	
11	Right-tailed Value	=FINV((100-J5)/100/2,F10,G10)	
12			
13	Confidence Interval Limits		
14	Lower Limit	=J7/J11	
15	Upper Limit	=J7/J10	
16			

4. Cell J10 uses the function FINV to find the left-tailed critical F-value for a specified confidence level. The function's first argument equals 100 minus the confidence level with this result divided by 100 and then divided by two. The second argument for FINV is equal to the degrees of freedom as given in cell G10 and the third is the degrees of freedom given in cell F10. Finally, the value from this function is divided into one. Thus, the entry for cell J10

is =1/FINV((100-J5/100/2,G10,F10).

5. Cell J11 also uses the function FINV to find the right-tailed critical F-value for a specified confidence level. The first argument is the same as that for cell J10. The second and third arguments are reversed from those of cell J10. Also, the value of the function is not divided into one. Thus, the entry for cell J11 is **=FINV((100-J5/100/2,F10,G10)**.

6. The lower confidence limit is computed in cell J14 by the formula **=J7/J11**.

7. The upper confidence limit is computed in cell J15 by the formula **=J7/J10**.

Figure 7.7 shows the numerical results for this example.

Table 7.7 Point Estimate and Confidence Interval
for Two Variances

	H	I	J	K	L
1					
2					
3					
4		Confidence Interval for a			
5		Confidence Level of	95	%	
6					
7		Point Estimate	0.96412		
8					
9		F Distribution Values			
10		Left-tailed Value	0.2002		
11		Right-tailed Value	4.99489		
12					
13		Confidence Interval Limits			
14		Lower Limit	0.19302		
15		Upper Limit	4.81565		
16					

In conclusion the point estimate of the ratio of the variance of the number of sales for stores without the posters to the variance of the number of sales for stores with the posters is 0.964116. The precision of this estimate is provided by the 95% confidence interval which is 0.193021 to 4.815652. In passing we would note that the interval includes the value 1.0 so we would conclude the variances do not differ significantly.

CHAPTER 8. ANALYSIS OF VARIANCE

8.1 The ANOVA: SINGLE FACTOR Analysis Tool

8.2 The ANOVA: TWO-FACTOR WITHOUT REPLICATION Analysis Tool

8.3 The ANOVA: TWO-FACTOR WITH REPLICATION Analysis Tool

This chapter continues our use of Excel for inferential statistics. In particular, the statistical procedure referred to as the **analysis of variance** (commonly called **ANOVA**) allows you to test for the equivalence of the population means of two or more populations with independent samples. You may recall that the procedure of Section 5.2 of Chapter 5 was used to test for the equivalence of the population means of only two populations with independent samples. It utilized a t-test for the analysis. On the other hand, ANOVA utilizes a F-test and can be used if you have two populations or more than two. For the two population situation, the results of the two-tailed t-test and that for the F-test are exactly alike. This is true both for the critical value approach and the p-value approach to hypothesis testing.

Excel provides three separate ANOVA analysis tools. These correspond to the three test situations usually discussed in business statistics textbooks. The first is the ANOVA: SINGLE FACTOR analysis tool presented in **Section 8.1** below. Single factor ANOVA is also called a one-way ANOVA It is used to analyze the equivalence of means for two or more **values** (sometimes called **levels**) of one **variable** (sometimes called **factor**). It requires that there be more than one observation for each of the values of the variable.

For example, you might wish to test the effectiveness of a number employee training programs by randomly assigning two or more employees to each program. For this situation, the variable (or factor) corresponds to the training programs and the values (or levels) are the different types of training programs. The result for an individual employee is an observation. The experimental structure of one variable with multiple levels and two or more observations per level is called a **completely randomized design**.

The second tool is the ANOVA: TWO-FACTOR WITHOUT REPLICATION analysis tool as discussed in **Section 8.2**. This is also called a two-way ANOVA without interaction. Again there is a single variable of interest but to test the effect of this variable, the sample observations are organized into **blocks**. Instead of obtaining independent observations for different levels as is done for the single factor situation of section 8.1, the observations are obtained from the same block. For example, the block might correspond to the same city, the same person or the same point in time. The experimental structure of this situation is called a **randomized block design**.

Section 8.3 presents the third tool the ANOVA: TWO-FACTOR WITH REPLICATION analysis tool. This is called a two-way ANOVA with interaction. It is used to analyze the equivalence of means for two or more values (levels) of two variables (factors). It requires that there be more than one observation for each combination of values of the two variables. For example, suppose the first variable is the training program for which there are five possible values, and the second variable is the sex of the employee for which there are two values. There are a total of ten (= 5 times 2) combinations of the two variables. For each of the ten combinations, two or more observations would be required to analyze it as a two-way ANOVA with interaction. This experimental structure is called a **two-way factorial design**.

The test situations for all three of these ANOVA tools are based on three key assumptions. They are that (1) the observations are obtained randomly and independently from the populations, (2) the observations are drawn from normally distributed populations and (3) the populations have a common variance.

8.1 THE ANOVA: SINGLE FACTOR ANALYSIS TOOL ─────────

We will consider the use of the ANOVA: SINGLE FACTOR tool through the following example.

Ms. Bearferd Lynn is the sales manager for Eves Valves, Inc. The firm markets their valves throughout the United States through sales representatives. Currently, Bearferd is considering three new compensation plans for the sales representatives. One includes only a salary, one includes both a salary component and a commission component and the third includes only a commission. In order to compare the effectiveness of the three plans, Bearferd randomly selects

24 sales representatives and randomly assigns eight to each compensation plan. The sales levels for the 24 representatives for the next 6 months is recorded.

To analyze the results using Excel you would proceed as follows.

1. Start Excel, enter the **Identification Material**, and then enter the labels and data in columns B and C as shown in Figure 8.1. Save the workbook file with the name ANOVA.

Figure 8.1 One-way ANOVA Example Data

	A	B	C	D	E
1		Analysis of Variance Examples			
2		Your Name			
3	Today's Date			File: ANOVA.xls	
4					
5		COMPENSATION PLAN INCLUDES			
6		Salary	Sal.&Com.	Commissn	
7		4500	4430	5810	
8		4580	4740	5420	
9		4200	4530	4800	
10		4860	4830	5100	
11		5040	5100	5460	
12		4740	4920	6180	
13		4320	4140	4680	
14		4410	4320	4620	
15					

2. From the menu bar select **Tools**, from the subsequent pull-down menu select **Data Analysis** and from the Data Analysis dialog box select **ANOVA: Single Factor**.

3. Fill in the entries of the ANOVA: Single Factor dialog box as shown in Figure 8.2. Notice that the input range includes the labels in the cells B6, C6 and D6.

4. The output will appear as shown in Figure 8.3. In this figure column B has been widened to allow the display of the full labels.

As you will note Excel provides the means and variances for each of the three compensation plans. In addition, it presents an analysis of variance table with the sample statistics for conducting an F-test for the following hypotheses.

$$H_0: \mu_1 = \mu_2 = \mu_3$$
$$H_a: \text{not all } \mu\text{'s are equal}$$

The **CRITICAL F-VALUE APPROACH** for the test requires you to compare the computed value for the F-statistic to the critical value for F. If the computed F is greater than the critical value of F, the null hypothesis is rejected. Otherwise the null hypothesis is not rejected. The critical value is the value from the F distribution corresponding to the alpha value specified in Figure 8.2 and the degrees of freedom for the numerator and the denominator of the F statistic.

Figure 8.2 ANOVA: Single Factor Dialog Box

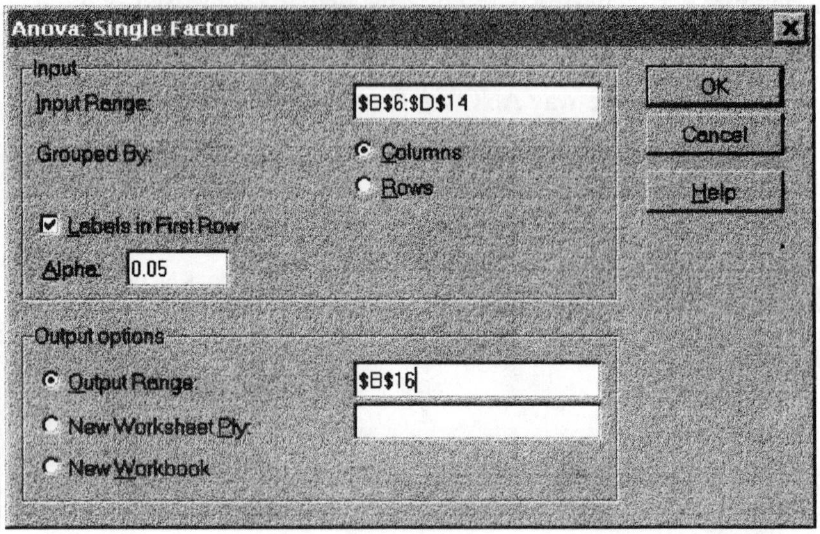

Anova: Single Factor

Input

Input Range: $B$6:$D$14

Grouped By: ⊙ Columns   ○ Rows

☑ Labels in First Row

Alpha: 0.05

Output options

⊙ Output Range: $B$16

○ New Worksheet Ply:

○ New Workbook

OK   Cancel   Help

Figure 8.3 Results for One-way ANOVA

Anova: Single Factor

SUMMARY

Groups	Count	Sum	Average	Variance
Salary	8	36650	4581.25	80412.5
Sal.&Com.	8	37010	4626.25	106169.6
Commissn	8	42070	5258.75	313955.4

ANOVA

Source of Variation	SS	df	MS	F	P-value	F crit
Between Groups	2296233	2	1148117	6.881303	0.005031	3.466795
Within Groups	3503763	21	166845.8			
Total	5799996	23				

For this example we note that the computed value for F is 6.881303 in cell F27 and the critical value is 3.466795 in cell H27 so we would reject the null hypothesis. Thus, we would conclude that the means are not equal. In other words, we conclude that the compensation plans have had an effect on the sales levels. You may wish to look into the F-distribution table in your textbook and ascertain that the critical F value for a significance level of 0.05 and a degrees of freedom for the numerator of 2 and for the denominator of 21 is 3.47.

For the **p-VALUE APPROACH** to the test, you will need to refer to Table 5.3 (or 5.5) of Chapter 5 to categorize the results. For our current example the p-value is given in cell G27 of Figure 8.3 as 0.005031. The categories of Table 5.3 (or 5.5) would classify the results as *highly significant*. Accordingly, we would again reject the null hypothesis that the means are equal. We would conclude that the compensation plans did have a statistically significant effect on the sales results.

8.2 THE ANOVA: TWO-FACTOR WITHOUT REPLICATION ANALYSIS TOOL

The experimental design of Section 8.1, a single factor completely randomized design, sometimes may not detect the difference in means. This result may occur because the variation among the individual experimental units, the sales representatives in the previous example, may mask the variation due to the factor, the compensation plans in the previous example. A second experimental design might be used to circumvent this problem. It is called a randomized block design. Its use is analogous to the use of a paired t-test (see Section 5.4 of Chapter 5) instead of a t-test for independent samples (Section 5.2) when testing the equivalence of two population means. Just as the paired t-test provides a more precise test than the t-test for independent samples, the randomized block design provides a more precise test than that of the completely randomized design. Excel's ANOVA: TWO-FACTOR WITHOUT REPLICATION analysis tool is used to analyze the results from randomized block design.

For our previous Eves Valves example, suppose it is known that the sales representatives with the most experience will sell more regardless of the compensation plan used. Thus, we might make the statistical test more sensitive if we would block the representatives into eight groups of three each according to their experience. We would say that the three representatives with the most experience comprise block one. Each of them would be assigned to a different one of the three compensation plans. The next three most experienced representatives would constitute block two. Each of them would be assigned to a different plan and so on until all 24 have been assigned to a compensation plan. As a result of the this type of assignment process, the representatives in each block should have about the same amount of experience. This type of experimental design would help remove the effect of experience on the sales results and improve the likelihood of detecting the actual differences among the three compensation plans.

To analyze this type of design with Excel for Ms. Lynn proceed as follows.

1. Start Excel, enter the **Identification Material**, and then enter the labels and data in columns B and C as shown in Figure 8.4. Note that we are using the second worksheet in the workbook named ANOVA. We selected the second worksheet by clicking on the tab towards the bottom of the Excel window labeled *Sheet2*. Save the workbook file with the name ANOVA.

Figure 8.4 Two-way ANOVA without Interaction Data

	A	B	C	D	E
1		Analysis of Variance Examples			
2			Your Name		
3	Today's Date			File: ANOVA.xls	
4					
5		COMPENSATION PLAN INCLUDES			
6	Experience	Salary	Sal.&Com.	Commissn	
7	Block 1	4860	5100	5810	
8	Block 2	5040	4920	6180	
9	Block 3	4740	4740	5420	
10	Block 4	4580	4830	5460	
11	Block 5	4410	4430	5100	
12	Block 6	4500	4530	4800	
13	Block 7	4320	4140	4680	
14	Block 8	4200	4320	4620	
15					

2. From the menu bar select **Tools**, from the subsequent pull-down menu select **Data Analysis** and from the Data Analysis dialog box select **ANOVA: Two-Factor Without Replication**.

3. Fill in the entries of the ANOVA: Two-Factor Without Replication dialog box as shown in Figure 8.5. Notice the input range includes the labels in the cells A6, B6, C6, D6 and A7 through A14.

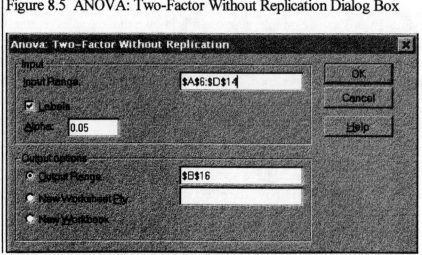

Figure 8.5 ANOVA: Two-Factor Without Replication Dialog Box

4. The output will appear as shown in Figure 8.6. In this figure column B has been widened to allow the display of the full labels.

Figure 8.6 Results for Two-way ANOVA without Interaction

	A	B	C	D	E	F	G	H
17	Anova: Two-Factor Without Replication							
18		SUMMARY	Count	Sum	Average	Variance		
19		Block 1	3	15770	5256.667	244033.3		
20		Block 2	3	16140	5380	483600		
21		Block 3	3	14900	4966.667	154133.3		
22		Block 4	3	14870	4956.667	205633.3		
23		Block 5	3	13940	4646.667	154233.3		
24		Block 6	3	13830	4610	27300		
25		Block 7	3	13140	4380	75600		
26		Block 8	3	13140	4380	46800		
27		Salary	8	36650	4581.25	80412.5		
28		Sal.&Com.	8	37010	4626.25	106169.6		
29		Commissn	8	42070	5258.75	313955.4		
30	ANOVA							
31		Source of Variatio	SS	df	MS	F	P-value	F crit
32		Rows	3017329	7	431047	12.40593	4.87E-05	2.764196
33		Columns	2296233	2	1148117	33.04386	4.99E-06	3.73889
34		Error	486433.3	14	34745.24			
35		Total	5799996	23				

As with the one-way ANOVA results of Figure 8.3, Excel provides the means and variances for each of the three compensation plans. In addition, it presents the means and variances for each of the eight blocks. The ANOVA table at the bottom of the output provides sample statistics for conducting two separate F-tests. One is a test to determine if means for the compensation plans differ or not. Specifically, the test hypotheses are

$$H_0: \mu_1 = \mu_2 = \mu_3$$
$$H_a: \text{not all } \mu\text{'s are equal}$$

The second F test is a test of whether there is a significant difference in the means of the eight blocks, that is, is there a block effect or not. For this example, the block effect would be the effect of sales experience on sales level. The test hypotheses for block effect are

$$H_0: \mu_1 = \mu_2 = \mu_3 \ldots = \mu_8$$
$$H_a: \text{not all } \mu\text{'s are equal}$$

The **CRITICAL F-VALUE APPROACH** to both these tests requires you to compare the computed value for the F-statistic to the critical value for F. If the computed F is greater than the critical value of F, the null hypothesis is rejected. Otherwise the null hypothesis is not rejected. The critical value is the value from the F distribution which corresponds to the alpha value specified in Figure 8.5 and the degrees of freedom for the numerator and the denominator of the F statistic.

From cell F32 of Figure 8.6 we note that the computed value for F is 12.40593 and from cell H32 the critical value is 2.764196 for the first F test, that is, the test to determine the effect of the compensation plans. Accordingly, we would reject the null hypothesis and conclude the compensation plans did have an effect. In a similar manner, we note the for the second F test that the computed value is 33.04386 in cell F33 and the critical value is 3.73889 in cell H33. Again the null hypothesis is rejected and we conclude there is definitely a block effect. The experience level of the sales representative does affect the sales level.

For the **p-VALUE APPROACH** to the test, you will need to refer to Table 5.3 (or 5.5) to categorize the results. For this example the p-value for the first test is given in cell G32 of Figure 8.6 as 4.87E-05 (or 0.0000487). The categories of Figure 5.3 would classify the results as *very highly significant*. Accordingly, we would again reject the null hypothesis that the means for the three compensation plans are equal. Similarly, the p-value for the second test in cell G33 is 4.99E-06 (0.00000499) so again we would reject the null hypothesis that the means for the eight blocks are equal.

8.3 THE ANOVA: TWO-FACTOR WITH REPLICATION ANALYSIS TOOL

The ANOVA: TWO-FACTOR WITH REPLICATION analysis tool is used to analysis the results from a two-way factorial experimental design. This design is used to explore the effect of two variables. It is somewhat like the randomized block design of Section 8.2. However for the randomized block design the focus is on one variable and a blocking variable for improving the precision of the test. It requires only one measurement for each of the cells in the design. For the two-way factorial experiment, the focus is on determining the effect of each of two separate variables and an interaction effect of the two variables. It requires two or more measurements for each of the cells.

Let us continue our example with Brearbert Lynn of Eves Valves, Inc. Suppose for sales purposes Eves Values has the country divided into four sales regions, Northeast, Southeast, Midwest and West. Furthermore, suppose Brearbert not only is interested in exploring the effect of the three compensation plans but she is also interested in the effect of the four sales regions and in the combined effect of compensation plan and geographic region. In order to test the significance of these three possible effects, Brearbert randomly selects 24 sales representatives. She then randomly assigns two representatives to each of the twelve possible combinations of compensation plan and geographic region. The sales levels for the 24 representatives for the next 6 months is recorded.

To analyze the results using Excel you would proceed as follows.

1. Start Excel, enter the **Identification Material**, and then enter the labels and data in columns B and C as shown in Figure 8.7. Note that we are using the third worksheet in the workbook named ANOVA. We selected the third worksheet by clicking on the tab towards the bottom of the Excel window labeled *Sheet3*. Save the workbook file with the name ANOVA.

Figure 8.7 Two-way ANOVA with Interaction Data

	A	B	C	D	E
1		Analysis of Variance Examples			
2		Your Name			
3	Today's Date			File: ANOVA.xls	
4					
5	SALES	COMPENSATION PLAN			
6	REGION	Salary	Sal.&Com.	Commissn	
7	Norhteast	4500	4430	5810	
8		4580	4740	5420	
9	Southeast	4200	4530	4800	
10		4860	4830	5100	
11	Midwest	5040	5100	5460	
12		4740	4920	6180	
13	West	4320	4140	4680	
14		4410	4320	4620	

---

2. From the menu bar select **Tools**, from the subsequent pull-down menu select **Data Analysis** and from the Data Analysis dialog box select **ANOVA: Two-Factor With Replication**.

3. Fill in the entries of the ANOVA: Two-Factor With Replication dialog box as shown in Figure 8.8. Notice that the input range includes the labels in the cells A6, B6, C6, D6 and A7 through A13.

4. The output will appear as shown in Figure 8.9. In this figure column B has been widened to allow the display of the full labels.

These ANOVA results provide the means and variances for each of the twelve possible combinations of compensation plan and geographic region. The ANOVA table at the bottom of the output provides sample statistics for conducting three separate F-tests. The first is a test to determine if the four geographic regions (labeled as **Sample** in cell A50) have a significant effect. Specifically, the test hypotheses are

$$H_0: \mu_1 = \mu_2 = \mu_3 = \mu_4$$
$$H_a: \text{not all } \mu\text{'s are equal}$$

Figure 8.8 ANOVA: Two-Factor with Replication Dialog Box

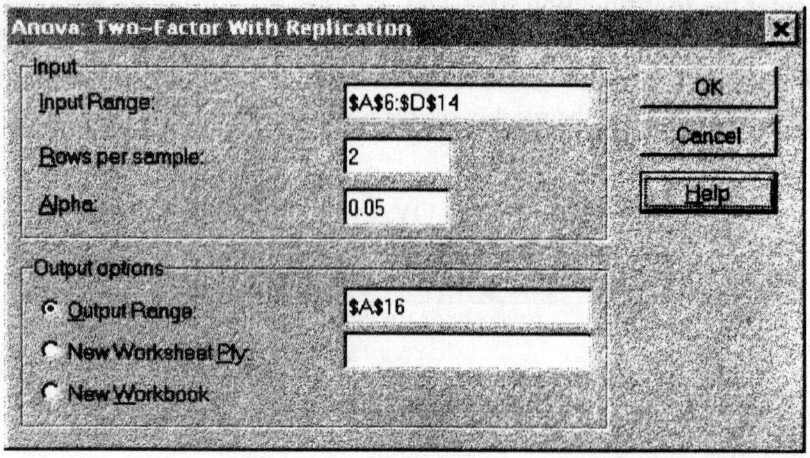

The second F-test is a test to determine if the three compensation plans (labeled as **Columns** in cell A51) have a significant effect. Specifically, the test hypotheses are

$$H_0: \mu_1 = \mu_2 = \mu_3$$
$$H_a: \text{not all } \mu\text{'s are equal}$$

The third F test is a test of whether there is a significant interaction or combined effect between the sales regions and compensation plans (labeled as **Interaction** in cell A52). The test hypotheses for the interaction effect are

$$H_0: \text{there is not an interaction effect between region and plan}$$
$$H_a: \text{there is an interaction effect between region and plan}$$

The **CRITICAL F-VALUE APPROACH** for these tests requires you to compare the computed value for the F-statistic to the critical value for F. If the computed F is greater than the critical value of F, the null hypothesis is rejected. Otherwise the null hypothesis is not rejected. The critical value is the value from the F distribution corresponds to the alpha value specified in Figure 8.8 and the degrees of freedom for the numerator and the denominator of the F statistic.

We note in Figure 8.9 that the computed F values both for the sales region (11.08462 in cell E50) and for the compensation plan (17.71899 in cell E51) are greater than their corresponding *F crit* values in cells G50 and G51. Accordingly, we would reject the null hypothesis in both cases. In other words, we conclude that the sales region and the compensation plan both have a significant effect on the six month sales results. On the other hand, the computed F value for the interaction effect of these two variables is 1.470002 in cell E52. It is smaller than the critical F value of 2.996117 in cell F52 so we do not reject the null hypothesis for this test. We conclude there is not a significant combined effect of sales region and compensation plan.

Figure 8.9 Results for Two-way ANOVA with Interaction

	A	B	C	D	E	F	G
16	Anova: Two-Factor With Replication						
17	SUMMARY	Salary	Sal.&Com.	Commissn	Total		
18	*Norhteast*						
19	Count	2	2	2	6		
20	Sum	9080	9170	11230	29480		
21	Average	4540	4585	5615	4913.333		
22	Variance	3200	48050	76050	321266.7		
23							
24	*Southeast*						
25	Count	2	2	2	6		
26	Sum	9060	9360	9900	28320		
27	Average	4530	4680	4950	4720		
28	Variance	217800	45000	45000	97800		
29							
30	*Midwest*						
31	Count	2	2	2	6		
32	Sum	9780	10020	11640	31440		
33	Average	4890	5010	5820	5240		
34	Variance	45000	16200	259200	268800		
35							
36	*West*						
37	Count	2	2	2	6		
38	Sum	8730	8460	9300	26490		
39	Average	4365	4230	4650	4415		
40	Variance	4050	16200	1800	41190		
41							
42	*Total*						
43	Count	8	8	8			
44	Sum	36650	37010	42070			
45	Average	4581.25	4626.25	5258.75			
46	Variance	80412.5	106169.6	313955.4			
47							
48	ANOVA						
49	rce of Varia	SS	df	MS	F	P-value	F crit
50	Sample	2154713	3	718237.5	11.08462	0.000896	3.4903
51	Columns	2296233	2	1148117	17.71899	0.000262	3.88529
52	Interaction	571500	6	95250	1.470002	0.26801	2.996117
53	Within	777550	12	64795.83			
54	Total	5799996	23				

For the **p-VALUE APPROACH** to these tests, you will need to refer to Table 5.3 (or 5.5) to categorize the results. For this example the p-value for the first test is given in cell F50 of Figure 8.9 as 0.000896 and that for the second test as 0.000262 in cell F51. The categories of Table 5.3 (or 5.5) would classify both of these results as *very highly significant*. Accordingly, we would again reject the null hypothesis for both tests. The p-value for the interaction effect test is 0.26801 in cell F52. We would categorize this as *not significant* and thus would not reject the null hypothesis.

This completes are discussion of the use of the three ANOVA data analysis tools provided by Excel. As mentioned in our introduction to this chapter, the F-test of this chapter is equivalent to the two-tailed t-test for population means of Chapter 5 for the two population situation. In the next chapter we will explore a similar situation for population proportions. We will see that the χ^2 test is equivalent to the two-tailed z-test for two population proportions of Chapter 6. We will see that the χ^2 test can also be used if there are more than two population proportions, and we will explore its use for another application.

CHAPTER 9. APPLICATIONS OF THE CHI-SQUARE STATISTIC

9.1   Goodness-of-Fit Test: Multinomial Distribution

9.2   Test of Independence: Contingency Tables

9.3   The PIVOT TABLE WIZARD
    9.3.1 One Variable Frequency Count
    9.3.2 Two Variable Frequency Count

In Chapter 7 we showed how the chi-square statistic could be used for statistical estimation and testing for population variances. In this chapter we demonstrate two additional hypothesis testing procedures which are based on the chi-square statistic. The first, the goodness-of-fit test for a multinomial distribution, is discussed in **Section 9.1**. The second, the test for independence using contingency tables, is discussed in **Section 9.2**. Both of these tests are performed on frequency count data. The multinomial goodness-of-fit test requires frequency counts for one variable. On the other hand, the contingency table test of independence requires frequency counts for a cross-tabulation for all combinations of values for two variables. Sometimes the frequency values are readily available. At other times, it is necessary to compute frequencies from a data set before conducting the test. For these instances, Excel provides a feature which makes the computation of frequencies somewhat easy. It is the PIVIOT TABLE WIZARD as presented in **Section 9.3**.

Before proceeding, we should mention that the tests of this chapter are generally used for **qualitative** or categorical data (measured on a nominal or ordinal measurement scale) as opposed to **quantitative** or numerical data (measured on an interval or ratio scale).   However, they can also be applied to the analysis of quantitative data.

9.1 GOODNESS-OF-FIT TEST:
MULTINOMIAL DISTRIBUTION————

Excel provides two statistical functions for conducting the multinomial goodness-of-fit test. The function CHIINV facilitates the critical χ^2-value approach to the test and CHIDIST facilitates the p-value approach to the test. We will demonstrate both approaches with the following example.

> Bib and Krit Waspork own B&K Ranch, Inc., which produces hay for ranches deep in the heart of the state of Zexas. They have thousands of customers to whom they provide five types of hay. In the past the proportion of their customers for the five types has been 0.16 for alfalfa, 0.09 for clover, 0.13 for timothy, 0.36 for mixture #1 and 0.26 for mixture #2. In planning for the upcoming season, they have asked a number of their customers their buying intentions. The result was 36 for alfalfa, 29 for clover, 27 for timothy, 55 for mixture #1 and 49 for mixture #2. B&K would now like to determine if these sample results indicate there has been a statistically significant change in their customer's requirements.

B&K's tabulation of their customers buying intentions could by done by hand. However, the PIVOT TABLE WIZARD of Excel can used to determine frequency counts such as this from a listing of the raw data. Thus, they could have used it as discussed in Section 9.3 to determine the necessary values.

We will develop a worksheet for computing the needed values for the hypothesis test. Proceed as follows.

1. Start Excel, enter the **Identification Material** in rows 1, and 2 of later Figure 9.2. Also enter the labels of rows 3, 10, 14 and 15 on the left-hand side of the worksheet and in rows 3 through 15 on the right-hand side of the worksheet. Enter the input values in cell C10, and cells A16 through A20, B16 through B20 and D16 through D20. Save the worksheet with the name CHI-SQR..

2. In cell H4 enter the formula to find the total observed frequencies. We will set this worksheet up to evaluate situations with up to 20 categories. Accordingly, the formula in cell H4 is **=SUM(B16:B35)** as shown in Figure 9.1.

3. Cell H5 is used to sum the hypothesized proportion inputs. These should sum to the value of 1.0. Any other value in this cell indicates the proportions are not correct. The formula in cell H5 is **=SUM(D16:D35)** since we are allowing for up to 20 categories.

Figure 9.1 Formulas for Chi-square Goodness-of-Fit Test

	E	F	G	H
1				
2	avid L. Eldredç		File: CHI-SQR.xls	
3	STATISTICAL			
4		Observed Frequency Su		=SUM(B16:B35)
5		Hypothesized Propor.Su		=SUM(D16:D35)
6				
7		Number of Categories		=COUNTA(A16:A35)
8		Degrees of Freedom		=H7-1
9				
10		Chi-square Test Statistic		=SUM(G16:G35)
11		Chi-square critical value		=CHIINV(C10,H8)
12		p-value for test		=CHIDIST(H10,H8)
13				
14		Expected	Chi-square	
15		Frequency	Value	
16		=$H$4*D16	=IF(F16>0,(B16-F16)^2/F16,0)	
17		=$H$4*D17	=IF(F17>0,(B17-F17)^2/F17,0)	
18		=$H$4*D18	=IF(F18>0,(B18-F18)^2/F18,0)	
19		=$H$4*D19	=IF(F19>0,(B19-F19)^2/F19,0)	
20		=$H$4*D20	=IF(F20>0,(B20-F20)^2/F20,0)	
21		=$H$4*D21	=IF(F21>0,(B21-F21)^2/F21,0)	
22		=$H$4*D22	=IF(F22>0,(B22-F22)^2/F22,0)	
23		=$H$4*D23	=IF(F23>0,(B23-F23)^2/F23,0)	
24		=$H$4*D24	=IF(F24>0,(B24-F24)^2/F24,0)	
25		=$H$4*D25	=IF(F25>0,(B25-F25)^2/F25,0)	

4. Cell H7 uses the function COUNTA to determine how many categories have been entered. The formula **=COUNTA(A16:A35)** counts the number of non-blank cells in the range A16 to A35.

5. The degrees of freedom for the chi-square statistic is one less than the number of categories. The formula **=H7-1** in cell H8 computes this value.

6. In cell H10 we compute the value for the chi-square statistic the formula **=SUM(G15:G35)**.

7. In cell H11 we compute the critical value for the chi-square distribution. It depends on the significance level of the test in cell C10 and the degrees of freedom in cell H8. The formula is **=CHIINV(C10,H8)**.

8. The formula in cell H12 computes the p value for the test. Its value depends on the test statistic value in cell H10 and the degrees of freedom. The formula is **=CHIDIST(H10,H8)**.

9. Cells F16 through F35 compute the expected frequencies. In cell F16 enter the formula **=$H$4*D16**. The absolute cell reference is used for cell H4 so this formula can be correctly copied. Copy the formula to cells F17 through F35.

10. Finally cells G16 through G35 compute the chi-square value for each category. Since we are setting the worksheet up to use an indefinite number of categories, we are forced to use an IF

statement to set the value equal to zero for the blank categories in the range. Thus, the IF statement computes the chi-square value for the non-blank categories. The formula for cell G16 is entered as **=IF(F16>0,(B16-F16)^2/F16,0)**. Copy the formula into cells G17 through G35.

The result of your efforts should appear as given in Figure 9.2. We now have the values necessary to conduct the test both with the critical χ^2-value approach and the p-value approach.

Figure 9.2 Results for Chi-square Goodness-of-Fit Test

	A	B	C	D	E	F	G	H	I
1			MULTINOMIAL GOODNESS-OF-FIT TEST						
2	Date: January 7, 1998				David L. Eldredge			File: CHI-SQR.xls	
3	INPUT DATA					STATISTICAL OUTPUTS			
4						Observed Frequency Sum		196	
5						Hypothesized Propor.Sum		1.000	
6									
7						Number of Categories		5	
8						Degrees of Freedom		4	
9									
10	Significance Level of Test=		0.05			Chi-square Test Statistic		11.600	
11						Chi-square critical value		9.488	
12						p-value for test		0.021	
13									
14		Observed		Hypthesized		Expected	Chi-square		
15	Category	Frequency		Proportion		Frequency	Value		
16	Alfalfa	36		0.160		31.36	0.6865		
17	Clover	29		0.090		17.64	7.3157		
18	Timothy	27		0.130		25.48	0.0907		
19	Mixture #1	55		0.360		70.56	3.4313		
20	Mixture #2	49		0.260		50.96	0.0754		
21						0	0.0000		
22						0	0.0000		
23						0	0.0000		
24						0	0.0000		
25						0	0.0000		

The null and the alternative hypotheses for this test are the following.

$$H_0: p_1 = 0.16, \ p_2 = 0.09, \ p_3 = 0.13, \ p_4 = 0.36, \ p_5 = 0.26,$$
$$H_a: \text{at least one of these proportions is incorrect}$$

The **CRITICAL χ^2-VALUE APPROACH** requires you to compare the computed value for the chi-square statistic to the critical value for chi-square. If the computed value is greater than the critical value, the null hypothesis is rejected. Otherwise the null hypothesis is not rejected. From Figure 9.2 we note that the computed chi-square value of cell H10 is 11.600 and the critical value of cell H11 is 9.488. Thus, we would conclude that not all the proportions are correct. In other words we would conclude that there has been a statistically significant change in B&K's customer's requirements.

For the **P-VALUE APPROACH** to the test, you need to refer to Table 5.3 (or 5.5) of Chapter 5 to categorize the results. For our example here the p-value given in cell H12 is 0.021. The categories of Table 5.3 (or 5.5) would classify these results as *significant*. Accordingly, we would again reject the null hypothesis. We would conclude there has been a change in the customers requirements.

You should save your completed worksheet for future use. Although you developed it for a particular test situation, it is completely general. Thus, you can use it for testing any specified set of proportion values. To use the worksheet, you only need to enter

1. The significance value in cell C10.

2. The categories beginning in cell A16. Since the worksheet is set up to utilize data in rows 16 through 35, all cells in column A through row 35 which **do not represent a category should be blank**. If not the number of categories computed in cell H5 will be incorrect.

3. The observed frequencies beginning in cell B16.

4. The hypothesized proportions beginning in cell D16. These should sum to 1.0. Cell H5 computes the sum of these so you may easily see that this is true or not.

Your worksheet will provide you with the values for conducting the hypothesis test for both the critical χ^2-value and the p-value approaches.

Before concluding this section let us point out **two special applications** of this test. First, it is commonly used to test for the **equivalence of a set of proportions**. The hypotheses for this are

$$H_0: p_1 = p_2 = p_3 = p_4 = p_5 = \ldots = p_k = 1/k$$
$$H_a: \text{at least one of the proportions is not equal}$$

The entries for the worksheet are as before except that the *Hypothesized Proportion* values are all equal to one divided by the number of proportions (i.e., 1/k).

The second special application is for the **two category situation**. For it the hypotheses are

$$H_0: p_1 = \text{a specified value}, \quad p_2 = 1\text{- the specified value}$$
$$H_a: p_1 \neq \text{a specified value}, \quad p_2 \neq 1\text{- the specified value}$$

These are equivalent to the Form I (two-tailed) hypotheses for testing one population proportion as given in Subsection 6.1.2 of Chapter 6. Thus, this situation can be tested using either the z statistic as in Chapter 6 or the chi-square statistic of this chapter. The two tests will always yield the same result.

9.2 TEST OF INDEPENDENCE: CONTINGENCY TABLES ──────

Three of Excel's statistical functions are useful for conducting the contingency table test of independence. The function CHIINV facilitates the critical χ^2-value approach to the test. Both the functions CHIDIST and CHITEST can be used to compute the p-value for the test. We will demonstrate the use of these functions by continuing the B&K Ranch example of Section 9.1.

As you may recall Bib and Krit produce hay for ranches deep in the heart of Zexas. In order to predict their customers' needs for the upcoming year they are attempting to determine if the type of hay a customer purchases is related to the primary type of livestock the customer raises. They have analyzed data for a sample of their customers noting the type of hay and the primary livestock for each customer. These results are shown in Table 9.1. They would now like to use the χ^2 test of independence to determine if there is a significant relationship between the two qualitative variables *type of hay* and *type of livestock*.

Table 9.1 Number of Customers Classified by Type of Hay and Type of Livestock

TYPE OF HAY	PRIMARY TYPE OF LIVESTOCK			
	Cattle	Horses	Emus	Sheep
Alfalfa	6	14	11	5
Clover	5	11	12	1
Timothy	2	7	9	9
Mixture #1	16	10	7	22
Mixture #2	14	16	9	10

Before developing our worksheet to conduct the test, we should make one comment regarding the data of Table 9.1. B&K would have had to analyze a list of customers in order to determine the number for each cell in the table. They might do this by hand. However, Excel provides an analysis feature which can be used to determine frequency count data from a listing of data. It is called the PIVOT TABLE WIZARD and is discussed in Section 9.3. Thus, B&K could have used it to compute the values for Table 9.1

We will now develop a worksheet for computing the needed values for the contingency table test of independence. You should continue with the CHI-SQR workbook from Section 9.1 but on *Sheet2*.

1. Enter the **Identification Information** in rows 1, and 2 of later Figure 9.5. Also enter the labels in rows 3 through 29. Enter the input values in cell E4, and in cells B9 through E13. Save the workbook CHI-SQR..

2. In cell E21 enter the formula to find the total observed frequencies. We will set this worksheet up to evaluate situations with up to 10 categories for each of the two variables. Accordingly, the formula in cell E21 is **=SUM(B9:K18)** as shown in Figure 9.3.

Figure 9.3 Beginning Formulas for Chi-square Test of Independence

	A	B	C	D	E
18					
19					
20	STATISTICAL OUTP				
21		Observed Frequencies			=SUM(B9:K18)
22					
23		Number of First Catego			=COUNTA(A9:A18)
24		Number of Second Cat			=COUNTA(B8:K8)
25		Degrees of Freedom			=(E23-1)*(E24-1)
26					
27		Chi-square Test Statis			=SUM(B48:K57)
28		Chi-square Critical Val			=CHIINV(E4,E25)
29		p-Value for Test			=CHIDIST(E27,E25)
30					

3. Cell E23 uses the Excel function COUNTA to determine how many categories have been entered for the first variable. The formula **=COUNTA(A9:A18)** counts the number of non-blank cells in the range A9 through A18.

4. Cell E24 determines how many categories have been entered for the second variable. The formula is **=COUNTA(B8:K8)**.

5. The degrees of freedom for the chi-square statistic is one less than the number of categories for the first variable times one less than the number of categories for the number of categories for the second variable. The formula **=(E23-1)*(E24-1)** in cell E25 computes this value.

6. In cell E27 we compute the value for the chi-square statistic. The formula is **=SUM(B47:K56)**. As before this formula is set up to evaluate situations with up to 10 categories for each of the two variables. We will create the table in the range B47 through K56 later.

7. In cell E28 we compute the critical value for the chi-square distribution. It depends on the significance level of the test in cell E3 and the degrees of freedom in cell E25. The formula is **=CHIINV(E4,E25)**.

8. The formula in cell E29 computes the p value for the test. Its value depends on the test statistic value in cell E27 and the degrees of freedom. The formula is **=CHIDIST(E27,E25)**.

9. As shown in Figure 9.4, Rows 31 through 43 present a table for computing the expected frequencies. To begin developing this table copy the contents of cells A6 through K18 to cells A31

through K43.   Also, copy cells A6 through K18 to cells A45 through K57 to provide the structure for the chi-square values table shown at the bottom of Figure 9.4.

Figure 9.4 Additional Formulas for Chi-square Test of Independence

	A	B	C
33	Category #1	=B8	=C8
34	=A9	=SUM(B$9:B$18)*SUM($B9:$K9)/$E$21	=SUM(C$9:C$18)*SUM($B9:$K9)/$E$21
35	=A10	=SUM(B$9:B$18)*SUM($B10:$K10)/$E$21	=SUM(C$9:C$18)*SUM($B10:$K10)/$E$21
36	=A11	=SUM(B$9:B$18)*SUM($B11:$K11)/$E$21	=SUM(C$9:C$18)*SUM($B11:$K11)/$E$21
37	=A12	=SUM(B$9:B$18)*SUM($B12:$K12)/$E$21	=SUM(C$9:C$18)*SUM($B12:$K12)/$E$21
38	=A13	=SUM(B$9:B$18)*SUM($B13:$K13)/$E$21	=SUM(C$9:C$18)*SUM($B13:$K13)/$E$21
39	=A14	=SUM(B$9:B$18)*SUM($B14:$K14)/$E$21	=SUM(C$9:C$18)*SUM($B14:$K14)/$E$21
40	=A15	=SUM(B$9:B$18)*SUM($B15:$K15)/$E$21	=SUM(C$9:C$18)*SUM($B15:$K15)/$E$21
41	=A16	=SUM(B$9:B$18)*SUM($B16:$K16)/$E$21	=SUM(C$9:C$18)*SUM($B16:$K16)/$E$21
42	=A17	=SUM(B$9:B$18)*SUM($B17:$K17)/$E$21	=SUM(C$9:C$18)*SUM($B17:$K17)/$E$21
43	=A18	=SUM(B$9:B$18)*SUM($B18:$K18)/$E$21	=SUM(C$9:C$18)*SUM($B18:$K18)/$E$21
44			
45	TABLE 3--CHI-SQL		
46	First		Second Category
47	Category #1	=B8	=C8
48	=A9	=IF(B34>0,(B9-B34)^2/B34,0)	=IF(C34>0,(C9-C34)^2/C34,0)
49	=A10	=IF(B35>0,(B10-B35)^2/B35,0)	=IF(C35>0,(C10-C35)^2/C35,0)
50	=A11	=IF(B36>0,(B11-B36)^2/B36,0)	=IF(C36>0,(C11-C36)^2/C36,0)
51	=A12	=IF(B37>0,(B12-B37)^2/B37,0)	=IF(C37>0,(C12-C37)^2/C37,0)
52	=A13	=IF(B38>0,(B13-B38)^2/B38,0)	=IF(C38>0,(C13-C38)^2/C38,0)
53	=A14	=IF(B39>0,(B14-B39)^2/B39,0)	=IF(C39>0,(C14-C39)^2/C39,0)
54	=A15	=IF(B40>0,(B15-B40)^2/B40,0)	=IF(C40>0,(C15-C40)^2/C40,0)
55	=A16	=IF(B41>0,(B16-B41)^2/B41,0)	=IF(C41>0,(C16-C41)^2/C41,0)
56	=A17	=IF(B42>0,(B17-B42)^2/B42,0)	=IF(C42>0,(C17-C42)^2/C42,0)
57	=A18	=IF(B43>0,(B18-B43)^2/B43,0)	=IF(C43>0,(C18-C43)^2/C43,0)
58			

10. In cell A34 enter the equation **=A9** so the contents of A34 will always be the entry in cell A9.

11. Copy the formula in cell A34 into cells A35 through A43. Note the cells corresponding to blank cells in the Observed Frequency Table will display a 0.

12. In cell B33 enter the formula **=B8**.

13. Copy the formula in cell B33 into cells C33 through K33. Note the cells corresponding to blank cells in the Observed Frequency Table will display a 0.

14. The cells within the Expected Frequency Table are equal to the corresponding row total of the Observed Frequency Table times the corresponding column total divided by the total of all the observed frequencies. We begin by entering in cell B34 an appropriate formula for copying into the remaining cells of the table. The appropriate formula requires that we used **mixed relative and absolute references** for computing the row sums and the column sums. The formula for cell B34 is **=SUM(B$9:B$18)*SUM($B9:$K9)/$E$21**. Note the first sum involves a relative row

reference and an absolute column reference. The second sum has an absolute row reference and a relative column reference. Finally, the reference to cell E21 has absolute references for both row and column. (Note: if you are using the **F4** key to change a relative reference to an absolute reference, one click will change both row and column to absolute, two clicks will change just the column and three clicks will change just the row.)

15. Next copy the contents of cell B34 into all the remaining cells in the range from B34 through K43. This completes the development of the Expected Frequency Table.

16. As shown in Figure 9.4, Rows 45 through 57 present a table for computing the chi-square values for each of the individual terms. The structure of this table was copied in Step 9 above. In cell A48 enter the equation **=A9** so the contents of A48 will always be the entry in cell A9.

17. Copy the formula in cell A48 into cells A49 through A57. Note the cells corresponding to blank cells in the Observed Frequency Table will display a 0.

18. In cell B47 enter the formula **=B8**.

19. Copy the formula in cell B47 into cells C47 through K47. Note the cells corresponding to blank cells in the Observed Frequency Table will display a 0.

20. The computation within this table finds the difference between the observed frequency and the expected frequency for each cell. It then squares this difference and divides the result by the expected frequency. However, we are setting this worksheet up to use an indefinite number of categories. This requires that we use an IF statement to set the value equal to zero if the expected frequency is zero. Otherwise the computation would result in division by zero. The formula for cell B48 should be entered as **=IF(B34>0,(B9-B34)^2/B34,0)**.

21. Next copy the contents of cell B48 into all the remaining cells in the range from B48 through K57.

The result of your efforts should appear as given in Figure 9.5. If you successfully developed this worksheet yourself, you should have a feeling of accomplishment. You now have the values necessary to conduct the test of independence with both the critical χ^2-value approach and the p-value approach.

The null and the alternative hypotheses for this test are the following.

H_0: Type of hay is independent of type of livestock
H_a: Type of hay is not independent of type of livestock

The **CRITICAL χ^2-VALUE APPROACH** requires you to compare the computed value for the chi-square statistic to the critical value for chi-square. If the computed value is greater than the critical value, the null hypothesis is rejected. Otherwise the null hypothesis is not rejected. From Figure 9.5 we note that the computed chi-square value of cell E27 is 32.43923 and the critical value of

Figure 9.5 Results for Chi-square Test of Independence

	A	B	C	D	E	F	G	H	I	J	K	L
1				**CONTINGENCY TABLE TEST OF INDEPENDENCE**								
2	Date: January 8, 1998			David L. Eldredge						File: CHI-SQR.xls		
3	*INPUT DATA*											
4		Significance Level of Test=		0.05								
5												
6	**TABLE 1--OBSERVED FREQUENCIES**											
7	First		**Second Category**									
8	Category	Cattle	Horses	Emus	Sheep							
9	Alfalfa	6	14	11	5							
10	Clover	5	11	12	1							
11	Timothy	2	7	9	9							
12	Mixture #1	16	10	7	22							
13	Mixture #2	14	16	9	10							
14												
15												
16												
17												
18												
19												
20	*STATISTICAL OUTPUTS*											
21		Observed Frequencies Sum			196							
22												
23		Number of First Category			5							
24		Number of Second Category			4							
25		Degrees of Freedom			12							
26												
27		Chi-square Test Statistic			32.43923							
28		Chi-square Critical Value			21.02606							
29		p-Value for Test			0.00118							
30												
31	**TABLE 2--EXPECTED FREQUENCIES**											
32	First		**Second Category**									
33	Category	Cattle	Horses	Emus	Sheep	0	0	0	0	0	0	0
34	Alfalfa	7.898	10.653	8.816	8.633	0.000	0.000	0.000	0.000	0.000	0.000	0.000
35	Clover	6.362	8.582	7.102	6.954	0.000	0.000	0.000	0.000	0.000	0.000	0.000
36	Timothy	5.923	7.990	6.612	6.474	0.000	0.000	0.000	0.000	0.000	0.000	0.000
37	Mixture #1	12.066	16.276	13.469	13.189	0.000	0.000	0.000	0.000	0.000	0.000	0.000
38	Mixture #2	10.750	14.500	12.000	11.750	0.000	0.000	0.000	0.000	0.000	0.000	0.000
39	0	0.000	0.000	0.000	0.000	0.000	0.000	0.000	0.000	0.000	0.000	0.000
40	0	0.000	0.000	0.000	0.000	0.000	0.000	0.000	0.000	0.000	0.000	0.000
41	0	0.000	0.000	0.000	0.000	0.000	0.000	0.000	0.000	0.000	0.000	0.000
42	0	0.000	0.000	0.000	0.000	0.000	0.000	0.000	0.000	0.000	0.000	0.000
43	0	0.000	0.000	0.000	0.000	0.000	0.000	0.000	0.000	0.000	0.000	0.000
44												
45	**TABLE 3--CHI-SQUARE VALUES**											
46	First		**Second Category**									
47	Category	Cattle	Horses	Emus	Sheep	0	0	0	0	0	0	
48	Alfalfa	0.4560987	1.0515287	0.5408636	1.5286341	0	0	0	0	0	0	
49	Clover	0.2916755	0.6815137	3.3779029	5.0978821	0	0	0	0	0	0	
50	Timothy	2.5987493	0.1226184	0.8622449	0.9851281	0	0	0	0	0	0	
51	Mixture #1	1.2823942	2.4197108	3.1072665	5.8866479	0	0	0	0	0	0	
52	Mixture #2	0.9825581	0.1551724	0.75	0.2606383	0	0	0	0	0	0	
53	0	0	0	0	0	0	0	0	0	0	0	
54	0	0	0	0	0	0	0	0	0	0	0	
55	0	0	0	0	0	0	0	0	0	0	0	
56	0	0	0	0	0	0	0	0	0	0	0	

cell E28 is 21.02606. Thus, we would conclude that the type of hay is not independent of type of livestock. In other words, there appears to be a statistically significant relationship between the type of hay and the type of livestock for B&K's customers.

For the **P-VALUE APPROACH** to the test, you need to refer to Table 5.3 (or 5.5) of Chapter 5 to categorize the results. For our example here the p-value given in cell E29 is 0.00118. The categories of Figure 5.3 would classify these results as *highly significant*. Accordingly, we would again reject the null hypothesis. We would conclude there is a statistically significant relationship.

You should save your completed worksheet for future use. Although you developed it for a particular test situation, it is completely general. Thus, you can use it for conducting any test of independence between two variables. To use the worksheet, you only need to enter

1. The significance value in cell E4.

2. The categories for the first variable beginning in cell A9. The worksheet is set up to utilize data in rows 9 through 18 so all cells in column A through row 18 **which do not represent a category should be blank**. Otherwise the computation of cell E23 will be incorrect.

3. The categories for the second variable beginning in cell B8. The worksheet is set up to utilize data in columns B through K so all cells in row 8 through column K **which do not represent a category should be blank** so the value in cell E24 is correct.

4. The observed frequencies beginning in cell B9.

5. Your worksheet will provide you with the values for conducting the hypothesis test for both the critical χ^2-value and the p-value approaches.

Step 8 of the above procedure used the function CHIDIST to determine the p value of the test. Excel also provides the function CHITEST for determining the p value. This function has only two arguments, the range of the observed frequencies and the range of the expected frequencies. Accordingly, the use of this function would eliminate the need to explicitly compute (1) the degrees of freedom, (2) the chi-square values of the third table of Figure 9.5 and (3) the chi-square test statistic value. The function would implicitly perform all these computations. However such an approach would not provide the chi-square test statistic value for conducting the critical χ^2-value approach. To obtain this value it would be necessary to compute the degrees of freedom. Then you could use the CHIINV function with the p value and the degrees of freedom to find the chi-square test statistic value.

9.3 THE PIVOT TABLE WIZARD

Many statistical procedures previously studied require frequency count data for qualitative variables. For example, the descriptive procedures of Sections 2.2.2 and 2.2.3 in Chapter 2 and the inferential procedures of Chapter 6 and Sections 9.1 and 9.2. Excel provides a feature which easily computes frequency values from raw data. The feature is a special type of table called a Pivot Table which can be developed using the PIVOT TABLE WIZARD. This Wizard presents a series of dialog boxes which has the user specify (1) the location of the raw data, (2) the structure of the Pivot Table and (3) the format for the output.

To demonstrate, we will continue with the B&K Ranch example of the prior two sections of this chapter. To make the example manageable for you we will only use the small customer list given in Figure 9.6. This list only has three variables, customer number, type of hay and type of livestock, for 20 customers. However, the procedures which follow would still be appropriate if we had many more variables and thousands of customers. We will use these data first to obtain a one variable frequency count as required for the test of Section 9.1 and second to obtain a two variable frequency count as required for the test of Section 9.2.

Figure 9.6 Pivot Table Example Data

	A	B	C	D	E	F
1		B&K RANCH DATA FOR PIVOT TABLE				
2	Date: Jan. 10, 1998		David L. Eldredge		File: CHI-SQR.xls	
3		CUSTOMER	HAY	LIVESTOCK		
4		1453	Clover	Cattle		
5		1454	Mixture #1	Emus		
6		1455	Alfalfa	Sheep		
7		1456	Clover	Horses		
8		1457	Mixture #2	Horses		
9		1458	Alfalfa	Sheep		
10		1459	Mixture #1	Cattle		
11		1460	Mixture #1	Emus		
12		1461	Mixture #2	Sheep		
13		1462	Mixture #2	Sheep		
14		1463	Timothy	Cattle		
15		1464	Alfalfa	Horses		
16		1465	Mixture #1	Sheep		
17		1466	Mixture #2	Sheep		
18		1467	Clover	Horses		
19		1468	Mixture #1	Horses		
20		1469	Timothy	Cattle		
21		1470	Mixture #2	Emus		
22		1471	Timothy	Cattle		
23		1472	Clover	Horses		

9.3.1 One Variable Frequency Count

Suppose we wish to determine the frequency count data for a multinomial goodness-of-fit test such as conducted in Section 9.1. In particular, suppose we need to compute the frequency values from the customer list of Figure 9.6 to be entered in cells B16 through B20 of Figure 9.2.

We will continue with the CHI-SQR workbook from Section 9.2 but move to *Sheet3*.

1. Enter the **Identification Material** information in rows 1, and 2 of Figure 9.6. Also enter the labels in row 3 and the data in cells B4 through D23. Save the workbook CHI-SQR..

2. You need to specify for the Pivot Table Wizard the range for the data. This can be done in at least two ways. If the data range is not extremely large it is easiest to use the mouse to highlight the data range. **It is important that the data labels in row three be included in the highlighted range**. For larger data ranges, it may be easier to simply select any one cell in the data range and let Excel guess at the range of data you want to use (if the guess is wrong, it can be corrected in step 5 below). We have used the first approach for the small data range of Figure 9.6 to indicate the range from B3 through D23.

> **Excel 5 Note:** Excel 5's Pivot Wizard does not allow the data labels to be numbers.

3. From the menu bar select **Data** and from the subsequent pull-down menu select **PivotTable** as shown in Figure 9.7.

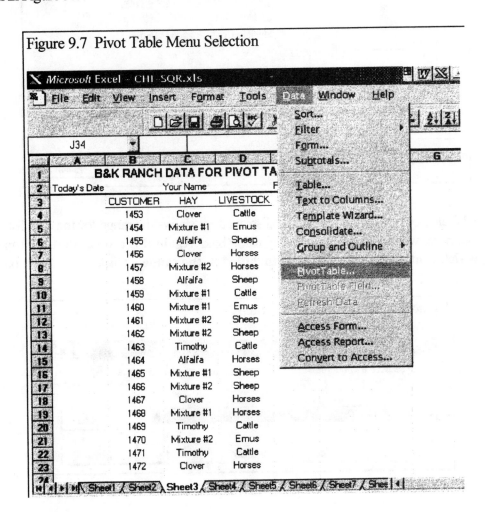

Figure 9.7 Pivot Table Menu Selection

4. The result will be the Step 1 dialog box for the Pivot Table Wizard as shown in Figure 9.8. It asks for the source of the data for the pivot table. For this step click on the option button for **Microsoft Excel List or Database** to indicate the data are internal to the current workbook and are located in one list on one worksheet.   Click on the **Next** command button.

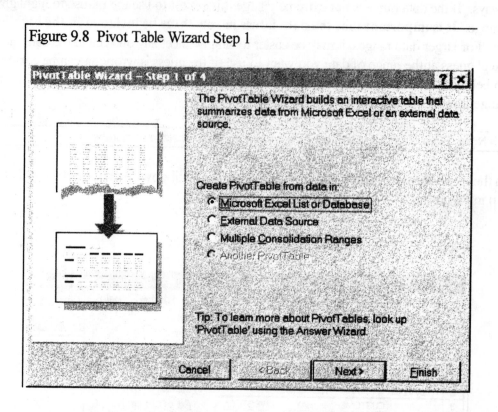

Figure 9.8 Pivot Table Wizard Step 1

5. The Step 2 dialog box of Figure 9.9 will be displayed. It shows the range for the data list. If this range is incorrect, we would correct it in the dialog box. **Again it is critical that the top row of the list, which contains the headings, be included in the range.**   Click on the **Next** button.

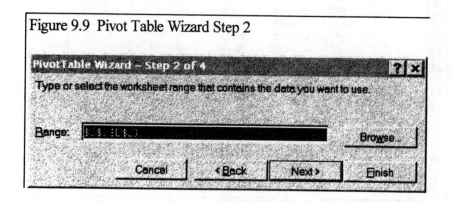

Figure 9.9 Pivot Table Wizard Step 2

6. The result will be the Step 3 dialog box as given in Figure 9.10. Whereas the first two steps specified the location of the raw data, this step specifies the structure of the pivot table. Figure 9.10 shows two general items. On the right-hand side it displays a command button for each of the three variables in the data range. On left-hand side it displays a pivot table with its four possible parts: PAGE, ROW, COLUMN and DATA. The idea is to use the mouse to drag and drop each of the variables to the appropriate part of the pivot table.

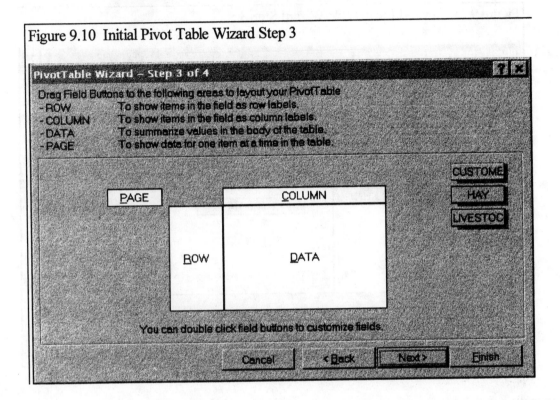

Figure 9.10 Initial Pivot Table Wizard Step 3

7. For our example, we wish to determine the number of customers for each of the five types of hay. To specify this we would move the mouse pointer to the **Hay** button, hold down the left mouse button, move the mouse pointer (which becomes a small rectangular button) to the *Row* part of the pivot table on the left and release the mouse button. The label *Hay* will appear above Row in the pivot table as shown in Figure 9.11. We repeat this dragging operation of the **Hay** button but release it on the *Data* part of the pivot table. The label *Count of Hay* will appear above Data in the table (see Figure 9.11). Excel has guessed that we wish to display the count of the number of hay customers. If it had guessed wrong we would proceed to Step 8 to modify it. If it guessed right we would proceed to Step 9 by clicking on the **Next** button.

8. If Excel does not display the desired summary measure in the Data section of the pivot table, double click on the summary measure which is shown in the data section. The result will be the Pivot Table Field dialog box as shown in Figure 9.12. The scrolling list box in the bottom left of the dialog box shows the 11 possible summary measures for a pivot table. We would select **Count,**

click on **OK** and then click on **Next** in the Step 3 dialog box. In passing we might note that you can modify the pivot data in further ways. If you select the **Options** button from the Pivot Table Field dialog box, an extension to the dialog box will be displayed. It includes a scrolling list of nine modifications which can be made to the data. For example, it allows you to convert the frequency counts to percentages.

Figure 9.11 Revised Pivot Table Wizard Step 3

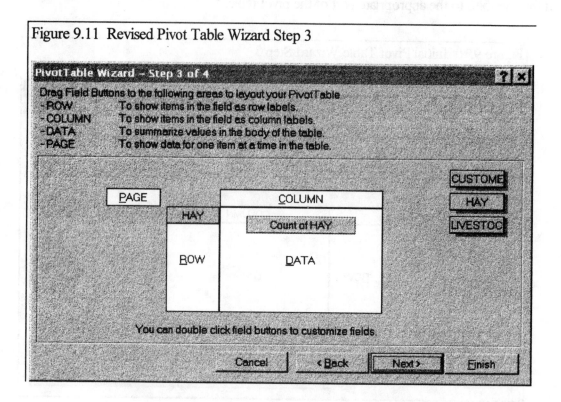

Figure 9.12 Pivot Table Field Dialog Box

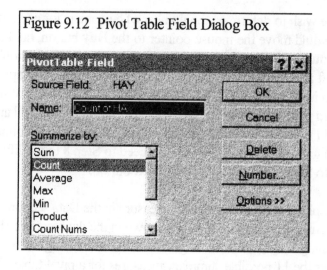

9. The result will be the Step 4 dialog box as given in Figure 9.13. As you will note there are six items to consider. The first two are in the upper right-hand corner. The first of these is the entry for the **Pivot Table Starting Cell**. As you will note from the figure, we have used cell F5 of the current worksheet. Below that entry is the **Pivot Table Name**. Excel has assigned the default name of *PivotTable1* which we have not changed. In the center of the dialog box are four check boxes. We have left two of them checked. They are **Grand Totals for Columns** and **AutoFormat Table**. The first asks for a total of all the frequencies and the second asks for the default format for the table (the format can easily be changed later if desired). The **Grand Totals for Rows** can either be checked or not since we have a single column of data. The **Save Data With Table Layout** should not be checked. Otherwise Excel will inflate the size of your Excel file by creating a duplicate copy of the data. Last click on **Finish** to produce the results of Figure 9.14.

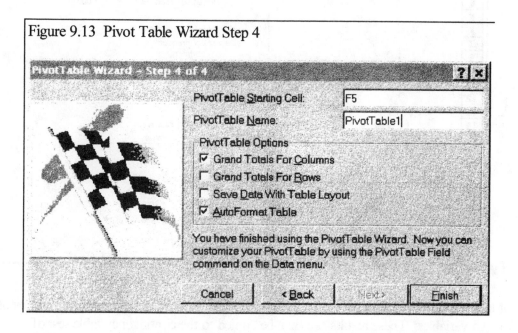

Figure 9.13 Pivot Table Wizard Step 4

Figure 9.14 Pivot Table Final Results

	A	B	C	D	E	F	G	H
1		B&K RANCH DATA FOR PIVOT TABLE						
2	Date: Jan. 10, 1998		David L. Eldredge		File: CHI-SQR.xls			
3		CUSTOMER	HAY	LIVESTOCK				
4		1453	Clover	Cattle				
5		1454	Mixture #1	Emus		Count of HAY		
6		1455	Alfalfa	Sheep		HAY	Total	
7		1456	Clover	Horses		Alfalfa	3	
8		1457	Mixture #2	Horses		Clover	4	
9		1458	Alfalfa	Sheep		Mixture #1	5	
10		1459	Mixture #1	Cattle		Mixture #2	5	
11		1460	Mixture #1	Emus		Timothy	3	
12		1461	Mixture #2	Sheep		Grand Total	20	
13		1462	Mixture #2	Sheep				
14		1463	Timothy	Cattle				

The frequency values in cells G7 through G 12 can now be copied to *Sheet1* of the CHI-SQR workbook to compute the values for the Multinomial Goodness-of-Fit test. If you do this, the results of Figure 9.15 will be obtained. How do these compare to those found in Figure 9.2 for the sample of size 196?

Figure 9.15 Pivot Table Chi-square Goodness-of-Fit Test Results

	A	B	C	D	E	F	G	H	I
1			MULTINOMIAL GOODNESS-OF-FIT TEST						
2	Date: January 7, 1998				David L. Eldredge		File: CHI-SQR.xls		
3	*INPUT DATA*				*STATISTICAL OUTPUTS*				
4						Observed Frequency Sum		20	
5						Hypothesized Propor.Sum		1.000	
6									
7						Number of Categories		5	
8						Degrees of Freedom		4	
9									
10	Significance Level of Test=		0.05			Chi-square Test Statistic		6.520	
11						Chi-square critical value		9.488	
12						p-value for test		0.164	
13									
14			Observed		Hypthesized		Expected	Chi-square	
15	Category		Frequency		Proportion		Frequency	Value	
16	Alfalfa		3		0.160		3.2	0.0125	
17	Clover		4		0.090		1.8	2.6889	
18	Timothy		5		0.130		2.6	2.2154	
19	Mixture #1		5		0.360		7.2	0.6722	
20	Mixture #2		3		0.260		5.2	0.9308	
21							0	0.0000	

9.3.2 Two Variable Frequency Count

The pivot table feature of Excel can also be used to produce a cross-tabulation for all combinations of values for two variables. These results can than be copied to the contingency table test of independence worksheet to compute the values for the test.

Suppose we wish to determine the frequency count for the test conducted in Section 9.2. In particular, suppose we need to compute the frequency values from the customer list of Figure 9.6 to be entered in cells B9 through E13 of Figure 9.5 for the B&K contingency table..

We will continue working on *Sheet3* of the CHI-SQR workbook.

1. Begin by highlighting the range of the data from cells B3 through D23. **Note that it is necessary that the variable names of row 3 be included in the range.**

2. From the menu bar select **Data** and from the subsequent pull-down menu select **PivotTable** as previously shown in Figure 9.7.

3. The result will be the Step 1 dialog box for the Pivot Table Wizard as shown in Figure 9.8. It asks for the source of the data for the pivot table. For this step click on the option button for **Microsoft Excel List or Database** to indicate the data are internal to the current workbook and is located in one list on one worksheet. Click on the **Next** command button.

4. The Step 2 dialog box of Figure 9.9 will be displayed. It shows the range for the data list. If this range is incorrect, we would correct it in the dialog box. **Again it is critical that the top row of the list, which contains the headings, be included in the range**. Click on the **Next** button.

5. The result will be the Step 3 dialog box as given in Figure 9.10. Whereas the first two steps of the PIVOT TABLE WIZARD specified the location of the raw data, this step specifies the structure of the pivot table. Figure 9.10 shows two general items. On the right-hand side it displays a command button for each of the three variables in the data range. On left-hand side it displays a pivot table with its four possible parts: PAGE, ROW, COLUMN and DATA. The idea is to use the mouse to drag and drop each of the variables to the appropriate part of the pivot table.

6. For our example, we wish to determine the number of customers for each of the twenty combinations of five types of hay and four types of livestock. To specify this we would move the mouse pointer to the **Hay** button, hold down the left mouse button, move the mouse pointer (which becomes a small rectangular button) to the *Row* part of the pivot table on the left and release the mouse button. The label *Hay* will appear above Row in the pivot table as shown in Figure 9.16. Next we would drag the **Livestock** to the Column part of the pivot table. The label *Livestock* will appear to the left of Column in the pivot table. Next we would repeat this dragging operation of the **Livestock** button but release it on the *Data* part of the pivot table (we could have used the Hay button a second time instead of the Livestock button a second time to obtain the same results). The label *Count of Livestock* will appear above Data in the table (see Figure 9.16). Excel has guessed that we wish to display the count of the number of customers. If it had guessed wrong we would proceed to Step 7 to modify it. If it guessed right we would proceed to Step 8 by clicking on the **Next** button.

7. If Excel does not display the desired summary measure in the Data section of the pivot table, double click on the summary measure which is shown in the data section. The result will be the Pivot Table Field dialog box as shown in Figure 9.12. The scrolling list box in the bottom left of the dialog box shows the 11 possible summary measures for a pivot table. We would select **Count**, click on **OK** and then click on **Next** in the Step 3 dialog box. In passing we might note that you can modify the pivot data in further ways. If you select the **Options** button, an extension to the dialog box will be displayed. It includes a scrolling list of nine modifications which can be made to the data. For example, it allows you to convert the frequency counts to percentages.

Figure 9.16 Pivot Table Wizard Step 3

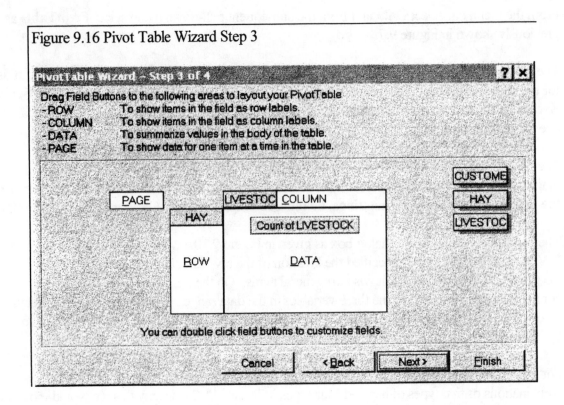

8.   The result will be the Step 4 dialog box as given in Figure 9.17. As you will note there are six
     items to consider. The first two are in the upper right-hand corner. The first of these is the entry
     for the **Pivot Table Starting Cell**. As you will note, we have used cell F15 of the current
     worksheet. Below that entry is the **Pivot Table Name**. Excel has assigned the default name of
     PivotTable2 which we have not changed. In the center of the dialog box are four check boxes.
     We have left three of them checked. They are **Grand Totals for Columns, Grand Totals for
     Rows** and **AutoFormat Table**. The first two ask for a total of the frequencies by column and row,
     and the third asks for the default format for the table (the format can easily be changed later if
     desired). The **Save Data With Table Layout** should not be checked. Otherwise Excel will inflate
     the size of your Excel file by creating a duplicate copy of the data. Last click on **Finish** to produce
     the results as shown in Figure 9.18.

Figure 9.17 Pivot Table Wizard Step 4

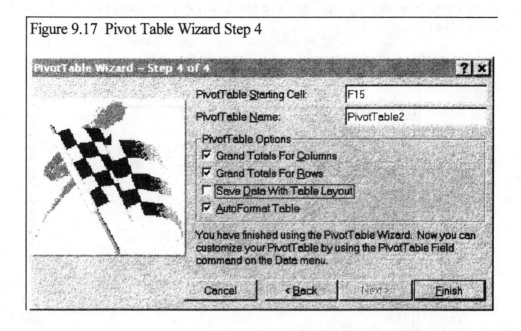

Figure 9.18 Pivot Table Final Results

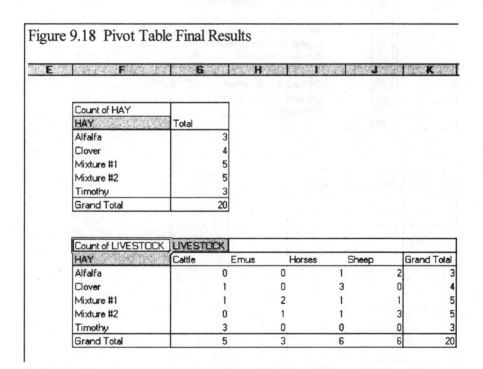

Count of HAY	
HAY	Total
Alfalfa	3
Clover	4
Mixture #1	5
Mixture #2	5
Timothy	3
Grand Total	20

Count of LIVESTOCK	LIVESTOCK				
HAY	Cattle	Emus	Horses	Sheep	Grand Total
Alfalfa	0	0	1	2	3
Clover	1	0	3	0	4
Mixture #1	1	2	1	1	5
Mixture #2	0	1	1	3	5
Timothy	3	0	0	0	3
Grand Total	5	3	6	6	20

The frequency values in cells G17 through J21 can now be copied to *Sheet2* of the CHI-SQR workbook to compute the values for the Contingency Table Test of Independence. If you do this, the results of Figure 9.19 will be shown. How do these results compare to those found in Figure 9.5 for the sample of size 196?

Figure 9.19 Pivot Table Test of Independence Results

	A	B	C	D	E	F
5						
6	TABLE 1--OBSERVED FREQUENCIES					
7	First		Second Category			
8	Category	Cattle	Horses	Emus	Sheep	
9	Alfalfa	0	0	1	2	
10	Clover	1	0	3	0	
11	Timothy	1	2	1	1	
12	Mixture #1	0	1	1	3	
13	Mixture #2	3	0	0	0	
14						
15						
16						
17						
18						
19						
20	STATISTICAL OUTPUTS					
21		Observed Frequencies Sum			20	
22						
23		Number of First Category			5	
24		Number of Second Category			4	
25		Degrees of Freedom			12	
26						
27		Chi-square Test Statistic			21.52222	
28		Chi-square Critical Value			21.02606	
29		p-Value for Test			0.04324	
30						

CHAPTER 10. REGRESSION ANALYSIS

10.1 Simple Linear Regression with TRENDLINE

10.2 Simple Linear Regression with the REGRESSION Analysis Tool

10.3 Multiple Regression with the REGRESSION Analysis Tool

10.4 Simple Non-linear Regression Analysis

Regression analysis may well be the most widely used statistical procedure. It is a statistical method for studying the relationship between two or more variables. One objective of a regression analysis is to arrive at a mathematical relationship which will predict values for one variable, called the **dependent variable**, based on the values for the remaining variables, called the **independent variables**. Since most business, industrial, governmental and social organizations need to forecast values for such things as demand, interest rates, inflation rates, prices, costs and so on, there is great interest in the use of regression analysis. Regression analysis with only one independent variable is called **simple linear regression**. On the other hand, if the analysis includes two or more independent variables, it is called **multiple regression**.

As a result of the widespread use of regression analysis, Excel includes a number of resources for performing the required computations and charting. These resources can be categorized into three groups: (1) the trendline feature for charts, (2) three data analysis tools and (3) twelve statistical functions The Trendline feature for charts facilitates the visual development of relationships for simple regression, that is, with one independent variable. The trendline feature can be used to develop relationships which are either linear or nonlinear.

In addition, Excel includes three data analysis tools for performing regression analysis and the closely associated procedure called correlation analysis. These tools are the REGRESSION Analysis Tool, the CORRELATION Analysis Tool and the COVARIANCE Analysis Tool. Finally, Excel includes twelve functions which facilitate the computations for regression analysis and correlation analysis through the use of the FUNCTION WIZARD. (For a listing and a description of these functions refer to the last twelve functions summarized in Appendix B.)

The capabilities of these three groups of resources duplicate each other in many aspects. The approach we take here is to introduce the student to those features which are the quickest and easiest to use for each part of the analysis. Accordingly, we first introduce in **Section 10.1** the use of the TRENDLINE feature for performing a simple linear regression analysis. We then consider in **Section 10.2** the added statistical results of the REGRESSION Analysis Tool for simple linear regression analysis. We continue with the use of the REGRESSION Analysis Tool in **Section 10.3** but for multiple regression. Finally, in **Section 10.4** we use both the TRENDLINE feature and the REGRESSION Analysis Tool for non-linear simple regression. Other resources are used in these four sections as needed to complete our analysis. For example, the function TREND is discussed in sections 10.1, 10.2 and 10.3 for forecasting values for the dependent variable, and the CORRELATION Analysis Tool is used in Section 10.3 to test for the condition called multicollinearity.

10.1 SIMPLE LINEAR REGRESSION WITH TRENDLINE

We will begin our consideration of regression analysis with the following example.

Ms. Laura Maura is the product manager for Nutrecal, a food supplement product. In order to prepare her marketing plan for next year, she needs to predict the demand for Nutrecal. She feels the best predictor of demand for Nutrecal is the amount spent on advertising. Accordingly, she has gathered data from eight test markets which show the advertising level in thousands of dollars and the corresponding sales level in thousands of dollars. She first wishes to find a simple linear regression relationship which will allow her to predict sales as a function of advertising level. To analyze her results using the trendline feature of Excel you would proceed as follows.

1. Start Excel, enter the **Identification Material**, and then enter the labels and data in columns B and C as shown in Figure 10.1. Save the workbook with the file name REGRESS.

2.   As was noted in Section 2.2 of Chapter 2, Excel's Chart Wizard can be used to create 15 types of charts. The XY (Scatter) type will be used to plot the data and compute the regression equation for this example. Move the pointer to the CHART WIZARD icon on the standard toolbar and

click once. (Note: If you have not used the Chart Wizard before you may wish to refer to Figures 2.8 through 2.12 given in Chapter 2 for Excel 7 and 5, and in Appendix C for Excel 8.)

Figure 10.1 Simple Linear Regression Example Data

	A	B	C	D	E
1		Regression Analysis Examples			
2		Your Name			
3	Today's Date		File: REGRESS.xls		
4					
5		ADVERT.	SALES		
6		74.0	900.0		
7		27.5	266.4		
8		169.0	1555.2		
9		497.0	4320.0		
10		270.5	2707.2		
11		44.5	439.2		
12		63.0	1209.6		
13		189.5	2966.4		
14					

3. The pointer will change to a small representation of a cross and a bar chart. Move it to cell E5 and click the mouse button. The Chart Wizard Step 1 dialog box will appear as shown in Figure 10.2.

Figure 10.2 Data Range for Scatter Diagram

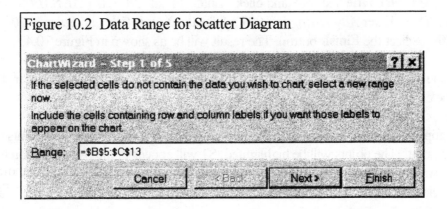

4. Enter the range B5:C13 in the **Range** text box either by keying or by clicking and dragging. Click on **Next**. The Chart Wizard Step 2 will appear (see Figure 2.8 in Chapter 2 or in Appendix C).

5. Use the mouse to select the **XY (Scatter)** chart and then select the **Next** button. The Chart Wizard Step 3 (see Figure 2.10) will appear.

6. Select format number **3** for Step 3 and the **Next** button to obtain Step 4 (see Figure 2.11).

7. For Step 4, make sure **Columns** is selected for **Data Series in** option. Click on the option button once or twice to select it. Select **Next** to obtain Step 5 of Figure 10.3.

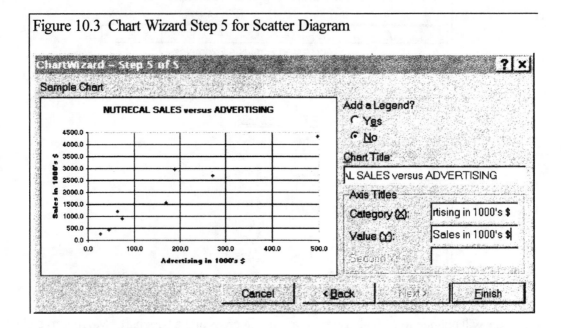

Figure 10.3 Chart Wizard Step 5 for Scatter Diagram

8. For the **Add legend** option select **No** by clicking once or twice on its option button. Move the pointer to the **Chart Title** text box and click. Enter the title *NUTRECAL SALES versus ADVERTISING*. Enter *Advertising in 1000's $* for the **X-axis title** and *Sales in 1000's $* for the **Y-axis title**. Select the **Finish** button. The result will be as shown in Figure 10.4.

9. Next double click inside the chart to activate it for editing. A cross-hatched border should appear around the chart.

10. To superimpose a line of regression on this scatter diagram, select the plotted points by clicking on any single point. The points will be highlighted, S1 will appear in the name box (on the left just above the worksheet) and the formula bar (on the right in the same line) will show that SERIES has been selected.

Excel 8 Note: The CHART WIZARD of Excel 8 (97) is significantly different from that of Excel 7 and 5. Step 9 above only requires a single click, and instead of a cross-hatched border the sizing handles are displayed. For Step 11 you should click on **Chart** instead of **Insert**, and on **Add Trendline** instead of just **Trendline**. Appendix C provides additional insights into the changes made to the CHART WIZARD for Excel 8.

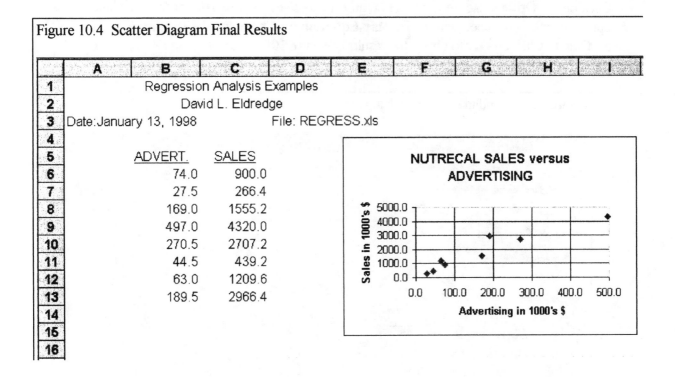

Figure 10.4 Scatter Diagram Final Results

11. Click on **Insert** from the menu bar and then click on **Trendline** on the pull-down menu.

12. Click on the **Type** tab, click on **Linear** for the Trend/Regression Type as shown in Figure 10.5.

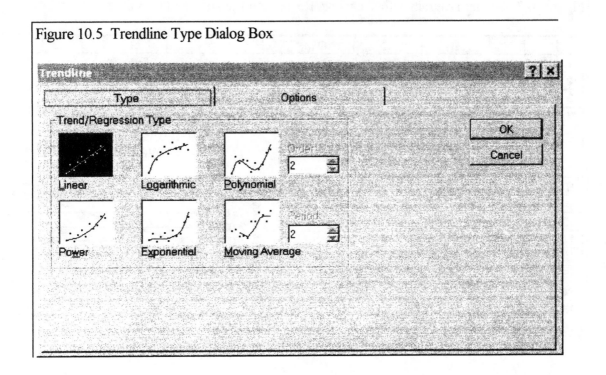

Figure 10.5 Trendline Type Dialog Box

13. Click on the **Options** tab. As shown in Figure 10.6, select **Automatic** for the Trendline Name option. Click to put checks in the **Display Equation on Chart** and the **Display R-squared Value on Chart**. Click on **OK** to obtain the results of Figure 10.7.

Figure 10.6 Trendline Options Dialog Box

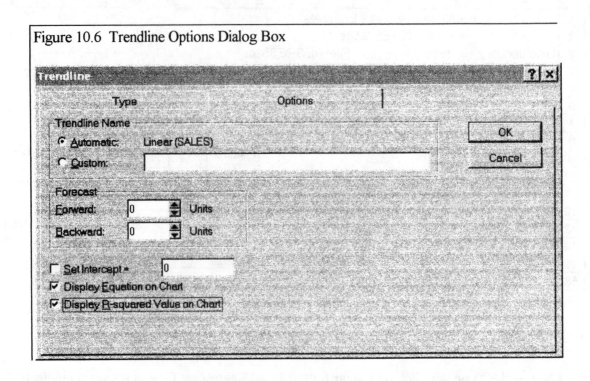

Figure 10.7   Scatter Diagram with Trendline, Regression Equation and R^2 Value

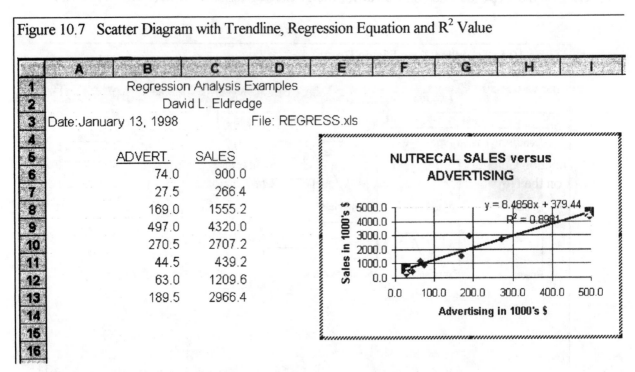

What do the results of Figure 10.7 mean? First, the best linear relationship for these data is the equation

$$y = 8.4858x + 379.44$$

where x is the advertising level in 1000's of dollars and y is sales in 1000's of dollars. Second, $R^2 = 0.8981$ suggests that 89.81% of the variability of the sales values about their average can be explained by changes in advertising. This indicates that the equation fits the data very well. There are more precise statistical measures of the goodness of fit of an equation to data as we will see in the next section. However, R^2, called the coefficient of determination, is a good single measure of the strength of the relationship.

In summary, this approach to simple linear regression analysis rather easily yields (1) a scatter diagram providing a visual interpretation of the relationship between two variables, (2) the equation for the best straight line relationship and (3) a good measure of how strong the linear relationship is.

Once a good fitting relationship has been found, it can be used to predict the average value for y for a specified value of x. There are a number of ways of doing this in Excel. One approach would be enter the regression formula in a worksheet cell and insert the value for the independent variable, x, into the formula. The cell would then display the predicted y value.

A second approach for predicting is to use the statistical function called TREND. The general format for this function is

=TREND(range of y values, range of x values, range of x values to be used for predicting)

Suppose we wish to make predictions for the above example for advertising levels of 100, 200, 300 and 400 thousand dollars. We would proceed as follows with the worksheet REGESS..

1. Enter the values 100, 200, 300 and 400 in cells B18 through B21.

2. Click on the FUNCTION WIZARD icon, *fx*, on the Standard Toolbar. The result will be the dialog box for Function Wizard - Step 1 of 2 (see Figure 3.7 in Chapter 3). Click on **Statistical** in the Function Category list box and scroll to and click on **Trend** in the Function Name list box. Click on the **Next** button. The Function Wizard Step 2 of 2 dialog box as shown in Figure 10.8 will be displayed on the screen.

3. Use the mouse or the keyboard to select the range of cells where the predicted y values are to appear, C18 through C21.

4. As shown in Figure 10.8 for the step 2 dialog box, enter the range for the y values, the range for the x values, and the range of x values to be used for predicting. The fourth text box labeled as *const* can be left blank (alternatively the word **True** or the number **1** can be entered for it) to indicate the constant is not to be forced to a value of zero. Click on the **Finish** button. The result will be the predicted y value for the first x value. To obtain functions for the remaining x values,

we need to edit the function so it is treated as an array.

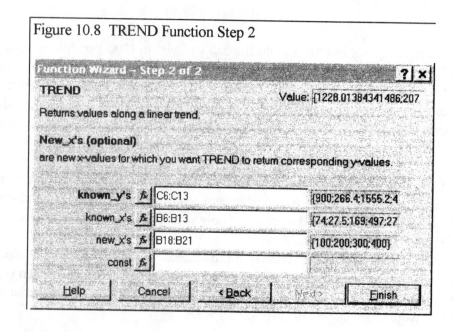

Figure 10.8 TREND Function Step 2

5. With the predicted y value cells (C18:C21) still selected, press the **F2** key to enter the **Edit** mode. Notice the word *Edit* appears in the status bar on the far left below the worksheet.

6. Press and hold the **Ctrl** and **Shift** keys and then press the **Enter** key. Curly brackets will be added around the TREND function statement and values will be computed for the second and subsequent predicted y values.   See Figure 10.9 for the predictions.

The above procedure provides the predicted y values for a number of specified x values. If you only wished to make a prediction for one x value, steps 5 and 6 would not be needed.

10.2 SIMPLE LINEAR REGRESSION
WITH THE REGRESSION ANALYSIS TOOL——————

The TRENDLINE feature for charts is a quick and easy method for obtaining a regression analysis as demonstrated in the prior section. However, its analysis results are rather limited, and it is only useful if there is one independent variable. In this section, we wish to demonstrate a second Excel resource for conducting a regression analysis, the REGRESSION analysis tool. It provides more complete results, and as we will see in Section 10.3, it can be used if there are more than one independent variable.

Figure 10.9 Predicted y Value Results

	A	B	C	
4				
5		ADVERT.	SALES	
6		74.0	900.0	
7		27.5	266.4	
8		169.0	1555.2	
9		497.0	4320.0	
10		270.5	2707.2	
11		44.5	439.2	
12		63.0	1209.6	
13		189.5	2966.4	
14				
15				
16				
17				
18		100	1228.0	
19		200	2076.6	
20		300	2925.2	
21		400	3773.7	

Let us return to the Nutrecal problem of Ms. Laura Maura from the prior section. As before she wishes to find a simple linear regression relationship which will allow her to predict sales as a function of advertising level. To analyze her results using the regression analysis tool you would proceed as follows after you have selected *Sheet2* in the REGRESS workbook.

1. Enter the **Identification Material**, and then enter the labels and data in columns B and C as previously shown in Figure 10.1. You may use Excel's **Copy** and **Paste** commands to copy the inputs of Figure 10.1 from Sheet1 to Sheet2. Save the workbook file with the name REGRESS.

2. From the menu bar select **Tools**, from the subsequent pull-down menu select **Data Analysis** and from the Data Analysis dialog box select **Regression**.

3. Fill in the entries of the Regression dialog box as shown in Figure 10.10. Notice that the input range includes the labels in the cells B5 and C5, and the **Labels** check box has a check in it. All four check boxes in the Residuals section are checked.

4. Click on **OK** and the numerical output shown in Figure 10.11 will be presented on the screen. In addition, two charts or plots will be shown to the right of the numerical output. These are shown in Figures 10.12 and 10.13. The charts are shown in a cascading format in which the plot title may be the only visible part of the bottom chart. You may move the top chart by dragging it with the mouse to an unused part of the worksheet so both can be viewed at once.

Figure 10.10 Simple Regression Analysis Tool Dialog Box

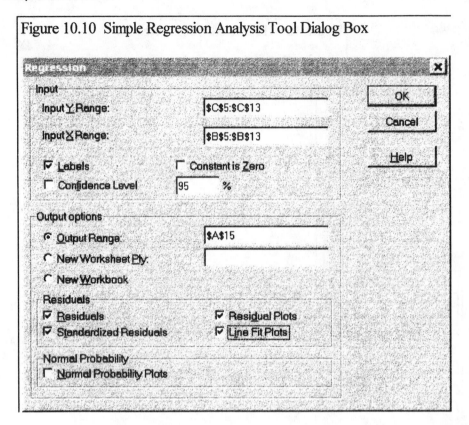

The numerical output of Figure 10.11 is presented in four parts from top to bottom. The top part labeled **Regression Statistics** presents the values for the coefficient of correlation, r but labeled as **Multiple R**, the coefficient of determination, r^2 labeled as **R Square**, the adjusted r^2 labeled as **Adjusted R**, the standard error of the estimate labeled as **Standard Error**, and the sample size labeled as **Observations**. The second part labeled **ANOVA** provides analysis of variance table output for the regression. The third part presents the regression coefficients together with statistics for evaluating the significance of the coefficients, such as the t statistic values, p-values and confidence intervals. Finally, the bottom part labeled **Residual Output** provides the predicted y values for each of the data points in the sample along with the residuals and standardized residuals.

Statistical values are given for testing the significance of the relationship with the p-value approach. From the ANOVA table we see the value for the F statistic is 52.86 in cell E26 with a corresponding *Significance F* value of 0.000344 in cell F26. The **Significance F** is the p-value for the overall regression relationship. Using the categories of Table 5.3 (or 5.5) in Chapter 5 we would categorize the relationship as *Very Highly Significant*. Thus, we would reject the null hypothesis. That is, we would conclude it is a good relationship based on the data we have.

Since this is a simple linear regression analysis we can reach the same conclusion based on the t statistic for the regression coefficient for advertising. We note from Figure 10.11 the advertising coefficient is 8.485774 in cell B32 with a t-statistic value of 7.270533 in cell D32 and a corresponding p value of

0.000344 in cell E32. For simple linear regression, the p value for the F statistic and for this t statistic will always be exactly the same. Thus, our conclusion is the same as in the previous paragraph.

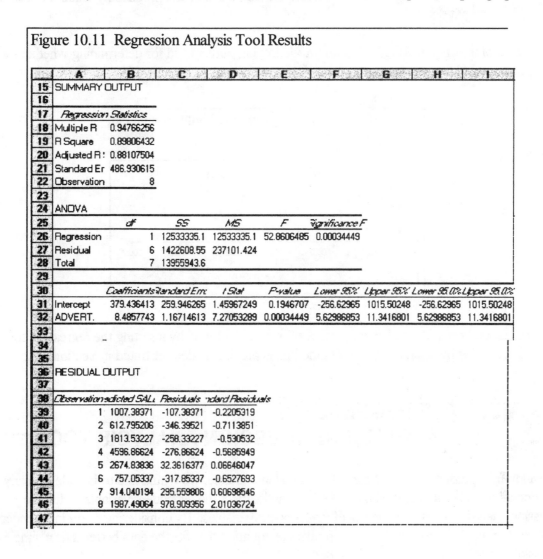

Figure 10.11 Regression Analysis Tool Results

	A	B	C	D	E	F	G	H	I
15	SUMMARY OUTPUT								
16									
17	*Regression Statistics*								
18	Multiple R	0.94766256							
19	R Square	0.89806432							
20	Adjusted R:	0.88107504							
21	Standard Er	486.930615							
22	Observation	8							
23									
24	ANOVA								
25		*df*	*SS*	*MS*	*F*	*ignificance F*			
26	Regression	1	12533335.1	12533335.1	52.8606485	0.00034449			
27	Residual	6	1422608.55	237101.424					
28	Total	7	13955943.6						
29									
30		*Coefficients*	*Standard Err*	*t Stat*	*P-value*	*Lower 95%*	*Upper 95%*	*Lower 95.0%*	*Upper 95.0%*
31	Intercept	379.436413	259.946265	1.45967249	0.1946707	-256.62965	1015.50248	-256.62965	1015.50248
32	ADVERT.	8.4857743	1.16714613	7.27053289	0.00034449	5.62986853	11.3416801	5.62986853	11.3416801
33									
34									
35									
36	RESIDUAL OUTPUT								
37									
38	*Observation*	*edicted SAL*	*Residuals*	*ndard Residuals*					
39	1	1007.38371	-107.38371	-0.2205319					
40	2	612.795206	-346.39521	-0.7113851					
41	3	1813.53227	-258.33227	-0.530532					
42	4	4596.86624	-276.86624	-0.5685949					
43	5	2674.83836	32.3616377	0.06646047					
44	6	757.05337	-317.85337	-0.6527693					
45	7	914.040194	295.559806	0.60698546					
46	8	1987.49064	978.909356	2.01036724					
47									

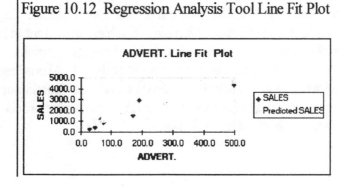

Figure 10.12 Regression Analysis Tool Line Fit Plot

The line fit plot of Figure 10.12 is similar to the scatter diagram of Figure 10.7. However, Figure 10.12 doesn't show a line of predicted y values. Instead it shows the predicted y value for each of the x values of the input data.

The residual plot of Figure 10.13 is useful for identifying outliers and for determining whether the assumptions underlying the regression analysis are met or not as discussed in your textbook.

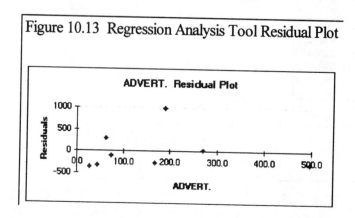

Figure 10.13 Regression Analysis Tool Residual Plot

As in the last section, predicted average values for y can be found by inserting the regression formula in a worksheet cell or by using the TREND function as previously demonstrated in Section 10.1.

10.3 MULTIPLE REGRESSION
WITH THE REGRESSION ANALYSIS TOOL

In developing a prediction equation for the dependent variable, we would like to include as many independent variables as can be shown to significantly affect the dependent variable. Multiple regression analysis allows any number of independent variables. By considering more independent variables, we would expect to develop a predictive equation that fits the data better than a simple linear regression equation.

For example let us reconsider the Nutrecal problem of Ms. Laura Maura. Suppose she feels there are independent variables other than advertising which are important in predicting the sales of Nutrecal. Suppose she identifies the other important independent variables as the price of the product and the number of sales representatives who sell Nutrecal. Accordingly, she would like to develop an equation which would allow her to predict sales as a function of advertising, price and number of sales representatives. To analyze her results you would proceed as follows after you have selected *Sheet3* of the REGRESS workbook.

1. Enter the **Identification Material**, and then enter the labels and data in columns B through E as shown in Figure 10.14. Note that the columns for the three independent variables are contiguous (next to each other) which is required by Excel's Regression Analysis Tool. Save the workbook file with the name REGRESS.

Figure 10.14 Multiple Regression Example Data

	A	B	C	D	E	F
1		Regression Analysis Examples				
2		David L. Eldredge				
3	Date: January 19, 1998			File: REGRESS.xls		
4						
5		SALES	ADVERT.	PRICE	SALE REPS.	
6		900.0	74.0	475	4	
7		266.4	27.5	475	7	
8		1555.2	169.0	450	5	
9		4320.0	497.0	400	5	
10		2707.2	270.5	400	4	
11		439.2	44.5	475	12	
12		1209.6	63.0	450	7	
13		2966.4	189.5	400	10	
14						

---

2. From the menu bar select **Tools**, from the subsequent pull-down menu select **Data Analysis** and from the Data Analysis dialog box select **Regression**.

3. Fill in the entries of the Regression dialog box as shown in Figure 10.15. Notice that the input range includes the labels in the cells B5 through E5, and the **Labels** check box has a check in it. All four check boxes in the Residuals section have been checked.

4. Click on **OK** and the numerical output shown in Figure 10.16 will be presented on the screen. In addition, six charts are shown to the right of the numerical output. These are shown in Figure 10.17. The charts are shown in a cascading format in which the chart title may be the only visible part of all except the top chart.

5. You can view each chart by bringing it to the top of the cascade stack. For example, click on the chart titled *SALES REPS. Residual Plot* to make it the active element. Then right click the chart to open a shortcut menu. Click on the menu selection **Bring to Front** and the result will be as shown in Figure 10.18.

Figure 10.15 Multiple Regression Analysis Dialog Box

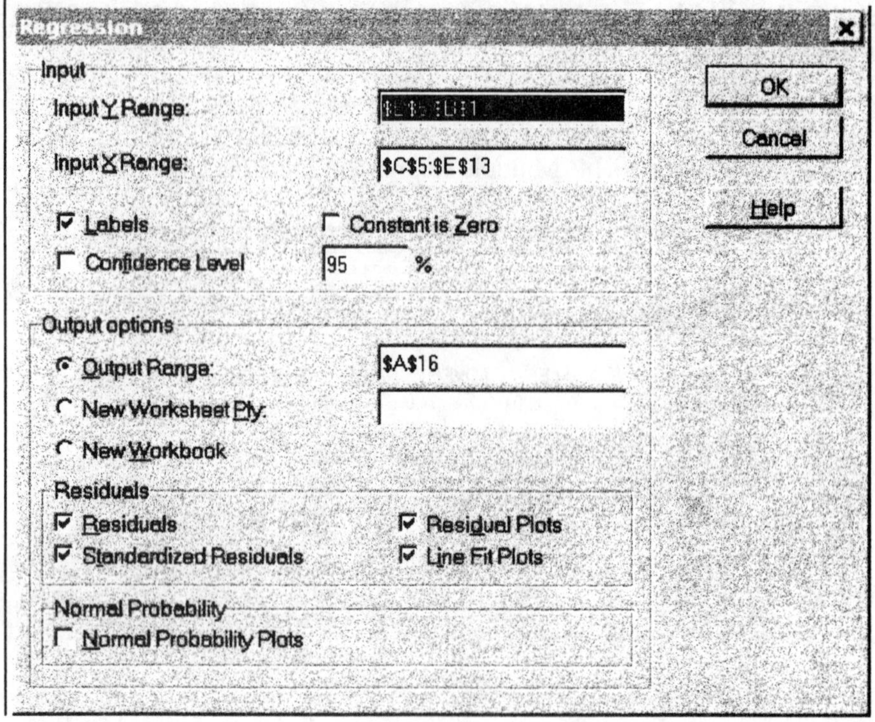

The numerical output of Figure 10.16 again includes four parts: *Regression Statistics, ANOVA,* regression coefficients with their statistics and *Residual Output.* From these results we conclude that the best straight line relationship is given by

Sales = 9063.101 + 5.199 * Advertising - 18.7265 * Price + 17.19767 * Sales Reps.

The R-Squared value of 0.976478 suggests that about 97.65% of the variability of the sales values about their average can be explained by changes in advertising, price and sales representatives.

From the ANOVA table of Figure 10.16, we note the F statistic value is 55.35 in cell E27 with a corresponding *Significance F* value of 0.001029 in cell F27. As before the *Significance F* is the p-value. Using the categories of Table 5.3 (or 5.5) of Chapter 5, we would categorize the relationship as *Highly Significant.* Thus, we would reject the null hypothesis that the relationship is not significant. That is, we would conclude we have found a good relationship based on the data we have.

Figure 10.16 Multiple Regression Analysis Example Numerical Results

	A	B	C	D	E	F	G	H	I
16	SUMMARY OUTPUT								
17									
18	*Regression Statistics*								
19	Multiple R	0.9881691							
20	R Square	0.9764782							
21	Adjusted R	0.9588369							
22	Standard E	286.4735							
23	Observatio	8							
24									
25	ANOVA								
26		df	SS	MS	F	*ignificance F*			
27	Regression	3	13627675	4542558.4	55.351782	0.0010292			
28	Residual	4	328268.27	82067.068					
29	Total	7	13955944						
30									
31		Coefficients	Standard Err.	t Stat	P-value	Lower 95%	Upper 95%	ower 95.0%	Upper 95.0%
32	Intercept	9063.1008	2688.4368	3.3711415	0.0280141	1598.7883	16527.413	1598.7883	16527.413
33	ADVERT.	5.1994475	1.3046588	3.9852929	0.0163289	1.5771264	8.8217685	1.5771264	8.8217685
34	PRICE	-18.72645	5.4854168	-3.413861	0.0269316	-33.95644	-3.496462	-33.95644	-3.496462
35	SALE REP	17.197669	41.534103	0.4140614	0.7000688	-98.11973	132.51506	-98.11973	132.51506
36									
37									
38									
39	RESIDUAL OUTPUT								
40									
41	Observation	redicted SAL	Residuals	dard Residuals					
42	1	621.58594	278.41406	0.9718667					
43	2	431.40464	-165.0046	-0.575986					
44	3	1600.8924	-45.69242	-0.1595					
45	4	4242.6338	77.36621	0.2700641					
46	5	3047.7613	-340.5613	-1.188805					
47	6	605.78359	-166.5836	-0.581497					
48	7	1084.1463	125.45368	0.4379242					
49	8	2729.792	236.60797	0.8259332					
50									

However, we need to examine the p-values for the individual regression coefficients to determine which of the independent variables are statistically different from zero. The p value for advertising in cell E33 is 0.016329 which suggests it is *significant*. That for price in cell E34 is 0.026932 and also *significant*. On the other hand, the p value for sales representatives in cell E35 is 0.700069 which suggests in is not significantly different from zero. Accordingly, we should rerun the regression with just the two independent variables, advertising and price.

The three line fit plots suggest similar conclusions. While the plots for advertising and for price suggest a linear relationship may be present, that for sales representatives does not suggest a relationship at all.

A final result which is useful here is the residual plots. As discussed in your textbook, these are useful for identifying outliers and for testing compliance with the assumptions underlying regression analysis.

Figure 10.17 Multiple Regression Analysis Example Output Plots

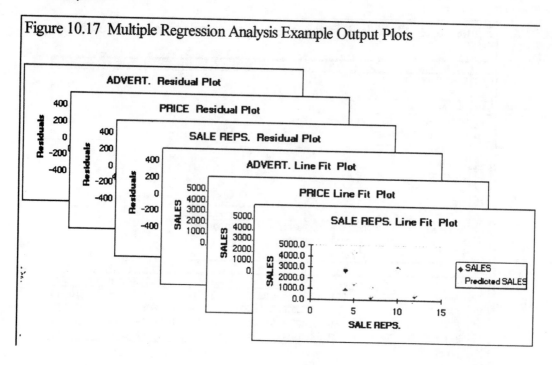

Figure 10.18 Multiple Regression Analysis Example Revised Output Plots

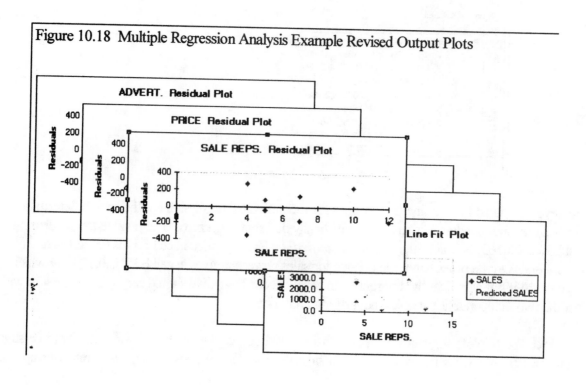

Once we have found a statistically useful relationship, we will want to use it to predict values for the dependent variable for specified values of the dependent variables. As in the two prior sections, predicted average y values can be made by entering the regression formula into a worksheet cell or by using the TREND function.

Finally, let us consider a problem associated with multiple regression analysis, namely, **multicollinearity**. This condition is present if two or more of the independent variables are positively or negatively correlated. One approach used to overcome the problem of multicollinearity is to examine the simple correlation coefficients between all the variables in the multiple regression analysis. Excel provides a data analysis tool for easily obtaining these correlation coefficient values. To use the CORRELATION Analysis Tool for our current example we would proceed as follows.

1. Select **Tools** from the menu bar, **Data Analysis** from the subsequent pull-down menu, and **Correlation** from the resulting dialog box. The result will be the dialog box shown in Figure 10.19.

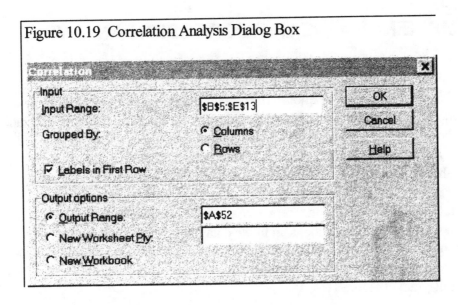

Figure 10.19 Correlation Analysis Dialog Box

2. Fill in the input range for all the variables including the labels. Click on **Columns** for the *Grouped By* selection, click on **Labels** in First Row, click on **Output Range** and enter **A52** as the upper left cell for the output range.

3. Click on **OK** and the matrix of correlation coefficients as shown in Figure 10.20 will be displayed in the worksheet.

Figure 10.20 Correlation Matrix for Example

	A	B	C	D	E	F
52		SALES	ADVERT.	PRICE	SALE REPS	
53	SALES	1				
54	ADVERT.	0.9476626	1			
55	PRICE	-0.933864	-0.815543	1		
56	SALE REF	-0.273658	-0.385553	0.1827193	1	
57						

The correlation coefficient of 0.9476626 in cell B54 between sales and advertising, and that of -0.933864 in cell B55 between sales and price suggest there is a relationship between the dependent variable sales and these two independent variables. This is consistent with the previous regression results of Figure 10.16 and with the line plots between these variables. However, the correlation coefficient value between advertising and price is given in cell C55 as -0.815543. This suggests these two independent variables may be collinear and may require further analysis as discussed in your textbook.

10.4 SIMPLE NON-LINEAR REGRESSION ANALYSIS

Oftentimes a scatter plot of a dependent variable, y, and an independent variable, x, will suggest the relationship between the two variables is not linear. For such situations Excel provides a feature for easily exploring the nature of the relationship. You may have noticed it while you were working through Section 10.1. Specifically in Figure 10.5 the **Trendline Type** dialog box includes logarithmic, polynomial, power and exponential relationships in addition to the linear relationship we used in Section 10.1. Accordingly, you may try various relationships through the trendline feature. (Note: the sixth option shown in Figure 10.5, Moving Average, is method for time series forecasting.)

To demonstrate how this is to be done we will continue with the example from Section 10.1. In that section we showed that a linear relationship fit the data very well. However, we can very easily evaluate the four other relationship forms available through the trendline feature in order to try to develop a better fit to the data. We can begin our investigation of non-linear relationships by returning to the scatter diagram of Figure 10.4.

1. Click on the **Sheet1** tab of the workbook named REGRESS.

2. Next double click inside the chart to activate it for editing. A cross-hatched border as was shown in Figure 10.7 will appear around the chart. (for Excel 8 see **Excel 8 Note** in Section 10.1.)

3. To superimpose a line of regression on this scatter diagram, select the plotted points by clicking on any single point. The points will be highlighted, S1 will appear in the name box (on the left just above the worksheet) and the formula bar (on the right in the same line) will show that SERIES

has been selected.

4. Click on **Insert** from the Menu Bar and then click on **Trendline** on the pull-down menu.

5. Click on the **Type** tab and click on **Logarithmic** for the Trend/Regression Type . (See Figure 10.5.)

6. Click on the **Options** tab. Select **Automatic** for the Trendline Name option and click to add check marks to the **Display Equation on Chart** and the **Display R-squared Value on Chart** (see Figure 10.6) check boxes. Click on **OK** to obtain the results of Figure 10.21. (Note the scatter diagram has been increased in size, and the equation and R^2 have been relocated to make it easier to read.)

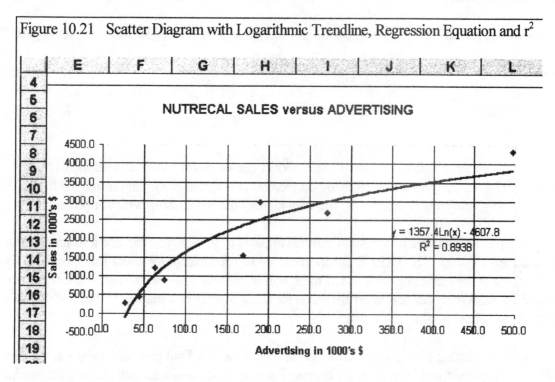

Figure 10.21   Scatter Diagram with Logarithmic Trendline, Regression Equation and r^2

As shown in figure 10.21, the relationship which was found is

$$y = 1357.4*Ln(x) - 4607.8$$

where Ln(x) is the natural logarithm of the advertising level in 1000's of dollars and y is sales in 1000's of dollars. Also, $R^2 = 0.8938$ suggests that 89.38% of the variability of the sales values about their average can be explained by changes in advertising. Although this indicates that the equation fits the data very well, it is slightly less than the 89.81% given in Figure 10.7 for the linear relationship.

By changing our selection in Step 5 above, we can also develop a polynomial relationship, a power relationship and an exponential relationship for these data. Moreover, the polynomial relationship option allows you to specify a quadratic relationship (order 2), a cubic relationship (order 3), a quartic relationship (order 4), and so on through order 6.

You may wish to try these other relationship forms on your scatter diagram. To do so, first move the mouse pointer so it is touching the line on the scatter diagram for the logarithmic curve. Then press the **Delete** key to eliminate (1) the curve, (2) the equation and (3) the R^2. Then repeat steps 2 thorough 6 above for the other relationship forms.

So that you may ascertain the correctness of your efforts, the results for four other forms is as follows.

Polynomial (order 2): $y = -0.0107 x^2 + 13.938 x + 0.0966$ $R^2 = 0.9276$

Polynomial (order 3): $y = 0.00006 x^3 - 0.0578 x^2 + 22.65 x - 326.48$ $R^2 = 0.9328$

Power: $y = 15.084 x^{0.9401}$ $R^2 = 0.9178$

Exponential: $y = 543.7 e^{0.0051 x}$ $R^2 = 0.6931$

As demonstrated the trendline feature of Excel allows you to explore five different forms of a regression relationship quite easily. Relying on the scatter diagram to visually assess the fit and on the value of R^2 to numerically assess the fit, you may identify the relationship which appears to be best.

Once you have decided which regression formula appears to fit best, you can use it to predict values of y for specified x values. The TREND function cannot be used except for linear relationships. Thus the easiest approach for predicting with one of these non-linear relationships, is to enter the regression formula in a worksheet cell and insert the value for the independent variable, x. The cell will then display the predicted y value.

As discussed in Section 10.2, Excel's **REGRESSION Analysis Tool** provides many more analysis results then does the trendline feature for charts. Each of these non-linear regression relationships demonstrated above can also be obtained through the use of the REGRESSION tool. The general approach is to transform the original x values into appropriate altered values which are then used with REGRESSION.

For example, if we would add a column of x-squared values and run the regression of the y variable as a function of both the x and the x-squared values, we could obtain the polynomial (order 2) relationship. The results of this transformation process for the polynomial (order 2) is shown in Figure 10.22 (this was done on *Sheet4* of the workbook named REGRESS).

Figure 10.22   Regression Analysis Tool Results for Polynomial (order 2)

	A	B	C	D	E	F	G	H	I
4	y	x	x²						
5	SALES	ADVERT.	AD--SQD						
6	900.0	74.0	5476.00						
7	266.4	27.5	756.25						
8	1555.2	169.0	28561.00						
9	4320.0	497.0	247009.00						
10	2707.2	270.5	73170.25						
11	439.2	44.5	1980.25						
12	1209.6	63.0	3969.00						
13	2966.4	189.5	35910.25						
14									
15									
16	SUMMARY OUTPUT								
17									
18	*Regression Statistics*								
19	Multiple R	0.9631251							
20	R Square	0.9276101							
21	Adjusted R	0.8986541							
22	Standard E	449.50417							
23	Observatio	8							
24									
25	ANOVA								
26		df	SS	MS	F	ignificance F			
27	Regression	2	12945673.6	6472836.8	32.035182	0.0014099			
28	Residual	5	1010270.01	202054					
29	Total	7	13955943.6						
30									
31		Coefficients	Standard Err.	t Stat	P-value	Lower 95%	Upper 95%	ower 95.0%	Upper 95.0%
32	Intercept	0.0966485	357.906404	0.00027	0.999795	-919.9295	920.12284	-919.9295	920.12284
33	ADVERT.	13.938258	3.9659742	3.5144602	0.0170194	3.7434138	24.133103	3.7434138	24.133103
34	AD--SQD	-0.010696	0.00748706	-1.428543	0.2125069	-0.029942	0.0085505	-0.029942	0.0085505
35									
36									
37									
38	RESIDUAL OUTPUT								
39									
40	Observation	dicted SAL	Residuals	dard Residuals					
41	1	972.95878	-72.9587764	-0.162309					
42	2	375.31022	-108.910222	-0.24229					
43	3	2050.1859	-494.985874	-1.101182					
44	4	4285.5067	34.4932847	0.0767363					
45	5	2987.7973	-280.597329	-0.624237					
46	6	599.16923	-159.969226	-0.355879					
47	7	835.75617	373.843828	0.8316804					
48	8	2257.3157	709.084315	1.577481					
49									

We note that the results of Figure 10.22 are as given above for trendline. In particular, the regression equation and value for R squared are

$$y = -0.010696\ x^2 + 13.938258\ x + 0.0966485 \qquad\qquad R^2 = 0.9276101$$

The results from Figure 10.22 in addition show the overall regression relationship is *highly significant* (the Significance F value is 0.0014099). However, the p-value for the x-squared term is 0.2125069 which means it is not significant and the p-value for the x term is 0.01070194 which means it is only *significant*.

We can use the REGRESSION Analysis Tool to obtain the results for polynomial relationships with higher order terms by including columns of x raised to the third power, x raised to the fourth power and so on. Furthermore, we can use the tool to obtain the exponential relationship by including a column of the natural logarithm of each x value. We would then run the regression of the y variable as a function of the column of natural logarithm of the x values.

This completes our exploration of the regression capabilities of Excel. We have shown how to use the **Trendline** feature, the **Regression Analysis Tool**, the **Correlation Analysis Tool** and the **Trend function**. We have not utilized a number of Excel's regression functions which are summarized in Appendix B. However, those we have not used duplicate to a large degree the capabilities of the items we have demonstrated.

CHAPTER 11. TIME SERIES FORECASTING

11.1 Identification of Appropriate Forecasting Methods

11.2 The MOVING AVERAGE Analysis Tool

11.3 The EXPONENTIAL SMOOTHING Analysis Tool

11.4 Linear Trend Projection with TRENDLINE

11.5 Non-linear Trend Projection with TRENDLINE

11.6 Choosing the Appropriate Forecasting Method

A time series consists of numerical data recorded over a period of time at regular intervals. Time series forecasting techniques are based on the premise that the factors which influenced patterns of activity in the past will continue to do so in the same manner in the future. Accordingly, time series forecasting techniques attempt to identify a pattern in the time series data which can be projected into the future.

Excel includes a number of resources for supporting time series forecasting. In **Section 11.1,** we discuss the use of CHART WIZARD for identifying forecasting methods which are appropriate for a particular time series. In sections 11.2 through 11.5, we present four time series forecasting methods which are readily available in Excel. **Section 11.2** presents the MOVING AVERAGE Analysis Tool and **Section 11.3** the EXPONENTIAL SMOOTHING Analysis Tool. In **Section 11.4,** we present the use of the TRENDLINE feature for charts for forecasting by linear trend projection. In **Section 11.5,** we present it for forecasting by non-linear trend projection. Finally in **Section 11.6,** Excel statistical functions are used to identify the best method for forecasting a time series.

11.1 IDENTIFICATION OF APPROPRIATE
FORECASTING METHODS ———

Most well-used time series forecasting methods consider a time series to be made up of the following four components.

1. Trend—a long-term upward or downward change in the time series
2. Cyclical—periodic increases and decreases which occur over a time period longer than a year
3. Seasonal—periodic increases and decreases which occur within a year
4. Irregular—remaining changes in the time series not attributable to the other three components

All time series forecasting methods assume there is an irregular component in the time series. In addition, some methods are appropriate when one or more of the first three components are also present. For example, some are appropriate for an irregular component and a trend component, some for an irregular and a cyclical component and some for an irregular and a seasonal component. In addition, some are appropriate for an irregular component and any combination of the three other components. On the other hand, other methods are appropriate when only the irregular component is present. These methods are called smoothing methods.

Both the moving average method of Section 11.2 and simple exponential smoothing of Section 11.3 are smoothing methods. Thus, they are most effective for a time series which does not have a trend, cyclical or seasonal component. The two trend projection methods of Section 11.4 and 11.5 are appropriate for time series with a trend component. Thus, the determination of whether to use the moving average or simple exponential smoothing methods as opposed to the two trend projection methods involves determining whether a trend is present in the time series. One way to make that determination is to chart the time series. A visual inspection of the time series plot can be used to determine if a trend appears to be present or not. This can be accomplished in Excel through the CHART WIZARD.

Let us consider the situation of Riper's Donuts which has been in operation for the past 6 years in Murville. Mr. Riper needs to forecast weekly sales of donuts in order to determine the amount of ingredients to purchase. He has collected sales data for the past 20 weeks. These have been entered into an Excel worksheet as shown in Figure 11.1. In addition, Figure 11.1 shows a chart of the sales data. The chart was obtained using the Chart Wizard. Briefly the procedure is as follows. (Note: If you would like to refer to the screen captures of this process you should refer to Figures 2.8 through 2.12 as given in Chapter 2 for Excel 7 and 5, and in Appendix C for Excel 8.)

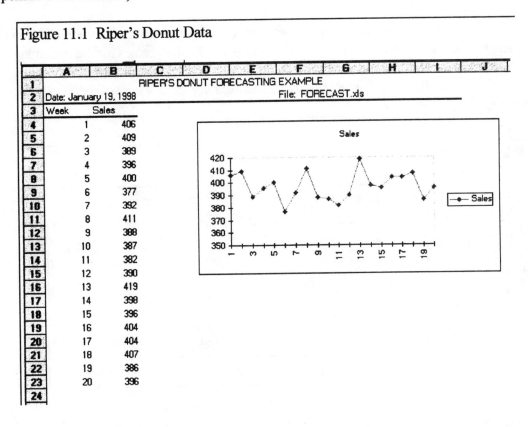

Figure 11.1 Riper's Donut Data

1. Use the mouse or the keyboard to highlight the sales data and label in cells B3 through B23.

2. Use the mouse to select the CHART WIZARD and move the chart pointer to cell D4.

3. Click the following for the 5 steps of Chart Wizard (these are for Excel 7 and 5—for Excel 8 see Appendix C for its 4 steps).

    Step 1—**Next**
    Step 2—**Line** and **Next**
    Step 3—**1 and Next**
    Step 4—**Next**
    Step 5—**Finish**

Quickly and easily we have obtained the line chart of the time series shown in Figure 11.1. Note we have not taken the steps necessary to provide a chart title, axes titles or other editing features. However, the resulting chart shows what we need to know. It indicates a time series which does not appear to have either an increasing or decreasing trend. The chart allows us to reach this conclusion although it wasn't apparent from an inspection of the numerical sales data. Based on this conclusion we would recommend that the moving average or simple exponential smoothing method would be most appropriate for these data.

Now consider a second example. Sandy Guyer, the athletic director of Bubeye State University, is wishing to forecast the average attendance at their home football games for the upcoming year. She has obtained the average attendance for the last 8 years and entered these data into an Excel worksheet as shown in Figure 11.2. Note that we have used *Sheet2* of the FORECAST workbook of Figure 11.1.

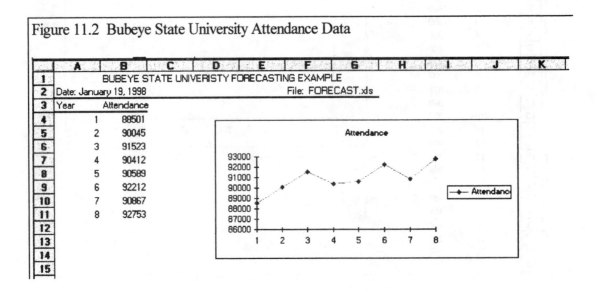

Figure 11.2 Bubeye State University Attendance Data

As before it is hard to draw a conclusion from the only numerical values. However, the chart shows an apparent increasing trend in the attendance data. Accordingly, the linear trend projection and the non-linear trend projection methods would be the most likely of our four time series methods for forecasting these data accurately.

11.2 THE MOVING AVERAGE ANALYSIS TOOL

We will use the MOVING AVERAGE Data Analysis Tool to forecast for the Riper's Donut example of Figure 11.2. Begin by removing the chart from the worksheet of Figure 11.1. Move the mouse pointer inside the chart and click once. Then press the **Delete** key and the chart will be deleted.

The procedure for forecasting these data using a 4-point moving average is the following.

1. From the menu bar select **Tools**, from the subsequent pull-down menu select **Data Analysis** and from the Data Analysis list box select **Moving Average**.

2. Fill in the entries of the Moving Average dialog box as shown in Figure 11.3. Notice that the input range includes the label in cell B3, and the **Labels** check box has a check in it. The entry for **Interval** refers to the number terms in the moving average. For this example it has a value of **4**. Neither the Chart Output nor the Standard Error boxes are checked.

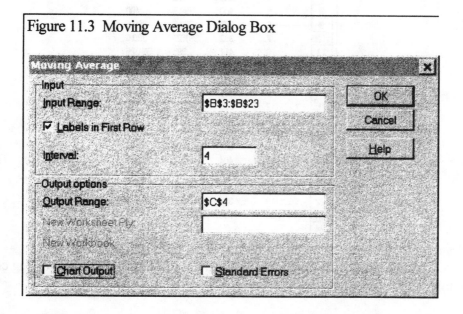

Figure 11.3 Moving Average Dialog Box

3. Click on **OK** and the numerical output shown in Column C of Figure 11.4 will be presented.

4. Enter the label **MovAvg** in Cell C3 and the label **Forecast** in Cell D3.

5. Each of the moving average values of Column C can be considered a forecast for the time period following it. These forecasts are shown in Column D. To obtain them, the entry =C7 is placed in Cell D8. This entry is then copied to cells D9 through D24 to compute forecasts for the remaining time periods including that for the 21st time period.

As shown in cell D24, the 4-point moving average forecast for the next period is 398.25. As discussed later we may want to explore values other than 4 for the number of points used in the moving averages.

11.3 THE EXPONENTIAL SMOOTHING ANALYSIS TOOL

We will now use the EXPONENTIAL SMOOTHING Data Analysis Tool to forecast for the Riper's Donut example of Figure 11.2.

Figure 11.4 Moving Average Results

	A	B	C	D
1			RIPER'S DONUT FOR	
2	Date: January 19, 1998			
3	Week	Sales	MovAvg	Forecast
4	1	406	#N/A	
5	2	409	#N/A	
6	3	389	#N/A	
7	4	396	400	
8	5	400	398.5	400
9	6	377	390.5	398.5
10	7	392	391.25	390.5
11	8	411	395	391.25
12	9	388	392	395
13	10	387	394.5	392
14	11	382	392	394.5
15	12	390	386.75	392
16	13	419	394.5	386.75
17	14	398	397.25	394.5
18	15	396	400.75	397.25
19	16	404	404.25	400.75
20	17	404	400.5	404.25
21	18	407	402.75	400.5
22	19	386	400.25	402.75
23	20	396	398.25	400.25
24				398.25

The procedure for forecasting these data using exponential smoothing with a smoothing constant value of 0.2 is the following.

1. From the menu bar select **Tools**, from the subsequent pull-down menu select **Data Analysis** and from the Data Analysis list box select **Exponential Smoothing**.

2. Fill in the entries of the Exponential Smoothing dialog box as shown in Figure 11.5. Notice that the input range includes the label in cell B3, and the **Labels** check box has a check in it. The entry for **Damping Factor** refers to the value of 1.0 minus the smoothing constant. Thus, its value is **0.8** for a smoothing factor of 0.2. Neither the Chart Output nor the Standard Error boxes are checked.

3. Click on **OK** and the numerical output shown in Column F of Figure 11.6 will be obtained.

4. Enter the label **Expo.Sm**. in Cell E3 and the label **Forecast** in Cell F3.

5. The exponential smoothing values of column F are the forecasts for the next time period. The formula in Cell F23 has been copied into Cell F24 to provide a forecast for the 21st time period.

As shown in cell D24, the forecast for the next period is 397.62689 based on simple exponential smoothing with a smoothing constant of 0.2.   As discussed later we may want to explore other values for the smoothing constant.

Figure 11.5 Exponential Smoothing Dialog Box

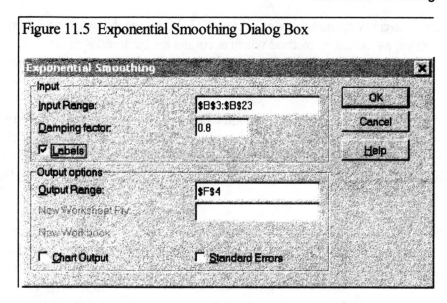

Figure 11.6 Simple Exponential Smoothing Results

	A	B	C	D	E	F	G
1			RIPER'S DONUT FORECASTING EXAMPLE				
2	Date: January 19, 1998					File: FORECAST.xls	
3	Week	Sales	MovAvg	Forecast	Expo.Sm.	Forecast	
4	1	406	#N/A			#N/A	
5	2	409	#N/A			406	
6	3	389	#N/A			406.6	
7	4	396	400			403.08	
8	5	400	398.5	400		401.664	
9	6	377	390.5	398.5		401.3312	
10	7	392	391.25	390.5		396.46496	
11	8	411	395	391.25		395.57197	
12	9	388	392	395		398.65757	
13	10	387	394.5	392		396.52606	
14	11	382	392	394.5		394.62085	
15	12	390	386.75	392		392.09668	
16	13	419	394.5	386.75		391.67734	
17	14	398	397.25	394.5		397.14187	
18	15	396	400.75	397.25		397.3135	
19	16	404	404.25	400.75		397.0508	
20	17	404	400.5	404.25		398.44064	
21	18	407	402.75	400.5		399.55251	
22	19	386	400.25	402.75		401.04201	
23	20	396	398.25	400.25		398.03361	
24				398.25		397.62689	

11.4 LINEAR TREND PROJECTION WITH TRENDLINE

When a visual inspection of a time series plot indicates a trend component is present, neither the moving average nor the simple exponential smoothing method will be effective in forecasting. Both of these smoothing methods will result in forecasts which usually lag the actual time series values.

The Bubeye State University example shown in Figure 11.2 does exhibit an obvious trend component. For such a time series, a forecasting method which accounts for the trend is necessary. Excel allows the easy use of two such methods. The linear trend projection method of this section and the non-linear trend projection method of the next section.

The linear trend projection method uses the method of least squares which forms the basis for simple linear regression analysis. Excel has a number of resources for performing the computations for a least squares fit. These include the TRENDLINE feature for charts as demonstrated in Section 10.1, the REGRESSION data analysis tool demonstrated in Section 10.2, and functions such as TREND which was used in Section 10.1.

Our feeling is that the most effective approach is based on the use of the trendline feature. It not only is quick and easy to use, it allows a visual inspection of the fit and the results are updated if the data for the problem change.

To demonstrate this approach let us return to the Bubeye State University attendance example.

1. Return to *Sheet2* of the FORECAST workbook. It should appear as shown in Figure 11.2.

2. Next double click inside the chart to activate it for editing. A cross-hatched border should appear around the chart (see Figure 11.7).

3. To superimpose a linear least squares fit line on this time series plot, select the plotted points by clicking on any single point. The points will be highlighted, S1 will appear in the name box (on the left just above the worksheet) and the formula bar (on the right in the same line) will show that SERIES has been selected.

4. Click on **Insert** from the Menu Bar and then click on **Trendline** on the pull-down menu.

Excel 8 Note: The CHART WIZARD of Excel 8 (97) is significantly different from that of Excel 7 and 5. Step 2 above only requires a single click, and instead of a cross-hatched border the sizing handles are displayed. For Step 4 you should click on **Chart** instead of **Insert**, and on **Add Trendline** instead of just **Trendline**. Appendix C provides additional insights into the changes made to the CHART WIZARD for Excel 8.

---

5. Click on the **Type** tab, click on **Linear** for the Trend/Regression Type (see Figure 10.5).

6. Click the **Options** tab. Select **Automatic** for the Trendline Name option (see Figure 10.6). Set the **Forecast Forward** spinner to **2** to ask for a projection two periods. Click to put a check in the **Display Equation on Chart** check box. Click **OK** to obtain the results of Figure 11.7.

This has very easily taken our time series plot and found the least squares line for these data. The plot allows us to visually evaluate how well the line fits the data. In Section 11.6 we will also compute a numerical evaluation of the fit.

Figure 11.7 Trendline Linear Least Squares Fit

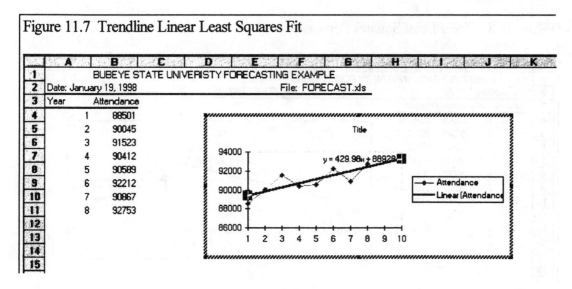

We may now use the least squares formula shown in Figure 11.7 to make a forecast for the next time period. We proceed as follows.

1. Key the label **Forecast** into Cell C3.

2. Key the number **9** in cell A12

3. Key the formula **=429.98*A4+88928** in Cell C4.

4. Copy the contents of Cell C4 into cells C5 through C12. The results will appear as shown in Figure 11.8.

The result is an estimate of the attendance based on the least squares formula for the nine years including the next year's estimate of 92,797.8.

11.5 NON-LINEAR TREND PROJECTION
WITH TRENDLINE————————

Frequently a time series plot will suggest a trend component which is not linear. For such situations Excel provides a resource for easily exploring the nature of the relationship. A reference to Figure 10.5 of Chapter 10, shows the TRENDLINE feature for charts includes logarithmic, polynomial, power and exponential relationships in addition to the linear relationship we used in Section 11.4. Accordingly, you may try any of these relationships through the trendline feature. (Note: the sixth option shown in Figure 10.5, Moving Average, could have been used in Section 11.2 above but it is less effective than the data analysis tool used in that section.)

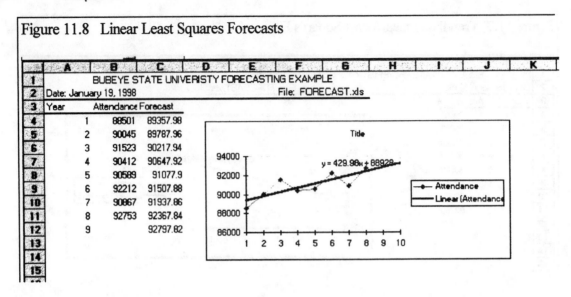

Figure 11.8   Linear Least Squares Forecasts

To demonstrate how this is to be done we will continue with the Bubeye State University example. We have shown that a linear trend fit the data quite well. However, we can very easily evaluate the four other relationship forms of TRENDLINE in order to try to develop a better fit to the data. To continue this example, we would proceed as follows.

1. Double click inside the chart as it appears in Figure 11.8. A cross-hatched border should appear around the chart such as shown in Figure 11.7.

2. Move the mouse pointer to the linear trend line shown in the figure and click once. The linear trend line will show a small square at its two ends to indicate it is ready for editing.

3. Press the **Delete** key in order to eliminate the linear trend line.

4. To superimpose a logarithmic least squares fit line on this time series plot, select the plotted points by clicking on any single point. The points will be highlighted.

5. Click on **Insert** from the menu bar and then click on **Trendline** from the pull-down menu.

6. Click on the **Type** tab, click on **Logarithmic** for the Trend/Regression Type (see Figure 10.5).

7. Click on the **Options** tab. Select **Automatic** for the Trendline Name option (see Figure 10.6). Set the **Forecast Forward** spinner to **2** to show a projection two periods into the future. Click to put a check in the **Display Equation** on Chart. Click on **OK** to obtain the results of Figure 11.9.

8. In order to compute the forecasts shown in Figure 11.9, enter the formula **=1573.5*LN(A4)+88777** in Cell C4 and copy it into cells C5 through C12.

Figure 11.9 Logarithmic Least Squares Forecasts

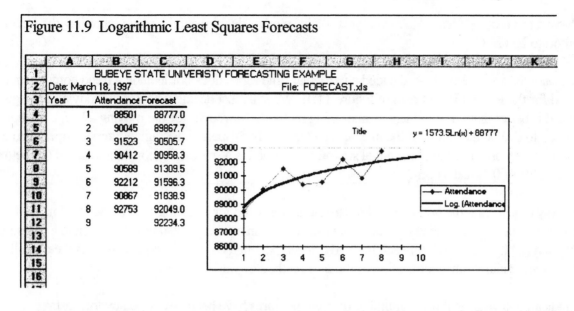

We can repeat the eight steps above to develop a polynomial relationship, a power relationship and an exponential relationship for these data. Moreover, the polynomial relationship option allows you to specify a quadratic relationship (order 2), a cubic relationship (order 3), a quartic relationship (order 4), and so on up to order 6.

You may wish to try these other relationships on your time series plot by repeating the 8 steps above for other Trend/Regression Types. For comparison the results for four other forms are the following.

Polynomial (order 2): $\quad y = -38.81\, t^2 + 779.26\, t + 88346$

Polynomial (order 3): $\quad y = 51.263\, t^3 - 730.85\, t^2 + 3419.3\, t + 85808$

Power: $\quad y = 88783\, t^{\,0.0174}$

Exponential: $\quad y = 88936\, e^{\,0.0047t}$

As demonstrated the trendline feature of Excel allows you to explore different forms of a least squares fit quite easily. In the following section we will consider how to decide what form best fits the data.

11.6 CHOOSING THE APPROPRIATE FORECASTING METHOD

In sections 11.2 through 11.5 we have explored a number of forecasting methods. As we outlined in Section 11.1, one of the considerations for choosing among them is the whether the time series appears to have a trend component. However, you still have other decisions to be made regarding the forecast method to be used.

For example, suppose we have decided a particular time series does not include a trend component as we did for the Riper's Donut data of Figure 11.1. We still must decide whether the moving average method is better than the exponential smoothing method. Moreover for the moving average method, we need to decide the length of the averaging interval.. Is a 4-period averaging interval superior to a 3-period, and so on? For the exponential smoothing method is a smoothing constant value of 0.2 better than a value of 0.3, and so on ?

One way of selecting the *best* overall forecasting method and for selecting the *best* values for parameters such as the averaging interval length and the smoothing constant is to compute a measure of the overall forecast error for each method or each parameter value. A comparison of the overall forecast error allows an identification of the *best* method or value.

As indicated in your textbook, a number of such measures have been developed by forecasting researchers. The three most popular are the mean absolute deviation (MAD), the mean squared error (MSE) and the mean absolute percentage error (MAPE). MAPE is most appropriate for comparing the predictive accuracy of *two or more time series*. Since we are interested in comparing *two or more forecasting methods or parameter* values for one time series, MAPE is not appropriate here.

Of the remaining two measures, MAD computes the average of the absolute difference between the actual time series values and their forecast values. MSE computes the average of the square of the difference between the actual and forecast values. The choice between these two methods depends on the importance of large differences. If avoiding large differences is very important, than MSE should be used. On the other hand, if you can afford to ignore a few extreme forecast errors provided the remaining forecast errors are small, than MAD should be used. The computations for MAD and MSE are almost identical. For MAD we find the absolute value of the forecast errors, and for MSE we square the forecast errors. We will demonstrate the use of MAD in our first example below and MSE in the second example.

Let us return to the Riper's Donut example. We will pick it up where we last left it in Figure 11.6.

1.   Click on the **Sheet1** tab at the bottom of the worksheet to return to the Riper's Donut example.

2.   Enter the labels **MA Error**, **ES Error** and **MAD =** in cells H3, I3 and G25 respectively.

3.   In cell H8 enter the formula **=ABS(B8-D8)** to compute the absolute value of the errors.

4.   Copy the formula in cell H8 to cells H9 through H23.

5.   In cell H25 enter the formula **=AVERAGE(H8:H23)**

6. In cell I5 enter the formula **=ABS(B5-F5).**

7. Copy the formula in cell I5 to cells I6 through I23.

8. In cell I25 enter the formula **=AVERAGE(I5:I23)**

The result will be as shown in Figure 11.10. Note that the two values for MAD are based on a different number of forecast errors. Each is the average of all the errors available for its specific forecast method. For the moving average method there are 16 error values and for the exponential smoothing method there are 19 error values. There is no error value for the forecast for period 21.

Figure 11.10 Riper's Donut Example MAD Computations

	A	B	C	D	E	F	G	H	I	J
1			RIPER'S DONUT FORECASTING EXAMPLE							
2	Date: January 19, 1998					File: FORECAST.xls				
3	Week	Sales	MovAvg	Forecast	Expo.Sm.	Forecast		MA Error	ES Error	
4	1	406	#N/A			#N/A				
5	2	409	#N/A			406			3	
6	3	389	#N/A			406.6			17.6	
7	4	396	400			403.08			7.08	
8	5	400	398.5	400		401.664		0	1.664	
9	6	377	390.5	398.5		401.3312		21.5	24.3312	
10	7	392	391.25	390.5		396.46496		1.5	4.46496	
11	8	411	395	391.25		395.57197		19.75	15.428032	
12	9	388	392	395		398.65757		7	10.657574	
13	10	387	394.5	392		396.52606		5	9.5260595	
14	11	382	392	394.5		394.62085		12.5	12.620848	
15	12	390	386.75	392		392.09668		2	2.0966781	
16	13	419	394.5	386.75		391.67734		32.25	27.322658	
17	14	398	397.25	394.5		397.14187		3.5	0.858126	
18	15	396	400.75	397.25		397.3135		1.25	1.3134992	
19	16	404	404.25	400.75		397.0508		3.25	6.9492007	
20	17	404	400.5	404.25		398.44064		0.25	5.5593605	
21	18	407	402.75	400.5		399.55251		6.5	7.4474884	
22	19	386	400.25	402.75		401.04201		16.75	15.042009	
23	20	396	398.25	400.25		398.03361		4.25	2.0336074	
24				398.25		397.62689				
25								MAD =	8.578125	9.210279

Based on these results we would conclude the 4-point moving average method is slightly more accurate than the exponential smoothing method with a smoothing constant of 0.2. Of course, we can also use the computation of MAD to determine if there is a better value for the number of points used in the moving average and a better value for the exponential smoothing constant.

Let us now return to the Bubeye State University example as shown in Figure 11.9. For it we will compare the linear and a quadratic trend projection forecast methods using MSE as an error measure. We will first use the linear relationship found in Section 11.4 and the quadratic relationship given in Section 11.5 to make forecasts. Next we will find MSE for each of these two projection methods.

1. Click on the **Sheet2** tab at the bottom of the worksheet to return to the Bubeye example.

2. Click inside the chart and press the **Delete** key to eliminate the chart.

3. Begin by entering the labels **LinearFore.**, **Quad.Fore.**, **Lin.Error**, **Quad.Error** and MSE in cells C3, D3, E3, F3 and D14 respectively.

4. In cell C4 enter the formula **=429.98*A4+88928** to compute the forecast of Figure 11.7.

5. In cell D4 enter the formula **=-38.81*A4^2+779.26*A4+88346** to compute the quadratic projection forecast as given in Section 11.5.

6. Copy the contents of cells C4 and D4 to cells C5 through D12.

7. In cell E4 enter the formula **=(B4-C4)^2** to compute the error squared value for the linear forecast.

8. In cell F4 enter the formula **=(B4-D4)^2** to compute the error squared value for the quadratic forecast.

9. Copy the contents of cells E4 and F4 to cells E5 through F11 (Not F12).

10. In cell E14 enter the formula **=AVERAGE(E4:E11)** to compute the average of the linear errors.

11. Copy cell E14 to cell F14 to compute the average of the quadratic errors.

The results will be as shown in Figure 11.11. The MSE values suggest that the quadratic method is a slight improvement over the linear method.

Figure 11.11 Bubeye Example MSE Computations

BUBEYE STATE UNIVERSITY FORECASTING EXAMPLE
Date: January 19, 1998   File: FORECAST.xls

Year	Attendance	LinearFore	QuadFore.	Lin Error	Quad Error
1	88501	89358.0	89086.5	734414.7	342751.7
2	90045	89788.0	89749.3	66069.6	87450.3
3	91523	90217.9	90334.5	1703181.6	1412556.0
4	90412	90647.9	90842.1	55658.2	184968.8
5	90589	91077.9	91272.1	239023.2	466557.3
6	92212	91507.9	91624.4	495785.0	345273.8
7	90867	91937.9	91899.1	1146741.1	1065292.3
8	92753	92367.8	92096.2	148348.2	431333.7
9		92797.8	92215.7		
			MSE =	573652.7	542023.0

CHAPTER 12. STATISTICAL QUALITY CONTROL CHARTS

12.1 $\bar{x}$ Chart for Controlling Process Average

12.2 R Chart for Controlling Process Variability

12.3 p Chart for Controlling Proportion of Defective Items

12.4 np Chart for Controlling Number of Defective Items

12.5 c Chart for Controlling Number of Defects per Unit

All processes in business and industry result in variation of the process outputs. In quality control, the causes of variation are classified either as **common (or chance) causes** or as **assignable (or special) causes**. Common causes are a number of randomly occurring events that are inherent to the process such as variations in materials, temperature, humidity and so on. Generally, these can be eliminated only by altering the process. On the other hand, assignable causes are specific events and factors which are usually temporary such as incorrect machine settings, cutting tool wear out, operator error and so on. These causes can be identified and eliminated. The primary objective of quality control is to detect and eliminate the assignable causes of process variation.

If the variation in process outputs is due only to common causes the process is considered to be **in control**. On the other hand, if some of the variation is due to assignable causes, the process is considered to be **out of control**. A number of statistical techniques have been developed to determine if a process is out of control. One of these is control charts.

A control chart consists of two major components. The first is a plot of a statistical value over time. The second is three lines superimposed on the plot. One of these is the centerline, a second is an upper control limit and the third the lower control limit. The **centerline (CL)** indicates the most likely value for the statistical value, the **upper control limit (UCL)** the largest expected value and the **lower control limit (LCL)** the smallest expected value. If all the plotted statistical values are randomly distributed between the two control limits, the process is considered to be in control. If the points are not randomly distributed between the two limits, the process is considered to be out of control.

A number of types of control charts have been developed to detect an out of control situation for various process outputs. Some of the more useful charts are those for detecting an out of control situation in the process average ($\bar{x}$ **chart**), in the process variability (**R chart**), in the proportion of defective items produced by a process (**p chart**), in the number of defective items produced by a process (**np chart**) and in the number of defects per unit produced by a process (**c chart**).

All of these five types of charts are based on averages for the statistical value of interest. The Central Limit Theorem (see Section 4.3 of Chapter 4) states that the probability distribution for representing the possible values for averages is the standard normal distribution. Accordingly, all five of these types of charts are based on the standard normal distribution. For all of them, the centerline is defined as the average or mean value, the upper control limit is defined as the mean plus three standard deviations, and the lower limit as the mean minus three standard deviations. From a table of the standard normal distribution, the probability that a value would fall outside these control limits can be found to be 0.0027 or about one-fourth of one percent. A very unlikely event when the process is in control.

The general process for constructing a control chart for each of the five types is the same. It includes

1. Entering into a worksheet the data values for the statistical output of interest ($\bar{x}$, R, p, np or c),
2. Computing an estimate of the mean and the standard deviation of the mean,
3. Setting the centerline (CL) equal to the mean, the upper control limit (UCL) equal to the mean plus three times the standard deviation, and the lower control limit (LCL) equal to the mean minus three times the standard deviation and
4. Charting the data values, centerline, upper control limit and lower control limit.

Accordingly, the five sections which follow present worksheets which are all quite similar. In **Section 12.1** we construct an $\bar{x}$ chart for controlling a process average and in **Section 12.2** an R chart for controlling process variability. These two charts usually are used in conjunction with each other to control a process output measured on a quantitative scale such as time, length, weight, and so on. A p chart for controlling the proportion of defective items produced by a process is developed in **Section**

12.3 and an np chart for controlling the number of defective items produced by a process in **Section 12.4**. These two charts provide the same type of results so usually either one or the other is used. Finally in **Section 12.5**, we demonstrate the use of Excel to develop a c chart for controlling the number of defects per unit produced by a process.

Since the development of these five charts is quite similar, we present the $\bar{x}$ chart in considerable detail. Then the subsequent four sections present primarily the differences from the discussion of this initial section.

12.1 $\bar{x}$ CHART FOR CONTROLLING PROCESS AVERAGE

We will use the following example to demonstrate the development of an $\bar{x}$ chart.

T&S Cakes, Inc., bakes and distributes cakes throughout the greater Terry Hut metropolitan area. The head baker, Granny Goose, attempts to produce cakes which weigh two pounds each. However, there is some variation in the cake weight which is monitored by Mr. Scotferd, T&S's quality control manager. During the most recent baking period, Scotferd took fifteen samples of four cakes each. The resulting 60 weights are given in cells B5 through E19 of the worksheet in Figure 12.1.

Figure 12.1 Data, Means and Ranges for T&S Cakes

	A	B	C	D	E	F	G	H	I	J	K
1					T & S CAKES, INC., EXAMPLE						
2	Date: January 22, 1998								File: QUALITY.xls		
3	Sample			Sample Values				Mean	Largest	Smallest	Range
4	Number	1	2	3	4	5	6				
5	1	1.6	2.0	2.4	1.9			2.0	2.4	1.6	0.8
6	2	2.0	2.0	2.2	1.8			2.0	2.2	1.8	0.4
7	3	1.9	2.3	1.6	1.8			1.9	2.3	1.6	0.7
8	4	2.4	2.4	2.2	2.3			2.3	2.4	2.2	0.2
9	5	1.7	2.1	1.8	2.2			2.0	2.2	1.7	0.5
10	6	1.6	2.0	2.0	2.2			2.0	2.2	1.6	0.6
11	7	2.3	2.3	1.9	2.5			2.3	2.5	1.9	0.6
12	8	2.2	2.2	1.8	1.6			2.0	2.2	1.6	0.6
13	9	1.7	2.2	2.1	1.9			2.0	2.2	1.7	0.5
14	10	2.2	2.2	2.0	2.3			2.2	2.3	2.0	0.3
15	11	2.1	2.4	2.4	1.6			2.1	2.4	1.6	0.8
16	12	2.1	2.2	1.8	2.0			2.0	2.2	1.8	0.4
17	13	2.3	1.8	1.8	2.4			2.1	2.4	1.8	0.6
18	14	1.7	2.4	2.2	2.2			2.1	2.4	1.7	0.7
19	15	1.7	1.8	2.1	1.7			1.8	2.1	1.7	0.4
20	16										
21	17										
22	18										
23	19										
24	20										
25	21										

We have set the worksheet up to accommodate the most usual situations. Typically the number of samples will be from 20 to 25 and each sample will include 4, 5 or 6 values. Accordingly, the worksheet allows values to be entered into rows 5 through 29 and columns A through G. For our example, we have used only 15 samples with 4 values each to minimize the number of values you will need to enter into the worksheet.

This problem will utilize two worksheets. On *Sheet1* as shown in Figure 12.1, we include the raw data and the computations for finding the sample means and ranges. The remaining computations and the construction of the $\bar{x}$ chart are given on *Sheet2*. The second sheet begins with the values for the sample means and ranges. This two-sheet setup allows you to begin either by entering the raw data into Sheet1 or by directly entering the sample means and ranges into the worksheet while bypassing the Sheet1 computations. The following procedure allows for either approach.

1. Start Excel and enter the **Identification Material** shown in rows 1 and 2 of Figure 12.1. Enter the labels and numbers in column A.

2. If you intend to enter the 60 data values, enter the remaining labels shown in rows 3 and 4 of Figure 12.1. Also enter the data values in the cells B5 through E19. If you wish to bypass entering the data and start by directly entering the sample means and ranges into the worksheet, you should **skip to Step 7**.

3. Enter the following formulas: **=AVERAGE(B5:G5)** in cell H5; **=MAX(B5:G5)** in cell I5; **=MIN(B5:G5)** in cell J5 and **=I5-J5** in cell K5 to find the mean and range for the first sample.

4. Copy the four formulas into rows 6 through 19 of their respective columns. The 15 sample means and 15 sample ranges will be computed for you.

5. Click on the *Sheet2* tab at the bottom of the worksheet. Enter the identification material in rows 1 and 2, and enter the labels and numbers in Column A as shown in Figure 12.2. (Alternatively you may copy this material from Sheet1 to Sheet2.)

6. Enter the formula **=Sheet1!$K5** in cell B5 (the single dollar sign is needed to facilitate copying later for the R chart). Enter the formula **=Sheet1!H5** in cell H5. Copy these two formulas into rows 6 through 19 of their respective columns. You should now **skip to Step 8** below.

7. **This step is only for those who have skipped here from Step 2 above**. Your *Sheet1* will look like Figure 12.2. Enter the sample ranges in rows 5 through 19 of column B and the sample means in rows 5 through 19 of column H.

8. Enter the remaining labels shown in row 4 of Figure 12.2.

9. Enter the six labels shown in cells D6 through D12 of Figure 12.2.

Figure 12.2 x̄ Chart Centerline and Control Limits for T&S Cakes

	A	B	C	D	E	F	G	H	I	J	K
1				T & S CAKES, INC., EXAMPLE							
2	Date: January 22, 1998								File: QUALITY.xls		
3	Sample							Mean	LCL	CL	UCL
4	Number	Range						1.98	1.65	2.04	2.44
5	1	0.8						2.00	1.65	2.04	2.44
6	2	0.4		Avg. of Sample Means		2.0		1.90	1.65	2.04	2.44
7	3	0.7		Average Range		0.5		2.33	1.65	2.04	2.44
8	4	0.2		A2 Factor		0.729		1.95	1.65	2.04	2.44
9	5	0.5						1.95	1.65	2.04	2.44
10	6	0.6		Lower Control Limit		1.65		2.25	1.65	2.04	2.44
11	7	0.6		Centerline		2.04		1.95	1.65	2.04	2.44
12	8	0.6		Upper Control Limit		2.44		1.98	1.65	2.04	2.44
13	9	0.5						2.18	1.65	2.04	2.44
14	10	0.3						2.13	1.65	2.04	2.44
15	11	0.8						2.03	1.65	2.04	2.44
16	12	0.4						2.08	1.65	2.04	2.44
17	13	0.6						2.13	1.65	2.04	2.44
18	14	0.7						1.83	1.65	2.04	2.44
19	15	0.4									
20	16										
21	17										

10. In cell F6 enter the formula **=AVERAGE(H5:H29)** in order to compute the average of the sample means. In cell F7 enter the formula **=AVERAGE(B5:B29)** to compute the average of the sample ranges.

11. Cell F8 contains the constant needed to convert the average of the sample ranges to the value for computing the 3-sigma control limits. It is the A_2 constant found in the table of control chart constants given in most business statistics textbooks. The value for A_2 depends on the number of observations in each sample. For four observations its value is 0.729 as indicated in Figure 12.2.

12. Cell F10 computes the lower control limit (LCL) with the formula **=F6-F8*F7**, cell F11 the centerline (CL) with the formula **=F6**, and cell F12 the upper control limit (UCL) with the formula **=F6+F8*F7**.

13. The values for the LCL, CL and UCL are to be repeated in columns I, J and K respectively. In cell I5 insert the formula **=$F$10**. We include the $ sign before the row and column designators to specify it as an absolute reference so it can be correctly copied later. In similar manner insert the formula **=$F$11** in cell J5 and **=$F$12** in cell K5.

14. Copy the formulas in cells I5, J5 and K5 into rows 6 through 19 of the respective columns. We now have the data for plotting the 15 means together with the LCL, CL and UCL in columns H, I, J and K.

15. We will use the CHART WIZARD to prepare the plot. As was noted in Section 2.2 of Chapter 2, Excel's CHART WIZARD can be used to create 15 types of charts. The **Line** type will be used to construct the $\bar{x}$ chart. Begin by highlighting the cells H5 through K19.

16. Move the pointer to the CHART WIZARD icon on the standard toolbar and click once. The pointer will change to a small representation of a cross and a bar chart. Move it to cell M5 and click the mouse button. The Chart Wizard Step 1 dialog box will appear as shown in Figure 12.3. (Note: If you have not used the CHART WIZARD before you may wish to refer to Figures 2.8 through 2.12 given in Chapter 2 for Excel 7 and 5, and in Appendix C for Excel 8.)

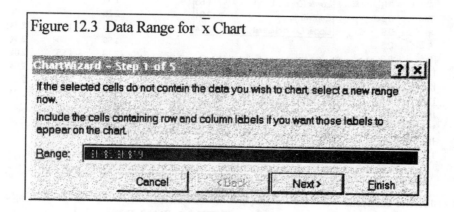

Figure 12.3 Data Range for $\bar{x}$ Chart

17. Verify that the data range is correct and click on the **Next** button. The Chart Wizard Step 2 will appear (see Figure 2.8 in Chapter 2 for Excel 7 or 5 and in Appendix C for Excel 8).

18. Use the mouse to select the **Line** chart and then select the **Next** button. The Chart Wizard Step 3 as shown in Figure 12.4 will appear.

19. Select format number **1** for Step 3 and the **Next** button to obtain Step 4 as shown in Figure 12.5.

20. For Step 4, make sure **Columns** is selected for **Data Series in** option since the data are in columns. Click on the option button once or twice to get a dot in it. Select **Next** to obtain Step 5 of Figure 12.6.

21. For the **Add legend** option select **No** by clicking once or twice on its option button. Move the pointer to the **Chart Title** text box and click. Enter the title *X-BAR CHART FOR T&S CAKES*. Enter *Sample Number* for the **X-axis title** and *Cake Weight in Pounds* for the **Y-axis title**. Select the **Finish** button. The result will be as shown in Figure 12.7.

Although the chart of Figure 12.7 presents all the data of a control chart, it requires editing for it to appear as a usual control chart . We can make three types of changes. First we can change the y-axis scale so the four plotted lines aren't all bunched at the top of the chart. Second, we can remove the

Figure 12.4 Chart Formats for Line Chart

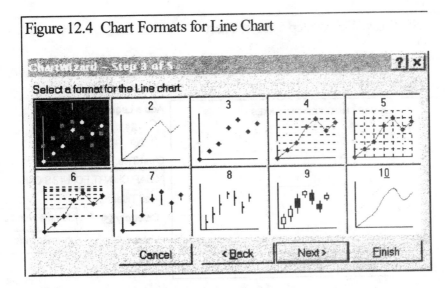

Figure 12.5 Chart Wizard Step 4 for $\bar{x}$ Chart

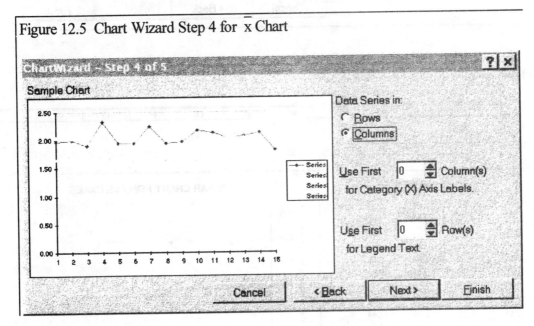

symbols from the LCL, CL and UCL lines. Third we can add a label to the LCL, CL and UCL lines. The result will be the form usually presented in textbooks. We demonstrate these changes by continuing with the procedure of this section.

22. Double click inside the chart to activate it. A cross-hatched border will be added to the chart.

> **Excel 8 Note:** The CHART WIZARD of Excel 8 (97) is significantly different from that of Excel 7 and 5. Step 22 only requires a single click, and instead of a cross-hatched border the sizing handles are displayed. Appendix C provides additional insights into the changes made to the CHART WIZARD for Excel 8.

Figure 12.6 Chart Wizard Step 5 for $\bar{x}$ Chart

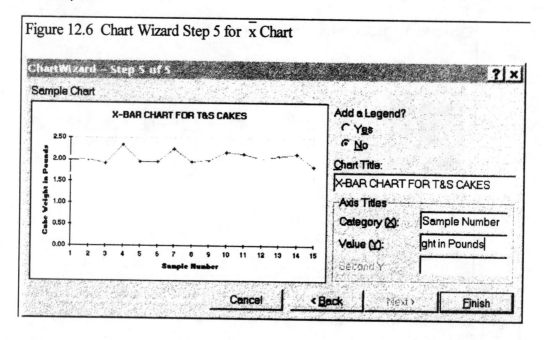

Figure 12.7 Initial Form of $\bar{x}$ Chart

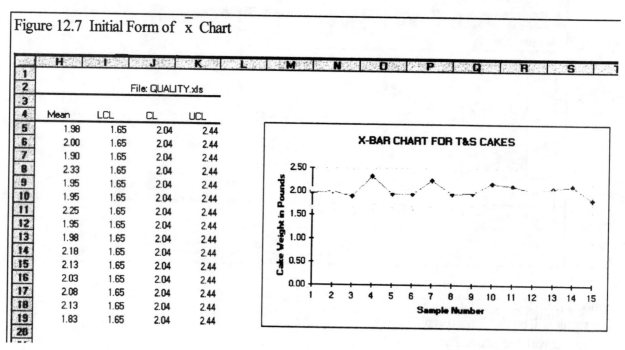

	Mean	LCL	CL	UCL
			File: QUALITY.xls	
4	Mean	LCL	CL	UCL
5	1.98	1.65	2.04	2.44
6	2.00	1.65	2.04	2.44
7	1.90	1.65	2.04	2.44
8	2.33	1.65	2.04	2.44
9	1.95	1.65	2.04	2.44
10	1.95	1.65	2.04	2.44
11	2.25	1.65	2.04	2.44
12	1.95	1.65	2.04	2.44
13	1.98	1.65	2.04	2.44
14	2.18	1.65	2.04	2.44
15	2.13	1.65	2.04	2.44
16	2.03	1.65	2.04	2.44
17	2.08	1.65	2.04	2.44
18	2.13	1.65	2.04	2.44
19	1.83	1.65	2.04	2.44

23. Click on the vertical axis. A black square will be appear at the top and the bottom of the axis to indicate it is active for editing.

24. Click on **Format** on the menu bar and click on **Selected Axis** on the subsequent menu. The Format Axis dialog box as shown in Figure 12.8 should appear.

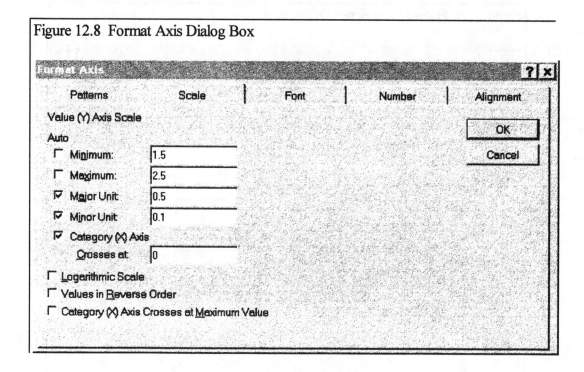

Figure 12.8 Format Axis Dialog Box

25. Click to remove the checks from two check boxes labeled **Auto Minimum** and **Maximum**.

26. Enter the number **1.5** in the minimum textbox and the number **2.5** in the maximum textbox. Then click on **OK**. The chart y axis will be revised as shown in later Figure 12.10.

27. Click once on the UCL line. A number of black squares show that the line is active.

28. Click on **Format** on the menu bar and click on **Selected Axis** on the subsequent menu. The Format Data Series dialog box as shown in Figure 12.9 should appear.

29. Click on the **Patterns** tab. For **Line** click on the option button **Automatic** and for **Marker** click on **None**. Click on **OK** and the UCL line will be displayed without symbols as shown in Figure 12.10. (You may also change the color, style or weight of the line within this dialog box. Some textbooks use dashed lines for the control limits.)

30. Repeat the steps 22 through 29 for the CL line and then again for the LCL line.

31. Next we will add labels to the UCL, CL and LCL lines using the Text Box feature of the Drawing Toolbar. To display this toolbar click the **Drawing** icon on the Standard Toolbar. The toolbar will

be displayed as shown at the very bottom of Figure 12.10.

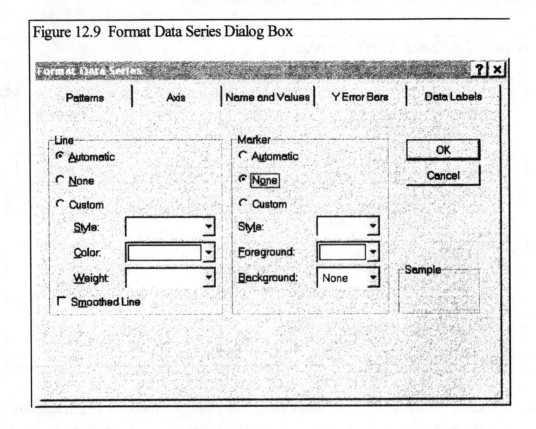

Figure 12.9 Format Data Series Dialog Box

32. Click on the **Text Box** icon on the drawing toolbar. The mouse pointer will become a small cross. Locate it near the UCL line where you want the text box to begin. Then press the left mouse button and move the mouse to open the text box and then release the mouse button. You may need to practice this operation.

33. After the box is open, you can type your label for the UCL line. If the box isn't large enough to display the entire label, click to activate the box and use the sizing handle to enlarge it.

34. If the text box does not blend into the chart because it has a border and/or its color is not the same as the chart, you can change these attributes. Click on the text box to make it active. Then click on **Format** from the menu bar, **Object** from the subsequent pull-down menu and **Patterns** tab for the Format Object dialog box. The left side of the dialog box allows you to change the border and the right side the fill color. Our final edited control chart is as shown in Figure 12.10.

This completes are discussion of the $\bar{x}$ chart. We will continue with this example in the next section for the development of a R chart for controlling process variability.

Figure 12.10 Final Edited Form of the $\overline{x}$ Chart

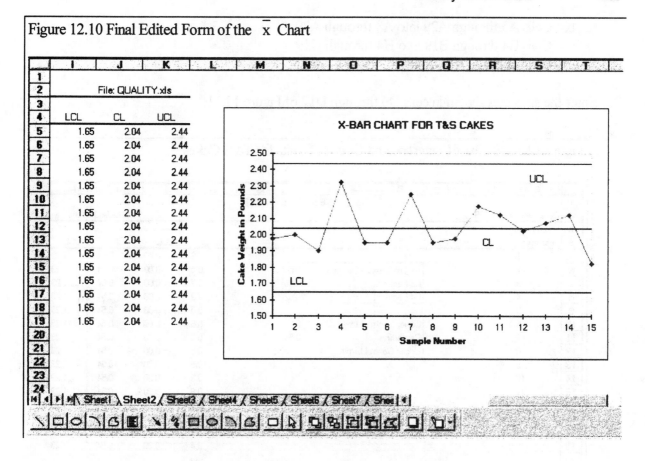

12.2 R CHART FOR CONTROLLING
PROCESS VARIABLILITY————

The R chart is used to monitor the variability of a process output just as the $\overline{x}$ chart is used to monitor the average value for a process output. Sample values of the range are plotted on the R chart. We conclude the process variability is out of control if the plotted sample values are not randomly distributed between the lower and upper control limits.

The procedure needed to develop an R chart is very similar to that given in Section 12.1 for the $\overline{x}$ chart. Accordingly, our presentation here will primarily indicate the differences in the two procedures. We will continue with the example of T&S Cakes of the prior section. The procedure assumes you have developed the worksheets of Figure 12.1 (*Sheet1*) and Figure 12.2 (*Sheet2*). The R chart computations of Figure 12.11 will be shown on *Sheet3*. However if you directly entered the mean and range values into the $\overline{x}$ chart worksheet of Figure 12.2 thus bypassing the first worksheet of Figure 12.1, your R chart computations of Figure 12.11 will be shown on *Sheet2*. We proceed as follows.

1. Copy from *Sheet2* to *Sheet3* (from Sheet1 to Sheet 2 if you bypassed Figure 12.1) the following.
    a. Rows 1 and 2 into rows 1 and 2

  b. Cells A3 through A29 into A3 through A29

  c. Cells B4 through B19 into H4 through H19

  d. Cells I4 through K19 into I4 through K19

2. Enter the six labels shown in cells D6 through D12 of Figure 12.11.

Figure 12.11 R Chart Centerline and Control Limits for T&S Cakes

	A	B	C	D	E	F	G	H	I	J	K
1					T & S CAKES, INC., EXAMPLE						
2	Date: January 23, 1998									File: QUALITY.xls	
3	Sample										
4	Number							Range	LCL	CL	UCL
5	1							0.8	0.00	0.54	1.23
6	2			Avg. of Sample Ranges		0.54		0.4	0.00	0.54	1.23
7	3			D3 Factor		0.000		0.7	0.00	0.54	1.23
8	4			D4 Factor		2.282		0.2	0.00	0.54	1.23
9	5							0.5	0.00	0.54	1.23
10	6			Lower Control Limit		0.00		0.6	0.00	0.54	1.23
11	7			Centerline		0.54		0.6	0.00	0.54	1.23
12	8			Upper Control Limit		1.23		0.6	0.00	0.54	1.23
13	9							0.5	0.00	0.54	1.23
14	10							0.3	0.00	0.54	1.23
15	11							0.8	0.00	0.54	1.23
16	12							0.4	0.00	0.54	1.23
17	13							0.6	0.00	0.54	1.23
18	14							0.7	0.00	0.54	1.23
19	15							0.4	0.00	0.54	1.23
20	16										

3. In cell F6 enter the formula **=AVERAGE(H5:H29)** in order to compute the average of the sample ranges.

4. Cells F7 and F8 contain the constants needed to convert the average of the sample ranges to the value for computing the 3-sigma control limits. These are the D_3 and the D_4 constants found in the table of control chart constants given in most business statistics textbooks. These values depend on the number of observations in each sample. For four observations the values are 0.000 and 2.282 as given in Figure 12.11.

5. Cell F10 computes the lower control limit (LCL) with the formula **=F6*F7**, cell F11 the centerline (CL) with the formula **=F6**, and cell F12 the upper control limit (UCL) with the formula **=F6*F7**.

6. We will use the CHART WIZARD to construct a **Line** chart. Begin by highlighting the cells H5 through K19.

7. You now need to repeat steps 16 through 21 of Section 12.1 in order to produce the initial R Chart. In Step 21 you should use the appropriate titles for the chart and for the Y-axis. (See

Figure 12.12.)

8. Repeat steps 22, and 27 through 34 (steps 23 through 26 are not needed for this plot) of Section 12.1 in order to edit your R chart into the final form as shown in Figure 12.12.

Figure 12.12 Final Edited Form of the R Chart

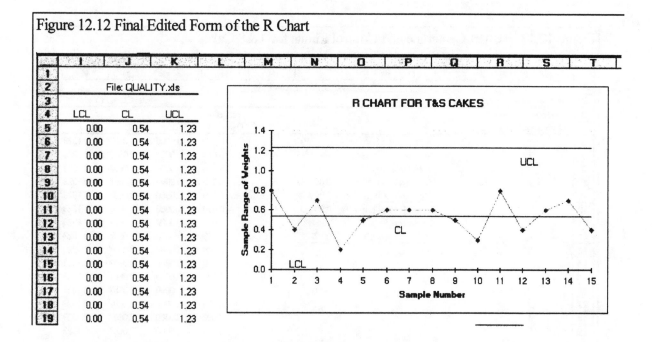

12.3 p CHART FOR CONTROLLING
PROPORTION OF DEFECTIVE ITEMS

Many times a quality characteristic for the output of a process can not be measured on a quantitative scale such as time, length or weight. For such situations, each item of output from the process may be classified as **defective** (nonconforming to specifications) or **nondefective** (effective or conforming to specifications). We can then monitor the quality of the process by analyzing either the proportion of defective items in a sample or the number of defective items in a sample. The control chart appropriate for monitoring the proportion of defective items is called the **p chart** presented in this section. The closely related control chart appropriate for monitoring the number of defective items is called a **np chart** and is presented in the immediately following section.

The procedure needed to develop a p chart is very similar to that given for the $\bar{x}$ chart and the R chart. We plot sample values between 3-sigma control limits to determine if the sample values have a random pattern within the limits.

We will again return to T&S Cakes, Inc. The ever discriminating Granny Goose wants every cake to have an acceptable frosting. However, it is not possible for her to personally inspect the large number of cakes produced each day by T&S. Consequently, she inspects a sample of 100 cakes each day and categorizes each cake as defective or not. Figure 12.13 presents the results for the last 15 days of her inspections. She would like to use these data to determine if the process is in control.

Figure 12.13 p Chart Centerline and Control Limits for T&S Cakes

	A	B	C	D	E	F	G	H	I	J	K
1					T & S CAKES, INC., EXAMPLE						
2	Date: January 23, 1998									File: QUALITY.xls	
3	Sample	Number						Proportion			
4	Number	Defective						Defective	LCL	CL	UCL
5	1	7		Size of Each Sample		100		0.070	0.0000	0.0607	0.1323
6	2	1		Number of Samples		15		0.010	0.0000	0.0607	0.1323
7	3	5		Total Defecitves		91		0.050	0.0000	0.0607	0.1323
8	4	9		Average Proportion		0.060667		0.090	0.0000	0.0607	0.1323
9	5	10		Std. Dev. for Avg. Prop		0.023872		0.100	0.0000	0.0607	0.1323
10	6	8		Lower Control Limit		0.000000		0.080	0.0000	0.0607	0.1323
11	7	6		Centerline		0.060667		0.060	0.0000	0.0607	0.1323
12	8	9		Upper Control Limit		0.132282		0.090	0.0000	0.0607	0.1323
13	9	2						0.020	0.0000	0.0607	0.1323
14	10	3						0.030	0.0000	0.0607	0.1323
15	11	10						0.100	0.0000	0.0607	0.1323
16	12	8						0.080	0.0000	0.0607	0.1323
17	13	3						0.030	0.0000	0.0607	0.1323
18	14	9						0.090	0.0000	0.0607	0.1323
19	15	1						0.010	0.0000	0.0607	0.1323
20	16										

We will develop our p chart on *Sheet4* of the workbook QUALITY as shown on Figure 12.13 (Sheet3 if you bypassed Figure 12.1). We proceed as follows.

1. Copy from *Sheet3* to *Sheet4* the following.
    a. Rows 1 and 2 into rows 1 and 2
    b. Cells A3 through A29 into A3 through A29
    c. Cells I4 through K19 into I4 through K19

2. Enter the labels in cells B3, B4, H3 and H4. Enter the data values in cells B5 through B19.

3. Enter the formula =B5/$F$5 in cell H5. Copy this formula into cells H6 through H19.

4. Enter the eight labels shown in cells D5 through D12 of Figure 12.13.

5. Enter into cell F5 the number of observations in each sample, **100**, and into cell F6 the number of samples, **15**.

6. In cell F7 enter the formula **=SUM(B5:B29)** in order to compute the total number of defectives.

7. The contents of cell F8 depend on whether the value for the proportion defective items when the process is in control is known or not. If this value is known, it should be entered into cell F8. If it is not known (as assumed for Figure 12.13), enter the formula **=F7/F6/F5**.

8. The formula for cell F9 computes the estimate for the standard deviation for the proportion defective. It is found from the formula **=SQRT(F8*(1-F8)/F5)**.

9. The LCL is equal to the estimate of the average proportion defective minus three times the standard deviation of the average proportion defective. However, the LCL can not be negative. Consequently, we must first determine if it is negative and set it equal to zero when it is. This can be accomplished with an **IF** function. The formula is **=IF(F8-3*F9<0,0,F8-3*F9)**.

10. Cell F11 computes the centerline (CL) with the formula **=F8**, and cell F12 the upper control limit (UCL) with the formula **=F8+3*F9**.

11. We will use the CHART WIZARD to prepare the p chart. Begin by highlighting the cells H5 through K19.

12. Repeat steps 16 through 21 of Section 12.1 in order to produce the initial p Chart. In Step 21 you should use the appropriate titles for the chart and for the Y-axis. (See Figure 12.14.)

13. Repeat steps 22, and 27 through 34 of Section 12.1 (steps 23 through 26 are not needed for this plot) in order to edit your p chart into the final form as shown in Figure 12.14.

Figure 12.14 Final Edited Form of the p Chart

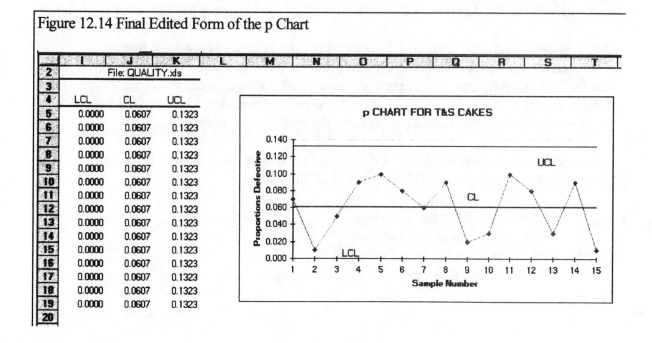

Our computations for the p chart have assumed that the number of observations in each sample is the same. However, a p chart can also be developed for situations when the number of observations is not the same for each sample. The worksheet of Figure 12.13 can be very easily modified to accommodate this. The modifications would include: (1) adding a column for sample size in column B, (2) finding the sum and the average for column B , (3) changing the formula in cell F8 to F7 divided by the sum of column B, (4) changing the denominator in cell F9 from F5 to the average for column B, and (5) changing the denominator in cell H5 from $F$5 to C5. Everything else would remain the same.

12.4 np CHART FOR CONTROLLING NUMBER OF DEFECTIVE ITEMS

The np chart offers an alternative to the p chart if all the samples have the same number of observations. It provides exactly the same information as the p chart. The only difference is that the number of defective items is plotted instead of the proportion of defective items. The choice between the two charts is a matter of personal preference provided the number of observations is the same for all samples.

As for the p chart, the **np chart** is applicable for situations when each item of output from a process may be classified as **defective** (nonconforming to specifications) or **nondefective** (effective or conforming to specifications). One approach to monitoring the quality of the process is to analyze the number of defective items in a sample with an np chart. The procedure needed to develop an np chart is very similar to that previously given for the x , R and p charts of the prior sections of this chapter. We plot sample values between 3-sigma control limits to determine if the sample values have a random pattern within the limits. Again we will consider the T&S Cakes example from the prior section.

The ever discriminating Granny Goose wants every cake to have an acceptable frosting. However, it is not possible for her to personally inspect the large number of cakes produced each day by T&S. Consequently, she inspects a sample of 100 cakes each day and categorizes each cake as defective or not. Figure 12.15 presents the results for the last 15 days of her inspections. She would like to use these data to determine if the process is in control.

We will develop our np chart on *Sheet5* of the QUALITY workbook as shown on Figure 12.15 (Sheet4 if you bypassed Figure 12.1). We proceed as follows.

1. Copy from *Sheet4* to *Sheet5* the following.
    a.   Rows 1 and 2 into rows 1 and 2
    b.   Cells A3 through B29 into A3 through B29
    c.   Cells I4 through K19 into I4 through K19

Figure 12.15 np Chart Centerline and Control Limits for T&S Cakes

	A	B	C	D	E	F	G	H	I	J	K
1					T & S CAKES, INC., EXAMPLE						
2	Date: January 23, 1998									File: QUALITY.xls	
3	Sample	Number						Number			
4	Number	Defective						Defective	LCL	CL	UCL
5	1	7		Number of Samples		15		7	0.0000	6.0667	13.2282
6	2	1		Total Defecitves		91		1	0.0000	6.0667	13.2282
7	3	5		Average No. Defective		6.06667		5	0.0000	6.0667	13.2282
8	4	9		Average Proportion		0.06067		9	0.0000	6.0667	13.2282
9	5	10		Std. Dev. for Avg. Prop		2.38718		10	0.0000	6.0667	13.2282
10	6	8		Lower Control Limit		0.00000		8	0.0000	6.0667	13.2282
11	7	6		Centerline		6.06667		6	0.0000	6.0667	13.2282
12	8	9		Upper Control Limit		13.22820		9	0.0000	6.0667	13.2282
13	9	2						2	0.0000	6.0667	13.2282
14	10	3						3	0.0000	6.0667	13.2282
15	11	10						10	0.0000	6.0667	13.2282
16	12	8						8	0.0000	6.0667	13.2282
17	13	3						3	0.0000	6.0667	13.2282
18	14	9						9	0.0000	6.0667	13.2282
19	15	1						1	0.0000	6.0667	13.2282
20	16										

2. Enter the labels in cells H3 and H4. Enter the formula **=B5** in cell H5. Copy this formula into cells H6 through H19.

3. Enter the eight labels shown in cells D5 through D12 of Figure 12.15.

4. Enter into cell F5 the number of samples, **15**.

5. In cell F6 enter the formula **=SUM(B5:B29)** in order to compute the total number of defective items. .

6. The average number defectives is computed in cell F7 with the formula **=F6/F5**, and the average number of proportion defective in cell F8 with the formula **=F7/100**.

7. The formula for cell F9 computes the estimate for the standard deviation for the number defective. It is found from the formula **=SQRT(F7*(1-F8))**.

8. The LCL is equal to the estimate of the number defective minus three times the standard deviation of the number defective but it can not be negative. As before, we use an **IF** function to test for negativity. The formula for cell F10 is **=IF(F7-3*F9<0,0,F7-3*F9)**.

9. Cell F11 computes the CL with the formula **=F7**, and cell F12 the UCL with the formula **=F7+3*F9**.

10. We will use the CHART WIZARD to prepare the np chart. Highlight cells H5 through K19.

11. You now need to repeat steps 16 through 21 of Section 12.1 in order to produce the initial np Chart. In Step 21 you should use the appropriate titles for the chart and for the Y-axis. (See Figure 12.16.)

12. Repeat steps 22, and 27 through 34 (steps 23 through 26 are not needed for this plot) of Section 12.1 in order to edit your np chart into the final form as given in Figure 12.16.

Figure 12.16 Final Edited Form of the np Chart

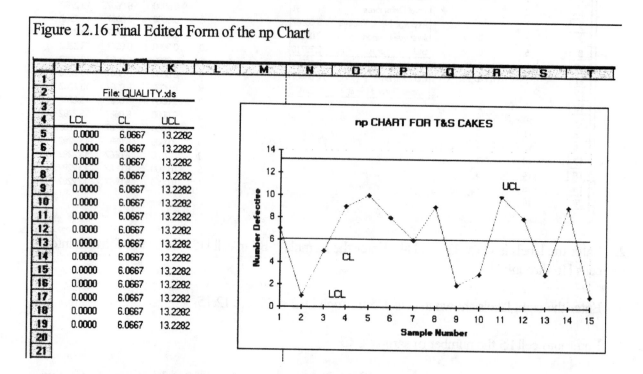

12.5 c CHART FOR CONTROLLING NUMBER OF DEFECTS PER UNIT

The p and the np charts monitor the proportion or number of defectives. Each item such as a T&S cake is simply classified as either being defective or not. However for some processes, it is possible for an output item to have more than one defect. For example, each cake might have a number of defects which can be counted. Accordingly, we could monitor the quality based on the **number of defects per unit** not the proportion or number defective items. This can be accomplished through a **c chart**.

Suppose the discriminating Granny Goose does count the number of defects she finds in each cake. The results she obtained for the last 15 samples is shown in column B of Figure 12.17. She would like to use these data to develop a c chart.

Again the basic procedure is to plot sample values between 3-sigma control limits to determine if the sample values have a random pattern within the limits. The primary way this chart differs from the four discussed above is in the computation of the standard deviation for determining the LCL and UCL values. The assumption behind the c chart is that the number of defects per unit is governed by the Poisson distribution.

We will develop our c chart on *Sheet6* of the QUALITY workbook as shown on Figure 12.17 (Sheet5 if you bypassed Figure 12.1). We proceed as follows.

1. Copy from *Sheet5* to *Sheet6* the following.
    a. Rows 1 and 2 into rows 1 and 2
    b. Cells A3 through A29 into A3 through A29
    c. Cells H4 through K19 into H4 through K19

2. Enter the labels in cells B3, B4, H3 and H4.

3. Enter the five labels shown in cells D7 through D12 of Figure 12.17.

Figure 12.17 c Chart Centerline and Control Limits for T&S Cakes

	A	B	C	D	E	F	G	H	I	J	K
1					T & S CAKES, INC., EXAMPLE						
2	Date: January 23, 1998									File: QUALITY.xls	
3	Sample	Number of						Number of			
4	Number	Defects						Defects	LCL	CL	UCL
5	1	1						1	0.0000	1.7333	5.6830
6	2	2						2	0.0000	1.7333	5.6830
7	3	3		Average No. Defects		1.73333		3	0.0000	1.7333	5.6830
8	4	4		Std.Dev.-No.of Defects		1.3165612		4	0.0000	1.7333	5.6830
9	5	2						2	0.0000	1.7333	5.6830
10	6	1		Lower Control Limit		0.00000		1	0.0000	1.7333	5.6830
11	7	4		Centerline		1.73333		4	0.0000	1.7333	5.6830
12	8	1		Upper Control Limit		5.68302		1	0.0000	1.7333	5.6830
13	9	3						3	0.0000	1.7333	5.6830
14	10	2						2	0.0000	1.7333	5.6830
15	11	0						0	0.0000	1.7333	5.6830
16	12	0						0	0.0000	1.7333	5.6830
17	13	1						1	0.0000	1.7333	5.6830
18	14	2						2	0.0000	1.7333	5.6800
19	15	0						0	0.0000	1.7333	5.6830
20	16										

4. Enter into cell F7 the formula **=AVERAGE(B5:B29)**.

5. In cell F6 enter the formula **=SQRT(F7)** to compute the standard deviation of the number of defects.

6. The LCL is equal to the estimate of the number of defects minus three times the standard deviation of the number of defects but can not be negative. The formula is **=IF(F7-3*F8<0,0,F7-3*F8)**.

7. Cell F11 computes the CL with the formula **=F7**, and cell F12 the UCL with the formula **=F7+3*F8**.

8. We will use the Chart Wizard to construct the c chart. Highlight cells H5 through K19.

9. Repeat steps 16 through 21 of Section 12.1 in order to produce the initial c Chart. In Step 21 you should use the appropriate titles for the chart and for the Y-axis. (See Figure 12.18.)

10. Repeat steps 22, and 27 through 34 (steps 23 through 26 are not needed for this plot) of Section 12.1 in order to edit your c chart into the final form as shown in Figure 12.18.

Figure 12.18 Final Edited Form of the c Chart

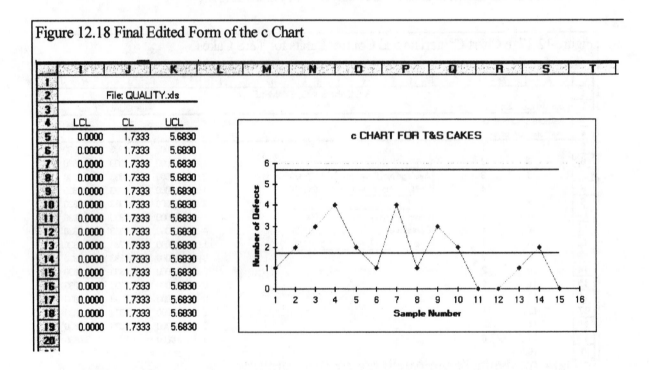

APPENDIX A. EXCEL DATA ANALYSIS TOOLS

What Are the Data Analysis Tools? Excel includes a collection of 19 data analysis tools. These provide analysis capabilities beyond Excel's inherent capabilities. Eighteen of these tools are for statistical applications. A discussion of the differences between these 18 statistical analysis tools and Excel's built-in statistical functions begins on the first page of Appendix B.

Where Can I Find the Data Analysis Tools? The data analysis tools are available in the component called the Analysis ToolPak which is an **add-in** program. Add-in programs are developed by companies other than Microsoft and can be added to Excel to increase its capabilities. Microsoft includes a number of add-ins, such as the Analysis ToolPak, with the Excel software it distributes. These must be added into Excel before they can be used within it.

Are the Data Analysis Tools Available on the Computer I am Using? The level of availability of the data analysis tools depends on the specific computer you are using. There are three possibilities.

1. The first possibility is that the Analysis ToolPak **(1) has been installed** and **(2) has been added** to the **Tools** pull-down menu. This means the data analysis tools are ready to use. To determine if this is your situation, click on **Tools** from the menu bar. If there is an entry near the bottom of the subsequent pull-down menu labeled **Data Analysis...**, the tools are ready to use. If it is not present, continue to the next possibility.

2. The second possibility is that the Analysis ToolPak **(1) has been installed** but **(2) has not been added** to the **Tools** menu. You must then add it to the menu. To determine if this is your situation and to add it to the menu, click on **Tools** from the menu bar. Then click on **Add-ins...** from the Tools pull-down menu. If the menu includes the selection **Analysis ToolPak** in the subsequent dialog box, you should click on the check box to its left to add a check mark to the box. (Note you are to add **Analysis ToolPak,** *not* **Analysis ToolPak-VBA**.) Next click on **OK** and the Analysis ToolPak will be added to the **Tools** menu and ready to use. If Analysis ToolPak is not an option on the add-ins dialog box, continue to the third possibility.

3. The third possibility is that the Analysis ToolPak **(1) has not been installed** and **(2) has not been added**. You must then first install it and second add it to the Tools menu. If this is your situation, you will need to exit from Excel and all other application programs and return to your computer's opening screen. Get your original diskettes or CD-ROM for Microsoft Office (or just Excel) and run the Setup program for it. Put the first CD or first diskette for your Microsoft Office software in the appropriate drive.

    a. Click on the **Start** command button and click on **Run** from the subsequent menu.

    b. The Run dialog box will appear on the screen. Assuming your CD or diskette is in drive D enter **D:\SETUP** in the text box and click on **OK**. (You may next get a dialog box indicating the Shortcut Bar is running. If so, click on **OK**.)

    c. The next dialog box will be labeled the **Microsoft Office—Set Up**. Click on the **Add/Remove** command button.

    d. The next dialog box is labeled **Microsoft Office—Maintenance**. Click to put a check mark in the **Excel** checkbox and to highlight Excel. Click on the **Change Option** button.

    e. The next dialog box is labeled **Microsoft Office—Microsoft Excel** . Click on the **Add Ins** button. Click on **Change Option**.

    F. The next dialog box is labeled **Microsoft Office—Add-Ins**. Click to put a check mark in the **Analysis ToolPak** (not Analysis ToolPak—VBA) check box and to highlight Analysis ToolPak. Click on **OK**.

    The installation program will now install the Analysis ToolPak. You can then start Excel. You will next need to add it to the Tools menu. Select **Tools**, then **Add-Ins** and put a check mark in the **Analysis ToolPak** check box and select **OK**. The Data Analysis Tools will now be available from the Tools pull-down menu.

How Do I Use the Data Analysis Tools? Once you have the Analysis ToolPak installed and it has been added to the **Tools** pull-down menu, you are ready to use these analysis tools. The tools are accessed by clicking on **Tools** on the menu bar and then clicking on **Data Analysis** on the subsequent pull-down menu. The result will be the Data Analysis dialog box with a scrolling list of the 19 data analysis tools (see Figure 1.6 of Chapter1). You then click on the name of the tool you wish to use and click on **OK**. A dialog box will then appear which allows you to enter the input range, output option and any other options required for the tool you have selected. If you are uncertain of an entry for a tool's dialog box, first click on **Help** (this is the Help in the tool's dialog box, not the Help in the prior Data Analysis dialog box with the scrolling list of the 19 tools). Next click on the button at the very end of the help topic message and the entries for the tool's dialog box will be described. Once the tool's dialog box is complete, click on **OK** and the output will appear.

For What Analyses Are the Data Analysis Tools Used? A presentation of the use of the data analysis tools is perhaps most helpful if it is given by category of analysis. Accordingly, the following list of the 18 statistical tools is by the type of statistical analysis each supports. The six categories used begin with *Descriptive Statistics* and end with *Time Series Forecasting*. The order of their presentation is that of a typical business statistics textbook. Within each category the tools are listed in the order they appear in this manual. The entry for each of the 18 statistical tools provides its name, its purpose and where its use is described within this manual. Further description of these is available through the Excel help facility. To access it, select **Tools** from the menu bar, **Data Analysis** from the subsequent pull-down menu, select the tool you wish to use from the resulting scrolling list, click on **OK** and click on **Help** in the next dialog box.

DESCRIPTIVE STATISTICS

Histogram—determines and graphs individual and cumulative frequencies for a one variable data set. It is presented in Section 2.1 of Chapter 2 and Section 4.3 of Chapter4.

Descriptive Statistics—generates a report of the values for 16 descriptive statistics such as the mean, median, mode, standard deviation, range, skewness and kurtosis for a one variable data set. It is presented in Section 3.1 of Chapter 3.

Rank and Percentile—produces a table of the ordinal and percentage rank of each value in a one variable data set. It is presented in Section 3.2 of Chapter 3.

SAMPLING FROM DISTRIBUTIONS

Random Number Generation—generates random values drawn from one of six possible probability distributions (also has a non-random selection called *patterned*). It is presented in Section 4.3 of Chapter 4.

Sampling—draws a random sample from a specified population for a single variable. This is the one statistical analysis tool not used within this manual.

HYPOTHESIS TESTING

t-Test: Two Sample Assuming Unequal Variances—performs a t-test on two independent samples to determine if the difference in the two population means is equal to a specified value (such as zero). This test is conducted under the condition that the two population variances are not known to be equal. It is presented in Section 5.2 of Chapter 5.

t-Test: Two Sample Assuming Equal Variances—performs a t-test on two independent samples to determine if the difference in the two population means is equal to a specified value (such as zero). This test is conducted under the condition that the two unknown population variances are known to be equal. It is presented in Section 5.3 of Chapter 5.

z-Test: Two Sample for Means—performs a z-test on two independent samples to determine if the difference in the two population means is equal to a specified value (such as zero). This test is conducted under the condition that the values of the two population variances are known, or the sample sizes are large so the normal distribution can be used to approximate the t distribution. It is presented in Section 5.3 of Chapter 5.

t-Test: Paired Two Sample for Means—performs a t-test on two paired (matched) samples to determine if the mean of the differences between the two population is equal to a specified values (such as zero). It is presented in Section 5.4 of Chapter 5.

F-Test: Two Sample for Variances—performs an F-test on two independent samples to determine if two population variances equal. It is presented in Section 7.2 of Chapter 7.

ANALYSIS OF VARIANCE

ANOVA: Single-Factor—performs a one-way analysis of variance to determine if two or more population means are equal . This test uses data from a *completely randomized* experimental design. It is presented in Section 8.1 of Chapter 8.

ANOVA: Two-Factor Without Replication—performs a two-way analysis of variance without interaction to determine if two or more population means are equal. This test uses data from a *randomized block* experimental design. It is presented in Section 8.2 of Chapter 8.

ANOVA: Two-Factor With Replication—performs a two-way analysis of variance with interaction to determine if two or more population means are equal. This test uses data from a *two-way factorial* experimental design. It is presented in Section 8.3 of Chapter 8.

REGRESSION AND CORRELATION

Covariance—creates a table of covariance values for all possible pairs of 2 or more independent variables. It is presented in Subsection 3.5.1 of Chapter 3.

Correlation—creates a table of correlation coefficients for all possible pairs of 2 or more independent variables. It is presented in Subsection 3.5.2 of Chapter 3, and in Section 10.3 of Chapter 10.

Regression—performs a simple linear regression analysis or a multiple regression analysis with up to 16 independent variables. It is presented in Sections 10.2, 10.3 and 10.4 of Chapter 10.

TIME SERIES FORECASTING

Moving Average—projects a time series based on the moving averages smoothing method. It is presented in Section 11.2 of Chapter 11.

Exponential Smoothing—projects a time series based on the simple exponential smoothing method. It is presented in Section 11.3 of Chapter 11.

APPENDIX B. EXCEL STATISTICAL FUNCTIONS

What Are the Statistical Functions? Excel includes hundreds of built-in functions. These are predefined formulas for performing frequently needed computations. Excel presents its functions in ten categories such as *Financial, Math &Trig, Database,* and *Engineering.* One of the ten categories is *Statistical*. The statistical category for Excel 7 and 5 lists 71 functions and that for Excel 8 (97) lists 80.

How Do the Statistical Functions and the Data Analysis Tools Differ? The statistical functions duplicate the capabilities of parts of the Data Analysis Tools discussed in Appendix A. However, there are differences in these two Excel features. These include the following.

- The results from the Tools are numbers, not formulas. Thus, a change in the input data analyzed by a Tool will not change the statistical results already computed by the Tool. To get the new results the Tool will have to be implemented again. In contrast, the output from a function is a formula. Accordingly, whenever the input data for the function are changed, the numerical results computed by the function are changed. (Note: Two of the Data Analysis Tools, MOVING AVERAGE and EXPONENTIAL SMOOTHING, are exceptions to this difference. These two tools do result in formulas, not numbers being entered into the worksheet. Also, the COVARIANCE tool results in formulas for two of its outputs, the variance for the two input variables.)

- The output from a Data Analysis Tool is formatted and labeled whereas that from a function merely presents the numerical results.

- A Tool generally provides the results which would be obtained from more than one function.

- Tools cannot be used in Excel formulas but statistical functions can.

How Do I Use the Statistical Functions? Access to the statistical functions is facilitated through Excel's FUNCTION WIZARD. If you click the icon on the Standard Toolbar which is labeled with the symbol *fx,* you will be presented with the Function Wizard dialog box (see Figure 1.7 of Chapter 1). The left side of the dialog box presents a scrolling list of the names of the ten function categories plus the selections *Most Recently Used* and *All.* If you click on the category **Statistical** in this scrolling list, the right side of the function dialog box will present a scrolling list of the 71 statistical functions for Excel 7 and 5, and 80 for Excel 8.

To select one of the statistical functions, highlight the function name by clicking on it in the right scrolling list. A brief description of the function will be displayed above the five command buttons at the bottom of the Function Wizard dialog box. Much greater detail about the selected function can be obtained by clicking on the **Help** command button in the lower left corner of the dialog box.

> **Excel 8 Note:** The dialog box is labeled as *Paste Function* instead of *Function 'Wizard – Step 1 of 2.* There are only three buttons at the bottom. The **Help button** has been replaced by a button for the **Office Assistant** (a question mark within a yellow balloon). The **Next button** has been replaced by an **OK button**. These serve the same purposes. The **Back** and **Finish** buttons are not needed.

If you click on the command button labeled **Next**, a second dialog box will be shown. Generally, this second dialog box will present one or more text boxes for keying the required values. Again help is available through the command button labeled as **Help**. Once the required text boxes are completed, click on the **Finish** button and the completed function will be entered into the active cell of the worksheet. The F2 keyboard key may be pressed in order to edit the function within the cell if it is necessary.

For What Analyses Are the Statistical Functions Used? The presentation of the use of the statistical functions is perhaps most helpful if it is by category of analysis. Accordingly, the following list of the 71 Excel 7 and 5 statistical functions is by the type of statistical analysis each supports. The 15 categories used begin with *Descriptive Statistics—Measures of Central Location* and end with *Regression and Correlation—Exponential Regression Analysis.* A sixteenth category at the end lists the nine additional functions which are given in the statistical function list for Excel 8.

The order of presentation of these first 15 categories is that of a typical business statistics textbook. Within each category the functions are presented in alphabetical order. The entry for each of the statistical functions provides its name and purpose. The use of many of these is demonstrated throughout this manual. Refer to the index to find the specific location for each function. Further description of the functions with examples of their use are available through the Excel help facility. To access it, select the FUNCTION WIZARD (the icon labeled with *fx* on the standard toolbar), next select the category **Statistical** and then select the specific function of interest. Finally, click on the **Help** command button.

> **Excel 8 Note:** Click on the Office Assistant (a question mark within a yellow balloon) button. Click on the Assistant's *Help with this feature* button and finally on its *Help on selected function* button.

DESCRIPTIVE STATISTICS—MEASURES OF CENTRAL LOCATION

AVERAGE—computes the arithmetic average (the usual mean)

GEOMEAN—computes the geometric mean (used for ratios, rates of changes and so on)

HARMEAN—computes the harmonic mean (rarely used in business applications)

MEDIAN—computes the median

MODE—computes the mode

TRIMMEAN—computes the trimmed mean (removes unusually small and/or large values)

DESCRIPTIVE STATISTICS—MEASURES OF VARIABILITY

AVEDEV—computes the average of the absolute deviations about the mean (**MAD**)

DEVSQ—computes the sum of the squared deviations about the mean

STDEV—computes the sample standard deviation (**n -1** in the denominator)

STDEVP— computes the population standard deviation (**N** in the denominator)

VAR—computes the sample variance (**n -1** in the denominator)

VARP—computes the population variance (**N** in the denominator)

DESCRIPTIVE STATISTICS—MEASURES OF SHAPE AND POSITION

KURT—computes the coefficient of kurtosis

SKEW—computes the coefficient of skewness

STANDARDIZE—computes the standardized value or z-score for a number

DESCRIPTIVE STATISTICS—SPECIFIC VALUES

LARGE—determines the kth largest value in a range (determines largest value if k is 1, the second largest if k is 2, and so on)

MAX—determines the maximum (largest) value in a range

MIN—determines the minimum (smallest) value in a range

SMALL— determines the kth smallest value in a range (determines smallest value if k is 1, the second smallest if k is 2, and so on)

DESCRIPTIVE STATISTICS—COUNTING

COUNT—counts the number of cells in a range which contain numeric values

COUNTA—counts the number of cells in a range which are not blank

FREQUENCY—determines the frequency distribution for data in a range

PERMUT—computes the number of permutations of n items taken k at a time (Excel also includes a combinations function, **COMBIN**, it is in the **Math & Trig** category)

DESCRIPTIVE STATISTICS—PERCENTILES AND RANKS

PERCENTILE—determines the kth percentile value of the values in a range (determines 10th percentile value if k is 0.1, 20th percentile if k is 0.2, and so on)

PERCENTRANK—determines the percentage rank in a range for a specified value (this is the inverse of the **PERCENTILE** function)

QUARTILE—computes the minimum value, maximum value or one of the three quartile values for a range

RANK—determines the rank of a number in a range of numbers

DISTRIBUTIONS—DISCRETE PROBABILITY DISTRIBUTIONS

BINOMDIST—computes either the individual probability value or the cumulative probability value for a specified random variable value for the binomial probability distribution

HYPGEODIST— computes the individual probability value (but not the cumulative probability value) for a specified random variable value for the hypergeometric probability distribution

NEGBINOMDIST— computes the individual probability value (but not the cumulative probability value) for a specified random variable value for the negative binomial probability distribution

POISSON—computes either the individual probability value or the cumulative probability value for a specified random variable value for the Poisson probability distribution

PROB— computes either the individual probability value for a specified random variable value or the total probability for a specified range for the random variable for a given discrete probability distribution

DISTRIBUTIONS—EXPONENTIAL AND NORMAL PROBABILITY DISTRIBUTIONS

EXPODIST— computes either the individual probability value or the cumulative probability value for a specified random variable value for the exponential probability distribution

NORMDIST—computes either the individual probability value or the cumulative probability value for a specified random variable value for the normal probability distribution

NORMINV—computes the random variable value for a specified probability value for the cumulative normal probability distribution

NORMSDIST—computes the cumulative probability value for a specified random variable value for the standard normal (mean of zero and standard deviation of one) probability distribution

NORMSINV—computes the random variable value for a specified probability value for the cumulative standard normal (mean of zero and standard deviation of one) probability distribution

DISTRIBUTIONS—DERIVED DISTRIBUTIONS

CHIDIST— computes the probability value for a specified random variable value for the chi-square distribution

CHIINV— computes the random variable value for a specified probability value for the chi-square distribution

FDIST—computes the probability value for a specified random variable value for the F distribution

FINV—computes the random variable value for a specified probability value for the F distribution

TDIST—computes the probability value for a specified random variable value for the t distribution

TINV—computes the random variable value for a specified probability value for the t distribution

DISTRIBUTIONS—OTHER CONTINUOUS PROBABILITY DISTRIBUTIONS

BETADIST—computes the probability value for a specified random variable value for the cumulative beta probability distribution

BETAINV— computes the random variable value for a specified probability value for the cumulative beta probability distribution

GAMMADIST— computes either the individual probability value or the cumulative probability value for a specified random variable value for the gamma probability distribution

GAMMAINV—computes the random variable value for a specified probability value for the cumulative gamma probability distribution

GAMMALN—computes the natural logarithm of the gamma function (not the gamma distribution)

LOGINV— computes the random variable value for a specified probability value for the cumulative lognormal probability distribution

LOGNORMDIST— computes either the individual probability value or the cumulative probability value for a specified random variable value for the lognormal probability distribution

WEIBULL—computes either the individual probability value or the cumulative probability value for a specified random variable value for the Weibull probability distribution

HYPOTHESIS TESTING AND CONFIDENCE INTERVALS

CHITEST—computes the p-value for the chi-square test of independence

CONFIDENCE—computes the sampling (or maximum) error (the half-width of the confidence interval) for a population mean using the z (standard normal) distribution

CRITBINOM—computes the critical value for hypothesis tests based on the binomial distribution

FISHER—computes the Fisher transformation for hypothesis tests

FISHERINV—computes the inverse of the Fisher transformation

FTEST—computes the p-value for the F test of the equivalence of two population variances

TTEST—computes the p-value for the t test of the equivalence of two population means for paired samples, for independent samples with equal variance or for independent samples with unequal variance

ZTEST—computes the p-value for the z (standard normal) test of one population mean with the population standard deviation either known or not known

REGRESSION AND CORRELATION—ASSOCIATION BETWEEN TWO VARIABLES

CORREL—computes the table of correlation coefficients (Pearson product moment correlation coefficients) for two ranges (this function is identical to **PEARSON**)

COVAR—computes the table of covariance values for two ranges

PEARSON—computes the table of correlation coefficients (Pearson product moment correlation coefficients) for two ranges (this function is identical to **CORREL**)

REGRESSION AND CORRELATION—SIMPLE LINEAR REGRESSION ANALYSIS

FORECAST—computes an estimated dependent variable value for a specified independent variable value based on a simple linear regression relationship

INTERCEPT—computes the value of the intercept for a simple linear regression

RSQ—computes the value for the coefficient of determination (the square of the correlation coefficient) for a simple linear regression

SLOPE—computes the value of the slope for a simple linear regression

STEYX—computes the standard error of the estimated y values for a simple linear regression

REGRESSION AND CORRELATION—MULTIPLE REGRESSION ANALYSIS

LINEST—performs a multiple (or simple) regression analysis and displays the regression coefficients and the additional regression outputs of the standard error for each of the regression coefficients, the coefficient of determination, the standard error of the estimated y values, the F statistic value and degrees of freedom, the sum of squares due to the regression and the sum of squares due to the error

TREND—computes estimated dependent variable values for specified independent variable values based on a multiple (or simple) regression relationship

REGRESSION AND CORRELATION—EXPONENTIAL REGRESSION ANALYSIS

GROWTH— computes estimated dependent variable values for specified independent variable values based on an exponential regression relationship

LOGEST—performs an exponential regression analysis (similar to **LINEST**, however the **LOGEST** relationship has the independent variables as exponents for the regression coefficients not multiplied times the coefficients as for the standard regression relationship used in **LINEST**)

ADDITIONAL STATISTICAL FUNCTIONS FOR EXCEL 8 (97)

- The following two functions have been **relocated from the Math & Trig** category of Excel 7 and 5 **to the Statistical** category of Excel 8

  COUNTBLANK— counts the number of cells in a range which are blank

  COUNTIF— counts the number of cells in a range which are not blank that meet a specified criterion

- The following seven functions have been **added to the Statistical** category for Excel 8. All seven return values for a range. The calculation includes numerical values, text and logical values such as FALSE and TRUE, not just numerical values. Text, empty cells and FALSE are evaluated as zero and TRUE is evaluated as one in the calculation.

  AVERAGEA— computes the arithmetic average (the usual mean) including text and logical values

  MAXA— determines the maximum (largest) value in a range including text and logical values

  MINA— determines the minimum (smallest) value in a range including text and logical values

  STDEVA—computes the sample standard deviation (**n -1** in the denominator) including text and logical values

  STDEVPA— computes the population standard deviation (**N** in the denominator) including text and logical values

  VARA—computes the sample variance (**n -1** in the denominator) including text and logical values

  VARPA—computes the population variance (**N** in the denominator) including text and logical values

APPENDIX C. EXCEL 8 (97) CHART WIZARD

The CHART WIZARD is used extensively in Chapters 2, 4, 10, 11, and 12 for developing statistical graphs and charts. The discussion in those chapters is for Excel 7. However, the Chart Wizard of Excel 8 (97) is significantly different from that of Excel 7 and Excel 5.   The differences are of a magnitude that an attempt to discuss them totally with notes within the chapters would interfere with the flow of manual. Accordingly, the purpose of this appendix is to present the revised CHART WIZARD as included in Excel 8.

Our approach will be to work through the frequency polygon example of Section 2.2 of Chapter 2. Thus, we repeat here Section 2.2 through the end of subsection 2.2.1 using the CHART WIZARD of Excel 8.

2.2 THE CHART WIZARD

Excel's feature called the CHART WIZARD can be used to create fourteen types of charts. Thirteen are listed in the scrolling list on the left of Figure 2.8. The fourteenth is at the bottom of the scrolling list and is hidden from view. It is the *Pyramid* chart which except for shape is similar to the *Cylinder* and the *Cone* shown in Figure 2.8. In Section 2.2, we demonstrate the use of four of the fourteen. The **XY (Scatter)** chart is used to develop both a frequency polygon for the example problem of Subsection 2.2.1 and a scatter diagram for the example of Subsection 2.2.4. In Subsection 2.2.2 another example is introduced. It is used to demonstrate the use of **Bar** chart, a **Column** chart and a **Pie** chart. In addition, Subsection 2.2.2 presents three-dimensional sub-types for the Bar, Column and Pie charts.

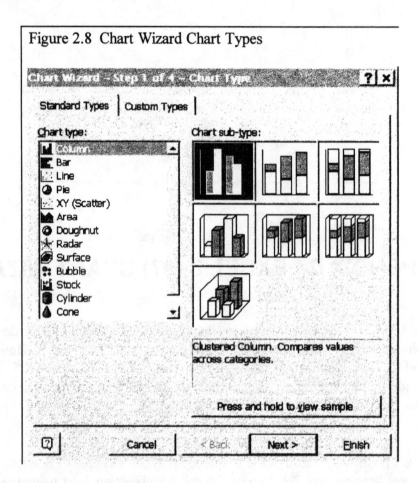

Figure 2.8 Chart Wizard Chart Types

2.2.1 Frequency Polygon

The XY (Scatter) chart can be used to create a frequency polygon for the *Cones Sold* example used throughout Section 2.1 above. You would proceed in the following manner.

1. Move the cell pointer to cell E25 and enter the label **Midpoint** and to F25 and enter the label **Frequency**.

2. In cells E26 through E33 enter the midpoints for the classes/bins of cells E6 through E13 as **15, 25, 35, . . . , 85.**

3. Copy the frequency values from cells F6 through F13 to cells F26 through F33. (You may wish to refer ahead to Figure 2.13 to see the results of Steps 1, 2 and 3.)

4. Highlight the range of cells from E25 through F33 by dragging.

5. Move the pointer to the CHART WIZARD icon on the standard toolbar and click once. The *Chart Wizard — Step 1 of 4—Chart Type* dialog box will appear as previously shown in Figure 2.8. If the **Standard Types** tab is not in front, click it.

6. Use the mouse to select the **XY (Scatter)** chart and then select the sub-type in the lower left corner of the Chart sub-types. See Figure 2.9. Click on the **Next** command button. The *Chart Wizard — Step 2 of 4—Chart Source Data* dialog box will be displayed as shown in Figure 2.10.

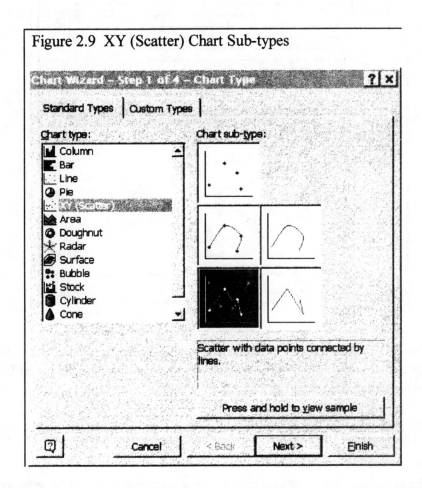

7. If the **Data Range** tab is not in front, click it. Check to make sure the data range is given as E25:F33 (as noted in Figure 2.10, Sheet1 may be referenced and the range given as absolute cell references). Make sure the **Columns** option button is selected for *Series in*. Click on the **Next** command button. The *Chart Wizard — Step 3 of 4—Chart Options* dialog box will appear as shown in Figure 2.11.

Figure 2.10 Chart Wizard Step 2, Chart Source Data dialog box

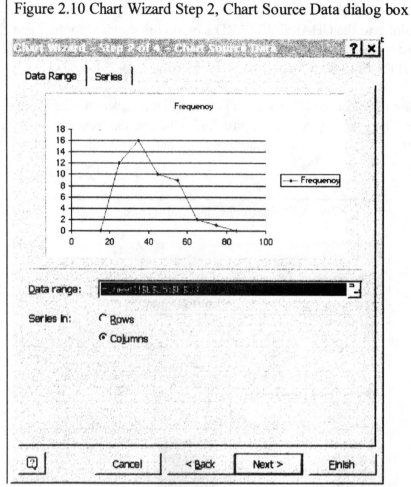

8. Click on the **Titles** tab if it is not in front. Move the mouse pointer to the **Chart title** text box and click. Enter the title *FREQUENCY POLYGON*. Enter *Class Midpoint* for the **Value (X) Axis** and enter *Frequency* for **Value (Y) Axis**.

9. Click on the **Axes** tab. Select the check boxes for both the **Value(X) Axis** and **Value (Y) Axis**.

10. Click on the **Gridlines** tab. All four check boxes shown should not be selected.

11. Click on the **Legend** tab. The check box *Show legend* should not be selected.

12. Click on the **Data Labels** tab. Select the option button for **None**. Click on the **Next** command button. The result will be the *Chart Wizard — Step 4 of 4—Chart Location* dialog box as shown in Figure 2.12.

13. Click on the option **As object in.** Click on the **Finish** command button. Click and drag the chart to a position beside the data. The result will be as shown in Figure 2.13.

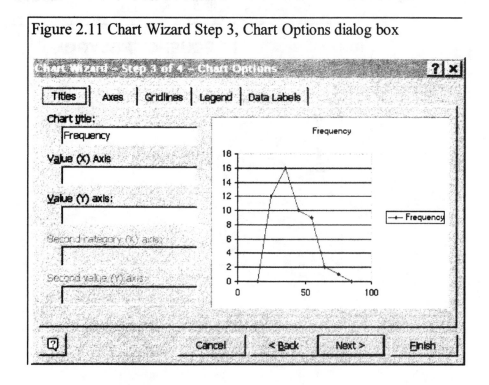

Figure 2.11 Chart Wizard Step 3, Chart Options dialog box

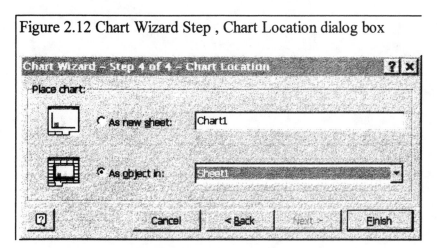

Figure 2.12 Chart Wizard Step , Chart Location dialog box

If you would like you can enlarge the chart as you did to get Figure 2.6 (refer to Chapter 2).

Figure 2.13 Frequency Polygon Final Results

Midpoint	Frequency
15	0
25	12
35	16
45	10
55	9
65	2
75	1
85	0

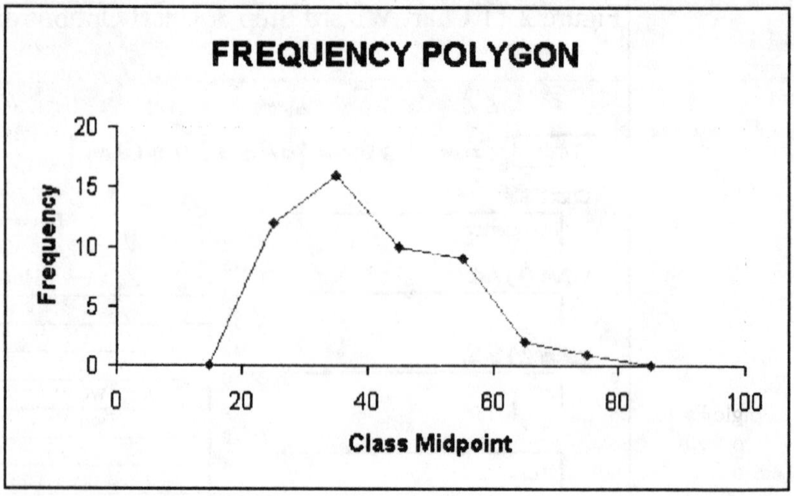

INDEX

263